Amye Reade

**Slaves of the sawdust**

Amye Reade

**Slaves of the sawdust**

ISBN/EAN: 9783744738767

Printed in Europe, USA, Canada, Australia, Japan

Cover: Foto ©ninafisch / pixelio.de

More available books at **www.hansebooks.com**

# Slaves of  the Sawdust.

BY
AMYE READE,
AUTHOR OF 'RUBY.'

LONDON: F V WHITE & CO.,
14 BEDFORD STREET, STRAND, W.C.

1893.

[*All Rights reserved.*]

TO

## ALFRED, LORD TENNYSON,

POET LAUREATE,

WHOSE DIVINE POETRY

AND

LOVE FOR HUMANITY HAS TOUCHED THE HEARTS OF ALL,

**This Book,**

WITH PERMISSION, IS

**Dedicated**

BY THE

AUTHOR.

TO

## ALFRED, LORD TENNYSON,

POET LAUREATE,

WHOSE DIVINE POETRY

AND

LOVE FOR HUMANITY HAS TOUCHED THE HEARTS OF ALL,

### This Book,

WITH PERMISSION, IS

### Dedicated

BY THE

AUTHOR.

# CONTENTS.

|  | PAGE |
|---|---|
| I.—ON THE NAB'S HEAD, | 1 |
| II.—WHANKS, | 11 |
| III.—LOOKING BACK, | 21 |
| IV.—MAKING AN ENEMY, | 31 |
| V.—ENVY AND HATRED, | 42 |
| VI.—NO JOY COMES UNMIXED, | 56 |
| VII.—'JACTA EST ALEA,' | 69 |
| VIII.—HORROX, | 77 |
| IX.—UNPROFESSIONALS, | 90 |
| X.—JOINING THE PROFESSION, | 101 |
| XI.—IN THE TRANSVAAL, | 111 |
| XII.—'MOTHER!' 'LEILA,' | 125 |
| XIII.—'MY AUNT'S MONEY,' | 136 |
| XIV.—'THE WAGES OF SIN,' | 146 |
| XV.—IN THE RING, | 160 |
| XVI.—MAD FOR LOVE, | 170 |
| XVII.—THE GOLDEN CORD IS BROKEN, | 178 |
| XVIII.—SHADOWS AND DUST, | 194 |
| XIX.—TOM TRIES HIS LUCK, | 200 |
| XX.—IN SACRED AISLE, | 212 |
| XXI.—A BROKEN PLEDGE, | 221 |
| XXII.—ANOTHER CHANGE, | 233 |
| XXIII.—BEHIND THE SCENES, | 243 |
| XXIV.—ON THE TRAIL, | 257 |
| XXV.—PAID IN FULL, | 269 |
| XXVI.—THE BEGINNING OF THE END, | 284 |
| XXVII.—DEATH UNSEEN, | 295 |
| XXVIII.—FINALE, | 304 |
| CHILD LABOUR, | 307 |

# *PREFACE.*

―o―

MUCH as I anticipated opposition to the indictment in my novel *Ruby*, in which I dealt with the cruelties employed in the training of young people for the amusements of thoughtless crowds, little did I expect that the selfish unbelief of some professing philanthropy would have been my greatest difficulty in arousing public sympathy for a long-suffering class, which are as yet practically helpless.

In their ill-judged supineness, some critics acted against me without examining the existence of the evil. I invited such examination from the public platform, and made such efforts as I deemed advisable, through my novel to teach the public the truth, which until then had been a dead secret. Further, I recommended them to inquire and assure themselves that my statements of the veritable horrors of the ring were positive realities.

My challenge was unheeded. They asserted, in their ignorance of circus life, that the conditions under which I described the children's sufferings were impossible, and in many instances I have been met with distrust and actual contradiction.

Some could not understand the brutality of men for the sake of gain. They had never put a foot 'behind the scenes,' yet they deemed themselves capable of judging that of which they knew nothing, and so declined to believe an accumulation of evidence. They deprecated any interference which might put an end to what they call amusement, but which I declare to be injustice and cruelty.

I have been severely blamed for representing, very mildly, the strong language daily used in connection with circus life. I maintain that I wrote no more than was necessary to point out the moral condition by which the girls are surrounded, but sentimentalists preferred that the evil should continue to exist rather than that it should be made known and redressed by public sympathy. Surely that which is too horrible to read should be regarded as too vile to live, and the language which has outraged their instincts cannot be less degrading to the young children's ears, when training for the circus, or the trapeze.

Is it not hypocritical to cry down that which is true, whilst erotic novels with profligate heroes abound in fashionable libraries and adorn the drawing-room, in order that fair and thoughtless women may while away the languid hours.

Yet these very people frequent the circus for

amusement, and enjoy seeing the poor spangled riders and acrobats straining their limbs into all kinds of unnatural postures, knowing as they know now, the frightful tortures they must have undergone to fit themselves for their performances.

Their selfishness is apparent, they withhold their sympathies, they call my careful statements of facts 'Sensation,' 'An advertisment,' 'An impossibility in a Christian country'—could I not write of such people that they are dull, unimpressible, and wanting in heart and moral courage?

It is true I drew a pitiful picture, I set down hard truths, truths which those who cry out about sweaters in the slums dare not have uncovered. I made known in *Ruby* a great deal, but there is more to divulge about the "slaves of the sawdust."

My mission shall be to tell it. I will go on until I have gained the protection I crave for those who perform wonderful feats for the pleasure of the people.

There is a dark phase in the lives of those who are engaged in the circus, but the light is beginning to break, the dawn is not very distant. For this end, I again place before my readers another tale, founded upon facts which I have personally verified.

With renewed vigour and perseverance, I am again directing my steps to the goal from which will arise the emancipation of these white slaves, and all my efforts will be directed to that great end, however remote it may appear to those who have found it so easy to consider my work far removed from the probabilities of truth.

I shall never weary waiting for victory; I shall never tire of my self-imposed task. I intend to dedicate all my faculties, all my time to win the cause of the young—no opposers shall obstruct my path, even if they dare to impute to me the stigma which must for ever rest on those who put idealism under the garb of truth.

AMYE READE.

*Christmas* 1891.

# *Slaves of the Sawdust.*

## CHAPTER I.

### ON THE NAB'S HEAD.

WHAT was that sound which broke the stillness of the summer day? Was it the call of someone in dire distress, or was it the hoarse cry of a seabird?

Repose, there seemed to be repose, everywhere, as far as the eye could see. Even the little village of Sandcliffe, with its quaint houses and wayside inn, was basking in the glorious heat of the July day. The unpaved street was almost deserted, for only a few cows, driven by a small boy, were to be seen lazily making their way to the farm upon the hill.

Now and again a shopkeeper peeped out of his door, for trade was slack and there was nothing to while away the long drowsy afternoon.

There were no strangers to attract attention, for Sandcliffe was too remote a place for holiday folk, and there was only a daily coach service between it and the town of Bayhaven, three miles away.

One summer, two great artists had come to paint a sea scene. Quite a flutter of excitement had been caused by their appearance, and the villagers made much of them. Indeed it was an event long to be remembered.

This summer-tide there were no artists to disturb the tranquillity of the good folks; so the days came and went with very little change in the monotony, which had grown habitual even to the young of the village. Sometimes a funeral, winding its way to the little Norman church, would give rise to lengthened gossips and discussions amongst the simple band left behind, or a village wedding lend a passing excitement to those who had known the bride's mother since baby days, had watched the bride, too, as she grew up a pretty, graceful maiden, who perchance had never been out of her village home, and who knew nothing of the restless, anxious world beyond.

A mile from these village homes the coast stretched down to the open sea, and a weird spot it was. During the winter days the waters frowned in angry majesty, and heavy grew the swell against the cold grey cliffs. Terrific was the roar of the waves as they broke against the pebbled shore; it seemed almost as if sky, cliffs, storm, and sea mated together, making the scene one of unabated fury.

But there were no storm clouds now chasing each other with angry force, the sweeping waters were resting, and only a murmur like a melodious chant was discernible, and that was but feebly heard from the shore, for the tide was down and there was a great expanse of golden sand stretching away before the blue waves, chaffing in idle play, could be reached. Further along, where the shore grew wider and more desolate, the murmur grew louder, for the waves broke against a mass of grey cragged rock, whose shattered peaks heaved from the water. At the ebb-tide they stood out in bold relief, but at the flow they were hidden by the waves. Sombre, beautiful as they were, stories were told by the villagers of the treacherous dangers of the Nab's Head Rock, for between the rock and the land an undercurrent flowed as the tide rose, and so insidious was it that a stranger could not guess from the gentle movement of the water of the terrible foe lurking beneath. On, on the current came, until the water grew black and deep, and the only way to the shore from Nab's Head Rock was through the Valley of Death.

The tide was rising now, and each moment the rock was growing less and less beneath the advancing tide, whilst the current between the shore and Nab's Head was running in with tremendous force. Soon all communication would be cut off, and the rock would be submerged for many hours.

Once again that strained, harsh cry was heard; it seemed to rise from the bosom of the sea, and then die away among the massive silent cliffs.

Again it came, fraught with anguish, almost heart-rending in its intensity. It could be no seabird, for the words, 'Help! help! I'm drowning!' uttered with passionate entreaty, reached the shore.

A rider had been galloping over the smooth sands, as yet untouched by the tide. He drew rein suddenly and listened; his boarhound uttered a long, low growl, he turned fiercely towards the dog.

'Be quiet, you brute, lie down.'

The animal obeyed his voice instantly, and crouched a few yards from the restive, panting horse. The rider glanced hurriedly around, shore—sand, sea, cliffs came under his rapid glance, but not until his eyes rested upon the rock did he perceive from whence the cry had arisen.

There he saw the flutter of a summer dress, an upturned face, white and drawn with acute agony and nameless terror. The owner of the face was clinging to the rugged rock with all her strength, whilst the sea encroached upon her every moment. The man saw that action must be prompt or it would be too late.

He struck his horse sharply with his whip, and the already nervous and excited animal plunged and reared, as if to resent such treatment, but a few sharp pricks from the spurs caused him to hasten his pace.

The girl had caught sight of the man, and she renewed her cry of distress.

'Help! help! I cannot reach the shore—save me!'

'Don't be afraid, Madame,' he shouted, 'I will come to you; my horse *shall* do it. Hold on tightly, do you understand?'

His authoritative tone reassured her, she was quite convinced that her danger was over, that he could really rescue her from her perilous position.

'I understand,' she replied faintly. Exhaustion was stealing over her, and this her rescuer seemed to realise.

'Hold on a little longer,' he shouted again; 'you shall soon be safe.'

The dog barked lustily when his master attempted to make his horse plunge into the deep water to reach the rock beyond.

Narrow as the crossing was, the animal refused to obey; he resisted bit and bridle, and the barking of the dog made him still more impatient and more eager to turn his back upon the sea.

'Hold your infernal noise!' the horseman shouted, and he stooped down and gave the dog a stinging cut with his whip. With a howl of pain the animal slunk away, and watched his master from afar with eager eyes.

Again he tried to put the horse to the water, but without success. He plunged again and again, backing on to the shore until his haunches almost touched the sandy beach.

The girl saw the affrighted horse from her vantage ground, and fear crept over her once again. Would the man's efforts to save her prove to be unavailing after all?

He did not call to her again, all his attention was directed to his horse. Oh! how long it seemed to her before he brought it once more to the water's edge, and yet it was scarcely a minute. He applied his spurs to the already bleeding flanks, and used his whip unmercifully. Neck, shoulders, and head came in for a shower of cruel cuts, until at length, with a neigh of terror, the horse plunged into the deepening sea. On, on he went, feeling his way cautiously and timidly, until the water reached beyond the girth, then he was carried by the current off his feet, and swimming became a necessity. At last, after many a struggle, he reached the more shallow water at the foot of the rock. There was just sufficient room for the horse to stand, and then his rider spoke.

'Now, Madame, do as I tell you quickly; delay will endanger our lives. Come as near me as you can, otherwise I cannot get a firm hold. You must be quick; it takes all my time to keep this beast quiet.'

She crept cautiously towards him, and in another moment he stretched over, and grasping her firmly round the waist, swung her on to the saddle before him and then wheeled the horse round shorewards. The task was not easy. With one hand he supported the girl, and with the other he held whip and bridle. To make matters more difficult, the horse plunged wildly, and splashed the water over them, blinding him with the spray. Sometimes the current carried them quickly forward, and to actually guide the animal was practically impossible.

The girl tried to thank him, but he bade her somewhat sternly to be silent.

Back again with his double burthen the horse fought his way through the treacherous current, until at length, almost exhausted, he felt the yielding sand beneath his hoofs. He stumbled once or twice on the loose shingle, and then the girl knew their terrible adventure was over.

Her rescuer lifted her from the horse as easily as if she had been a child, and then dismounting himself, he slipped the bridle over his arm and turned towards her. For a moment they stood in silence—a coyness came over the girl now the danger was averted and she found herself face to face with a stranger.

She was terribly agitated; he was calm, cool, and collected.

At last he spoke.

'Won't you sit down for a few moments, Mademoiselle, on that boulder close behind you and recover yourself?'

He had substituted Mademoiselle for Madame when he found she was a mere girl, perhaps scarcely eighteen years of age.

'You must be tired and wet too, I fear,' he added kindly. His tone of sympathy gave her confidence, and she looked up into his face.

What a pleasing picture he made standing there. A tall, dignified man, about thirty years of age, his dark flashing eyes and black hair served to show to greater advantage the rest of his fine features. A heavy black moustache half hid the haughty smiling mouth. But how firm he looked: vigour and energy of mind were clearly perceptible, and an observant person could hardly describe his face as sincerely kind. Handsome beyond a doubt, but there was something undefined, something which baffled description, which would make the decision hardly in his favour. But the girl only saw his manly beauty, and without knowing it her heart yielded to the lavish touch of nature, and she contemplated him as she would have done anything else which inspired her with admiration.

'Yes, I am very tired,' and she sat down on the boulder gratefully. 'I was so frightened. How good you were to save me.' She paused, her eyes filled with tears. After a struggle she continued: 'I am so very, very grateful.' She put out her hand, and as he took it he noticed how white and elegant it was, and he wondered who the fair-haired girl could be who had been left to the mercy of the waves.

'It has been a great pleasure to serve you. I am deeply thankful I came in time to be of use.'

He smiled bewitchingly as he spoke, his eyes beaming with genuine admiration as he looked down on the pretty girlish face.

'You are very good to say so, but it was all my own fault. I fell asleep, and when I awoke the waves which had been so far away before were close upon me. I called again and again, but no reply came. Then I thought I was lost, when suddenly you came up and saved me. You might have been drowned too. How brave you were!'

'You think so,' he replied in his rich, decisive tones, 'but I assure you it was nothing after all. Any man would do as much to gain the thanks of one so fair as you.' He raised his hat and bowed.

She smiled, but did not reply. She was not

prepared for compliments, least at all from a stranger, yet they pleased her.

Brave and stern he looked, whilst the shadows played around him—a man born to be a hero, if the Fates had not denied him such glory—a man who would have defied life and death, if such could be possible; but he possessed one peculiar faculty, of which he was very proud, and that was his power of inspiring fear, yet with passionate love, when he chose he used this influence with great force. This spell he now cast over the young girl before him.

'Be quiet, sir, do you hear, be quiet.' He turned to the horse with a scowl. 'You brute,' he had been about to say, but discretion came to his aid and he substituted 'sir.'

'"Fleetfoot" is so impatient,' he continued. 'I've had a pretty tough time of it coming from Bayhaven; he is young and fresh.'

'"Fleetfoot," what a pretty name,' and for the first time she turned to give the animal a searching look. 'You should call him "Rubicon" after to-day, because he has crossed the small stream coming from the sea. The water we came through will do for the "Rubicon," and you,' she hesitated, 'can be Cæsar, you are as courageous as he.'

A smile broke over his countenance at her words, that fascinating smile which had won more hearts than gold.

As she spoke something hot and moist licked her hand, and she turned round to see a large dog close upon her.

'Oh, you beauty!' she exclaimed, with sudden joy in her voice. 'I suppose he belongs to you?'

'Yes; his name is "Athol." He's a splendid beast. Are you fond of dogs?'

'Very, but I don't think you can be,' she

answered shyly. 'I saw you struck him with the whip; his cry of pain came to me on the rock, and poor "Fleetfoot," you lashed him cruelly—oh, it was horrible, horrible!' and she shuddered as she spoke.

'I am afraid young ladies don't quite understand horses with vile tempers,' he remarked severely. 'Do not you think a human life is of more consequence than that of a horse? Could I have let you drown,' he added more gently, 'because my horse refused to take the water? "Fleetfoot," or "Rubicon" as you wish him called, must obey his master.'

She felt somewhat nettled by his manner, and yet she was captivated by his strong will and absolute power.

'I do not wish him called "Rubicon,"' she replied quietly. 'You must think me very rude to have suggested a change in the name of your horse, but I do think he could have crossed the stream just as easily had you shown him more mercy. Shakespeare says: "Mercy becomes the monarch better than his crown." Do you ever read Shakespeare?'

'I have no time, Mademoiselle; I wish I had,' he replied gravely.

'I always carry a tiny copy of one of his plays,' and she pulled one from her pocket as she spoke and held it up for his inspection.

'May I look at it?' He took it from her, and then, as if by accident, he turned to the fly-leaf and read her name, Leila Gurney.

She watched him as he turned the wet leaves backwards and forwards, his diamond ring flashing in the light, and a pale flush spread over her face. She had forgotten her name was in the book, but it was too late now—he had seen it.

'Thank you,' he added, as he handed her back the tiny volume. 'Do you often come down here by the sea? It must be nice in the early morning, cool and refreshing.'

'Yes, I come every day, but generally in the afternoon, never in the morning.'

Unsuspectingly she had given the man just the information he wished for, and to his next question she replied just as truthfully.

'You live down in this place, I suppose?'

'No, I am here for the summer. I lodge at Green's Cottages up in the village, but it is dreadfully dull,' she added sadly. 'I have no friends—not even a dog or a horse—not a soul with whom I can exchange ideas. It is miserable.'

'I am sure it must be,' he replied. 'You're very young to be so much alone.'

She rose from the boulder, caressing the dog as she did so. She paused and looked seawards. The Nab's Head could not be seen now. A grey mist was skimming along deep down on the horizon, and the ships with their brown sails looked like big birds with expanded wings against the sky.

Nearer to the shore the sun's rays were steeping the clouds with gold, and breasting the waves with colour, making their edges glittering and ruddy.

'Well, good-bye,' and once again she put out her hand, 'good-bye, and thank you a thousand times for saving my life. I only wish I could give you some recompense for all you have done, but I own nothing of value that I could offer you. I wish I did.'

He took her hand gently, a thrill went through her at his touch; he noticed how the flush rose to her cheeks as he said good-bye.

Then he turned towards the horse.

'"Rubicon," we must go home,' he said, mounting quickly, and then whistling to his dog, he looked at the beautiful girl standing on the shore.

'Good-bye, Mademoiselle,' he called, and then lifting his hat he rode off in the direction of the town.

What a change had come over her life in those few short minutes, and as she hurried to her cottage home everything seemed brighter and more cheerful. Her life hitherto had been so dull, such a blank, that any change gave her intense pleasure.

This stranger had come, and pleasant visions of his fine, handsome face and gentle manners haunted her thoughts as the one bright star of her life.

Who was he she wondered? He had given her no clue, not even his name; that was a mystery still unrevealed.

With half rapture and half sorrow she thought of him, for her heart was full. Was it good-bye for ever she wondered?

Shadows and dreams of happiness had made up her lonely life; this perchance was only the flash of a meteor, come and gone and lost like the rest.

Then she remembered he was but a stranger.

---

## CHAPTER II.

### WHANKS.

QUIETLY the horse wended his way over the smooth, firm sands. He might have been riderless for the interest that was taken in his movements. The fright of crossing the water, together with the severe treatment he had undergone, had reduced his spirits considerably, and he was content to make the homeward journey at a slow pace. His master could have been in no haste, for spur and whip were idle for once.

The rider's thoughts were far away from the scene around him. He had for a time forgotten the rippling waves and the glories of the summer day. He had forgotten his horse and dog, so each went their own way.

Fancy had cast her glamour over him, making futurity more bright even for him. Such thoughts rarely if ever came to gladden his life. Hope had never painted unfading happiness in his mind, and no centre of special love had made his life an earthly heaven.

But he could not forget the bright, beautiful girl, with her wealth of short golden hair falling in loose curls around her shapely head; her soft, tender eyes, raised so gently when she spoke; the trusting, winsome manner, so girlish, so exquisitely natural.

There was grace in every action of the supple limbs, but it was when she smiled that her beauty was the most attractive. He wondered, if she was so beautiful now, what would her perfections be later when maturity had completed nature's bounteous gifts. How grateful she had been to him for saving her life, how warm in her gratitude had been the grasp of her tiny hand. Then his thoughts wandered to her loneliness, and he wondered gravely why she was friendless amongst strangers, and a feeling something akin to sympathy came over him.

His heart was smitten, his admiration grew with his thoughts of her, his passions were stirred to the very depths of his nature, he almost loved the girl with the golden hair. He must see her again, and that soon. He must learn more about his newly-found friend. Might she not be the one appointed to gratify the one ambition of his hard, stern life? He would try to win her for himself. Yet his scheme might fail. The girl might be a ward in Chancery, or there might be a guardian ready to put his foot down to prevent the girl coming to meet him. If she had had a father or mother surely she would have mentioned them after her narrow escape from death.

She was a lady, he was sure of that, although her dress was simple and somewhat shabby. Perhaps she was alone in the world—a girl with an income just removed from starvation.

Dwell as he might on the fairest picture his life had ever seen, deeper grew the mystery as to who could be the lovely girl found on the Nab's Rock.

Emilio Castelli was by profession an equestrian manager. He had filled that position for years in many of the great Continental and English circuses. He had been successful in all his undertakings, and had made considerable sums of money from time to time. He was now equestrian manager and ringmaster at Deval's Royal Circus, besides which he owned a troupe of performing horses which were almost world renowned. These were the attraction which filled the circus at every town they visited, and Castelli drew large amounts from the treasury every week.

He was a man who understood his duties thoroughly, and he expected those brought into contact with him to do the same. Those who knew him in social life thought him cold, unfriendly, and severe, and he was no favourite with the artistes or those engaged about the circus. But it was in his professional career that his full force of character was delineated. If one of his equestrian pupils became faulty in his tricks the dark eyes grew brilliant with suppressed passion, his thin lips grew set and white, his face became crimson and then pale, and great purple veins stood out on his broad forehead. Swiftly and with force he would raise the long thonged whip and administer cruel castigation for very slight errors.

To him an animal quivering with pain and trembling with anguish was no uncommon sight. He was hardened to the cruelty which embittered the lives of the poor weary horses. Their tortures and misery were nothing to him. Did they not bring him gold? In his capacity as ringmaster he showed little mercy, treating men and women with the same severity. Once when a great lady rider had come from a Continental circus, and all the men about the place raved of her beauty and her talents, he smiled at their infatuation and treated the fair equestrian with scanty ceremony. He was master of the ring, and he made her understand that, and none dared to dispute his right.

But a simple girlish face had suddenly impressed him, and for the first time in his life a woman's image lived in his mind to the exclusion of all else. Extremes meet in some natures, and with a mighty bound invade the heart with great force, thus beginning a virtue or a vice.

Years before Emilio Castelli had made up his mind that if he married he would marry a lady, a woman far removed from the associations of the ring, and this restless ambition had increased with time, and now perhaps the opportunity had come and the Fates would be propitious and give him the girl he had rescued from the waves. But his train of happy thoughts were interrupted. The horse stumbled over a loose stone, and with an oath Castelli checked him, and then awoke to the fact that he was close to the town. He pulled out his watch. It was growing late. He urged the horse on more quickly.

'If I am not there to the moment,' he murmured, 'something is sure to go wrong.' Up the crowded thoroughfare he rode, never slackening his speed until he reached the street where he lodged. Suddenly he reined in his horse, for in the roadway there was gathered a motley crowd, cheering two men who stood fighting in their centre. One of them fell, and his antagonist was upon him in a second. The roughs grew excited and yelled out,—

'Go it, Tim! Lay on to him! Keep him down! You've got him! Give him gruel!'

Some of the onlookers caught sight of the rider and shouted to their comrades,—

'Here's the boss from the circuss. There'll be a darned good row now. Let's clear out.'

Some of the wisest followed this advice, but many lingered to see 'it out.'

In a moment Castelli realised that one of his grooms was implicated in the quarrel.

'What's all this about?' he shouted. 'Stand on one side or I'll ride over you,' and suiting his action to his word he turned the horse into their midst.

Scrambling, fighting for the path to ensure their safety, they dispersed rapidly, but the two men still remained in the road, Tim Baker resolute and dogged, his companion lying on the ground, dust begrimed and without his hat.

'Get up, you fool!' roared Castelli. 'Get up!' The man looked up at his angry master and tried to rise. 'And clear out of the way, you blackguard!' he hissed, as he turned towards Tim Baker.

'The road ain't yours,' replied the man sullenly. 'Your groom ain't worth punching. Let him take that and be ——.'

He raised his heavy hobnailed boot to kick his opponent, but Castelli was too quick for him.

'Oh, that's your game, is it? Kick a man when he's drunk,' and before the man could realise his position Castelli had seized him by the collar, and lifting him off his feet, swung him across the street, where he fell into the gutter, whilst the loafing crowd cheered heartily. One boy, to obtain a better view, had climbed up a lamp post, and called out, 'There's beauty and the beast on a 'oss. Three cheers for the circuss,' after which refined speech he slid to the ground.

Castelli rode up to his door and sent a boy to his landlady to tell her he wanted her son to take his horse to the stables at the circus. Then dismounting, he waited for his man, who was coming slowly up to where he stood.

'Is the dog to come with the horse?' asked a youthful voice meekly, as if afraid to venture the question.

'No; be off,' replied Castelli shortly. 'So you can manage to walk straight now you're master has come home, can you, you drunken fool?' he said as the groom approached him. 'Come upstairs to my room.'

The man did not reply, but followed his master to his apartments.

Castelli's groom and personal attendant, known in the circus by the name of Whanks, was a great favourite with all of them. He had travelled with many of the large circuses, and had visited all the chief European cities. When he had been engaged by Castelli, his name caused much amusement amongst the artistes and in the stables. For a time he put up with the banter, and then one evening he told a group of his fellows why he was called 'Whanks.'

'You may laugh and jeer at me,' he said, 'but there's a sad reason why I like the name. Some years ago I was one of the attendants belonging to a celebrated troupe of acrobats. One of them, a little fellow, became awfully fond of me—he were a wee little chap, but spry, and sharp as a needle. Sometimes I would take him oranges, apples or cakes unbeknown to his trainer. One day after a rehearsal he comes to me and says: "Carl"—I was Carl then—"Carl, when I was at home my father called me 'Whanks.' I loved him the best in all the world, and when he died no one called me 'Whanks' again. I love you, Carl, almost as much as my father loved me, so may I call you 'Whanks'? Poor little fellow, he was only nine years old, but after that he always called me Whanks, and the rest of the troupe took it up. One night when the "show" was on at a circus in Vienna one of the bars snapped and Franz fell with a thud to the sawdust beneath. He never moved, but lay there like a log. They carried him out, and he died in my arms. Once, just before the last, he opened his eyes and said feebly: "Whanks, am I much hurt?" That was the only time he spoke. You've jeered at the name a goodish deal, but maybe you will not, now you know how I got at it.'

The grooms and stablemen turned away, and one or two of them murmured 'Poor little chap!' Soon the story spread, and no smile or sneer ever betrayed itself to the owner of the dead child's name.

Whom Castelli's Whanks had originally been no one knew. He never mentioned, within anyone's recollection, either his father or mother, or where he had been brought up. The only relation he ever spoke of was an aged aunt, who had promised to leave him what little money she possessed, together with her cottage and effects, and of this small prospective fortune Whanks was never tired of talking. It was his one thought, his daydream. His chums in the circus were delighted to stand him 'drinks,' for then the estimation of his coming wealth rose considerably, and much fun they had at the expense of him and his money. Unfortunately these drinks became very frequent, and his master had often threatened to discharge him. But when he was sober he was so useful and handy that he was forgiven and retained. His love for children and animals was excessive, and many a weary apprentice, both boys and girls, owed a debt of gratitude to Whanks for little acts of kindness shown them at their rehearsals. Every horse and dog at the circus loved him, and even 'Bruin' was more tractable with him, and often when the great rough bear refused to enter the ring to practise his tricks Whanks was called upon to induce him to do as he was bidden, and the animal became at once more docile. Thus it was that Whanks was too handy about the place to be dismissed.

Castelli knew his worth, but he never let his man forget that *he* was master, and never spared him for the sake of past good services.

When they reached Castelli's apartments, his master laid his riding-whip on the table, and then turning to his man, fiercely asked,—

'What the devil do you mean by getting tight? Can't I leave you for an hour without your running to the "pub," you besotted fool? The sooner you clear out of our show and drink yourself to death the better!' and he threw a look of disgust and contempt upon the shrinking shamefaced man before him.

'I couldn't help myself, sir, indeed I couldn't. Even when I got outside that blessed "pub" I says,

"No, I won't go in," and the rest says, "Whanks, be a man!" I—'

'A man, indeed,' broke in Castelli; 'a beast you mean.'

'Begging your pardon, sir, I says to them, "Not to-day, mates," and was a-moving off when one of our stablemen says, "One drink can't hurt you, Whanks, unless you're a fool."'

'Just what you are,' replied Castelli severely.

'I can't help it, sir; them men worrits my life out. All day long it's "Whanks come here or go there and give us a help," till I'm blowed if I knows what I am doing.'

'You know the way to that cursed bar fast enough. You ought to be ashamed of yourself, getting drunk and fighting in the street; you're a disgrace to the show. What do you suppose will be the end of it?'

'I wish I could tell you, sir, but I can't, so there's an end to that. I makes up my mind I'll never take another glass, and I says to myself, "I'll never get drunk again, never," and then someone comes along friendly like and I goes as far as the "pub" corner with them, and they persuades me against my will, sir, to have just one glass, and all of a sudden like I feels like as if I was swimming in the sea, and—'

The sea—that recalled the bright vision of the afternoon to Castelli's mind, and he exclaimed angrily,—

'Here, stop that infernal rubbish, and do not quote the sea to me. You tell me you can't help getting drunk, but look here,' and he stepped quite close to him, 'look here, you idiot, mark my words, let me catch you drunk once again and out you go neck and crop, remember that; and now be off to your work, you lazy, good-for-nothing loafer.'

'I am very sorry, sir,' replied the man in a penitent tone, and something like tears glistened in his eyes. 'When I get my aunt's money I shall—'

'You and your blessed aunt go to blazes. Be off, I tell you, or I will fling you down the stairs. Go,' he roared, 'do you hear?'

The man walked to the door, and then he turned a pathetic face to his infuriated master.

'You won't send me away this time, sir, will you?' he pleaded. 'I couldn't leave you and the horses and the old place. I'll never get drunk again, sir, never.'

'Once more, *will* you be gone, and shut the door after you if you are sober enough.'

Whanks closed the door, and as he walked slowly down the stairs he took a red handkerchief from his pocket and wiped away the tears that ran down his cheeks. 'The master's right, I am a fool. I've only got what I deserved; but I can't leave him, somehow I can't, although his tantrums are awful to put up with. If I had only got my aunt's money I'd never ask him for another blessed quid, but I'd stay on at the show all the same.'

He sighed, and went heavy-hearted to his work. His 'chums' noticed his downcast looks, and they guessed 'there'd been a jolly big row between him and his master,' but they wisely refrained from alluding to the subject.

Castelli, having expended his wrath, sat down to a hurried tea, and again his thoughts went back to the fair girl he had met. He could not forget her; he wondered where she was, what she thought of him, and if they should ever meet again.

'It's time I had a wife, I think,' he said to himself. 'What a beastly muddle everything is in. I'm sick of it all.'

Certainly his surroundings were not very pleasing to the eye—sofas and chairs were strewn with papers, circus bills, and posters, under the easy-chair boots and shoes lay thrown together—it was plain that no one ever tried to give the place a look of home. It was unmistakably 'apartments for a single gentleman.'

Castelli pushed his cup from him, rose from the table, lit a cigar, and started for the circus. In another hour a delighted audience were witnessing the performance of 'Castelli's performing horses,' and admiring their sleek coats and wonderful feats, and a buzz of delight went round from stalls to pit, and pit to the gallery. Their trainer, too, came in for a share of the admiration so lavishly offered. His winning smile, his graceful bearing, the fascinating manner were positive pleasures to his people, and when he offered some sugar to his horses in the ring, and spoke to them so gently, he received a perfect ovation, and then he looked more handsome still, with a flush of triumph resting on his face. He was *so* kind the people thought. Had they forgotten there was another picture called *Behind the Scenes?*

## CHAPTER III.

### LOOKING BACK.

LEILA GURNEY having got rid of her saturated garments, and having arrayed herself in a dressing-gown, sat down in a low chair by the bedroom window. The afternoon had been very adventurous and fatiguing, so she wished to sit quietly for a time to rest and think.

Before her stretched the pretty rustic garden, from whence came sweet odours, borne on the summer air, of roses, lilies, and lavender. Each offered their fragrance and their beauty.

Generally these gifts of the bounteous earth had given her the greatest pleasure, but they were unheeded now. She was wondering what would have been said had her dead body been washed up on the shore at the ebb-tide. She tried to picture how her father would have received the news, and if he would have cared so very much. Perhaps he would have grieved a little when he heard she was dead. Then her thoughts reverted to her brother Tom—dear, faithful, loving Tom! She could imagine *him* reading her father's letter telling him of the accident, and in foreign lands alone he would mourn and fret for a sister very dearly loved. It was the one joy of her life to know how his heart yearned towards her.

More serious thoughts followed, and she leant back in her chair and rested her head upon her small white hand. Supposing she had been drowned, where would she have been now? It was difficult for her to realise what the boundary between life and death must be. She could form no idea of the great void where the soul speeds on its last flight. And yet how near she had been to that awful veil which separates this world from the realms beyond the grave. She shuddered at the thought of the stillness of death, of her youth and life nearly lost, with only eternity in all its vagueness before her when earthly hopes had perished.

She was young enough not to wish for the pure and perfect rest of heaven. She had no longing for the land where all is gladness and the weary cease to sigh. If her life had been like a sail in a storm, the brightness of youth had made happy beams, and she had no wish to die. How thankful she was that the dark cloud which overshadowed the future had rolled away and left her life—she was so young to die.

There had been times when Leila Gurney would have resigned her life without a sigh; days upon which no light seemed to break through the gloom; hours when her lonely agony seemed too intense to be borne. She would have left life in those days willingly, but now she was changed. Something seemed to have come over her suddenly, just as the sun shines after the storm has passed.

Was not this change due to the young and handsome man who had inspired her with such admiration? To herself she wondered why she felt so interested in him, and why she could not forget his gracious smiles and kindly words of sympathy.

It was the first spark of love, but she did not know it as yet, when it was a pleasant dream, but the spell would break some day, and the bud spread and open its petals to the light, and then it would blossom into all the beauties of true love.

But she would have smiled if Cupid had whispered 'it is Love.'

Leila Gurney was just eighteen years of age; her life had been very far from happy—trouble had played a far more prominent part than joy or innocent pleasures, which girlhood has the right to demand. Her father, Charles Gurney, had been a very prosperous stockbroker, living in a good-sized house in Weymouth Street, Portland Place. When Leila and her brother Tom, two years her junior, were children, every luxury and indulgence was showered upon them by their fond father.

He had been past middle life when he brought

his handsome bride to Weymouth Street. But no young lover could have bestowed half the love and care upon his sweetheart that Charles Gurney did upon his young wife. Her wishes were his first consideration, her whims and fancies the pleasure of his life to gratify. Nothing was too much trouble to win her thanks or gain a smile from her lips. He was blind to all her faults, and when he came to find that she loved pleasure seeking abroad more than her home, and that admiration from the outside world delighted her better than his genuine praise, he put it down to being 'only natural' for one so young and beautiful, and he consented ungrudgingly to anything which made her happy.

She was his life, his all, and when a daughter was born to him he gave it none of the affection which he considered due to the mother. His love for the child was great because it was hers, but the baby girl must not steal the attentions which belonged solely to her mother. Her husband had wished that the child should be called Ida, because it had been his mother's name, and her memory was very precious to him; but his wife had fixed her mind on Leila, and as in all things his wife had her way the child was christened Leila. Her selfishness was so great that she would not even add his choice of a name to hers. She hated the idea of her husband interfering; besides, what was *his* mother to her? It never struck her that love for the son should surely engender some respect for the woman he called mother. In spite of all his love, and care, all his efforts to make her life one perpetual ray of sunshine, she would not please him by calling her child, and his, by the name he loved so dearly. At first her refusal vexed him considerably, but he banished from his mind any unkindly thoughts which arose. After all, a woman had every right to call her daughter by the name she liked the best, and Leila was very poetical and pretty, and so the shadow passed away. He had one hope, however, and that was that the baby girl would be the means of keeping his wife more at home. He was so fond of a domestic life that the constant round of pleasures had become the bane of his existence. But the advent of the child, he found, made no difference to the mother's gay life, and when two years afterwards a boy, Tom, was born, to his inexpressible grief, he saw the two children growing up left entirely to the charge of servants.

Graver trouble, however, was at hand. His income, although large, was not sufficient for constant extravagances, and at a time of life when he should have been enjoying more rest he had to redouble his energies and work harder to meet the constant demands made upon him for his wife's debts. He at last took a partner to help him, and for a time matters seemed brighter, and Charles Gurney hoped to pull another fortune together, for the sake of the woman who kept him toiling that she might spend and make merry.

But a very dark day was approaching, a day when he came home to find his wife fled—gone to her destruction and ruin, desecrating the sacred name of wife, and leaving a curse, and a shame almost too heavy to be borne by the husband and hapless children.

She had chosen in preference to her home, and to the purity of his love, the villainous overtures of her husband's partner. The tall, handsome, brilliant Herbert Clifford had come between her and those who had loved her so tenderly.

With winning smiles the seducer had won her from her vows, he had flattered her, offered her false words of devotion. It was nothing to him that she was giving up home, husband, and children. He did not care if in the after years she cursed him for teaching her to sin. She would be disgraced for ever, he knew that, but the pleasure would be his, the penalty hers alone.

She forgot the retribution to come. His fair speeches made her forget to think of a day when the villain would tire of his victim, and leave her alone to face the cruel coldness of the world—a woman branded with shame as the faithless wife, the dishonoured mother.

Leila Gurney was fifteen years of age, and her brother Tom thirteen, when the terrible trouble fell upon them. Both were old enough to realise the horror of their position. A certain sympathy was bestowed on them for the loss of their mother, but it was not the same kind of feeling which neighbours show when death has left children to mourn for those they loved. There were no tender words, no shake of the hand, no eyes dimmed with tears, and no offers of help were made to the lonely girl and boy.

The people who had been such dear friends of their mother were very sorry for them, but they kept aloof themselves, and took care that their children did the same.

These slights wounded Leila's and Tom's sensitive natures most cruelly, and to avoid the gaze of the curious they sat together alone, and only ventured out when the stars shone and the darkness grew over the great city. Their father's love for his erring wife turned to the bitterest hate; the channels of his heart, through which such adoration had coursed, were choked with anger, disappointment, and revenge. He had been so devoted to her that the loss seemed doubly cruel. She had deserted him after all the sacrifices he had made for her happiness.

He never attempted to trace the fugitives; he lost heart, health, and spirits. His business grew neglected, he showed no more love for home or children, he cared no longer how his affairs went. Was he not disgraced in the eyes of all the world? But there was one feeling which remained—a feeling of revenge, if such it could be called. His wife had dishonoured him and left him for another, but that other should never be able to bestow his name upon her; such as she had become she should remain to the end of her life. He would not divorce her, he would not give her her freedom. She had brought shame on the name of Gurney, let her bear it and no other to her death, and to this resolve he was steadfast.

Matters became worse, money came in slowly, and then he called his girl and boy together and told them he was a ruined man, that the home must be broken up at once, that delay would only make things worse for them all, and that Tom could not return to Harrow, and that he must put out of his mind all hopes of Oxford.

A few days later they bade good-bye to the only home they had ever known, and life began in a country cottage, with their father and one servant. Briarhill was a lonely, dull spot far away from the haunts of man. There they could eke out their fallen fortunes unknown to those who had been their friends in prosperous days. An old church, an ancient grammar school, and a cluster of houses formed the small town, if it could be called by such a name. The inhabitants had known each other all their lives, and were not prepared to venture on acquaintance with strangers. This suited Charles Gurney, who had become morose and gloomy—sitting hours in the tiny garden smoking, and never addressing a word to those about him. Fortunately for his children the greatest love existed between them, and they helped each other to bear their troubles bravely. Tom was sent to the grammar school by his father, but Leila was left to her own devices until the evening, when her brother devoted his time to her education.

But after a while the story of his mother's sin leaked out, and his schoolfellows chaffed him continually. Being proud and haughty, he resented this treatment. One day the affair came to a crisis. He turned on his tormentors, and fought for his name and his honour. One boy in particular, the bully of the school, came in for such treatment at Tom's hands as he had never experienced before. He did not appear at school again for a week, but Charles Gurney was requested to remove his son from the school.

For months after this Tom wandered about at home utterly miserable and sick at heart. At last he wrote to an old Harrow schoolfellow, whose father was a Transvaal merchant and had started a store at Malan, on the road from Durban to Pretoria. This merchant knew the actual position of the youth, and felt keenly for his sufferings. Thinking he would do better away from surroundings which made him dwell on his family disgrace, he offered to take him as an assistant to his manager at the store, where everything, from a drink to a pair of boots, was sold to the Boers and travellers.

When Charles Gurney was asked if he could spare his son he replied in the affirmative, but with such careless grace was the consent given that Tom felt his absence would be a pleasure rather than a pain to his father. He knew why, for often in the glad days he had praised Tom for his likeness to his mother. 'You're more like her,' he would say, 'than your sister. Just her eyes and expression, Tom, my boy.'

Was it any wonder that his father no longer wished that ever living picture to be daily before him, reminding him of his beautiful wife, now worse than dead to him?

Before Tom sailed he made his sister a vow that, if he lived so long, he would come home when he was older and take revenge on the man who brought about the ruin of all their hopes and happiness.

After her brother had left Leila began to droop. She became tired and weary of the awful monotony, worse a thousand times since Tom had gone; there were no long walks for her now, all day she wandered about alone. Her father never talked to her, indeed he seemed to ignore her presence. At last she grew so ill and weak as to attract the attention of the doctor, who had been called in to see her father upon two occasions.

'Gurney, if you don't send your daughter to the seaside I am afraid she will go into a decline; her case seems to me critical. Can't you manage it?'

So spoke Dr Burton one fine sunny day in early June.

'It's no use telling me that,' replied Charles Gurney. 'I've no one to send her with, and then it is expensive, and my income is so very limited. I can't do it, doctor,' he continued irritably.

'I am afraid you will *have* to use your income to bury her, then, very shortly, and as to having no one to send her with, I can manage that. Let her go to Sandcliffe; it's a quiet place, and she can have rooms with an old servant of mine who is married and has a pretty cottage there. My wife and the little ones went there two years ago; everything is cheap, clean, and comfortable. May I arrange that, Gurney, so as to save you time and trouble?'

He pleaded hard for the delicate, lonely girl, who was fretting her life away in such uncongenial surroundings.

'If you like to take the trouble, of course you can. I sha'n't. I should think there's too much of the mother in the girl to make it desirable to send her away alone to the seaside,' he added ungraciously.

So it was decided, and a few days later she was enjoying the bracing air of Sandcliffe, happier in mind, healthier in body. She had written to Tom such a long letter, and sent him, with her love, five pounds, just half the cheque put into her hands by the good doctor's wife the day she left.

'There are lots of little things you may need, my dear,' Mrs Burton had said, 'and that will make you less troublesome to your father.'

The girl had blushed, stammered her thanks, and shed a tear or two at the unexpected kindness, and gone her way—a way so free, so unfettered, that health and spirits would soon return to the young life, at least so the doctor and his wife hoped, for they pitied her deeply.

But father and friends were soon to be forgotten. Had not a bright star arisen, which lighted her path and left all else in gloom? It shone upon her mind, her heart, her very inmost soul. She could see nothing else, think of nothing but the radiant future before her.

But the star might wane, and what of the darkness then? Would it not be terrible after the shining light?

It shone—she never dreamt of the waning.

## CHAPTER IV.

MAKING AN ENEMY.

Three or four weeks had sped their course since Leila had been rescued from the Nab's Head Rock. To her it had been a very happy time, for Castelli had been her daily companion. Somehow or other he had found out the time of her strolls, and whenever possible had ridden over to Sandcliffe. It was an acquaintance which grew unconsciously; their appreciation of each other's society had so far been of a tacit nature.

She had been so lonely, so weary of her monotonous life that she had come to recognise him as a delightful companion. It was so pleasant to have someone to make her a consideration and to plan pleasures to cheer at least some hours of the solitary days.

One August morning he had ridden over on 'Rubicon,' bringing with him 'Athol' and Whanks. When he arrived at Sandcliffe sands he dismounted, and calling his dog, he dispatched Whanks with the horses to the village inn, then he sauntered along the beach to the trysting place. She was there before him. Truly she was a picture fit for the canvas of some great artist, he thought, as he advanced towards her, with her plain dress of pure white, unrelieved by colour excepting a bunch of crimson roses placed in her girdle, and her large hat, with the golden curls just resting on her classic brow.

He thought her most beautiful as she came forward to meet him, with a blush mantling her happy face, and giving a lustre to her wondrous eyes.

He would like to have kissed her, but he controlled the wish.

'Good morning, Leila.' He raised his hat, and gave her one of his winning smiles, as he gazed at her with fond admiration. 'I have not kept you waiting. I want a long chat with you to-day. What do you say if we stroll on towards the Downs? Are you tired?'

'Oh, no,' she replied gleefully, for was not the prospect of a walk with him the one bliss of her cheerless life. 'But where is " Rubicon,"' she added suddenly. 'Have you and " Athol " walked from Bayhaven? What a lovely creature he is. I love him so much.'

'Do you?' he asked, smiling again. '" Athol " is lucky to have won your love, but you see he is crab hunting now, and I fear does not appreciate the honour so much as he should. My groom has " Rubicon " up at the inn. I wanted to be free to-day. In the meantime he will have a feed of corn before his journey home.'

Together on the shingly beach, under the steep rugged cliffs they sauntered, he holding her hand for fear she should trip. Suddenly he paused.

'Leila, let us sit down.' There was something unusual in his tone, and she looked up into his face. She saw then how grave he was. They sat on a flat waterworn stone, and then he explained to her very gently who he was, and his occupation. She listened attentively, and he was delighted to find that her smile did not fade, that no disappointment or disgust overshadowed her face. When he ceased speaking she replied,—

'How clever you must be to ride in a circus. I have been to several, but not since I grew up. May I come to Bayhaven and see the circus there, and all your horses? I should so enjoy it,' she added with emphasis.

'Some day, Leila. You must wait just a little while. You see there is no train to bring you home. It must be some time when I can drive you back. Would you like that?'

'Yes,' she answered quietly.

His voice sounded like music to her ears, so rich, so gentle, yet so firm and kind.

'Leila,' he continued, 'I have grown very fond of you, very fond, and knowing that I belong to a circus, do you think you could return me some affection, or would my profession debar me from all such hope? All my future happiness depends upon your reply. In society, I know, we are counted as outcasts, but we have hearts, all the same, and can love despite the sawdust and the ring.'

He stopped speaking and looked to see what effect his words had upon his lovely companion. He showed none of the nervousness of an ardent love. He waited her reply calmly, and with a quiet dignity worthy of a king.

She did not answer for a moment, but her cheeks grew crimson, and she toyed restlessly with some stones she had picked up whilst he was speaking.

'There is nothing wrong in being engaged in a circus, is there?' she asked archly. 'I should like it beyond anything. I love horses and riding, but,' and she became very shy, 'I do *like* you very, very much.'

He kissed her as she spoke, and she did not resist it.

'Can you change "like" into "love," Leila?' he asked. 'That is what I want to know.'

'Yes,' she answered, getting still more confused 'but—'

'But what, my beauty?' he asked, putting his arm around her and drawing her closer to him.

'There's Tom,' she added. 'I always tell Tom everything. You know how I love him,' she said simply.

He had foreseen this difficulty and had his reply ready.

'Don't you think Tom would be glad to hear you were comfortably married? Do you not suppose it would be a great anxiety off his mind to know his sister was happy? Leila, he would advise you to marry the man you love if he were here. That should be sufficient guide for you.'

'But I should like to ask him before I decide to return your love. I must write to Tom, indeed I must.'

'Leila, dearest Leila, won't you be my wife, and let me care for you and love you? It will be time enough to tell Tom and your father when we are man and wife.'

She shook her head gravely.

'It will not do. I could not deceive Tom for all the world.'

'Is that your determination?' he asked her severely.

She noticed the change in his voice, but she held firmly to her desire.

'Yes, I am quite determined, quite. I can do nothing without Tom's advice.'

'So you will risk my happiness and yours for the sake of a boy's opinion. He cannot know what is best for you. Once more, my darling, will you be my wife?'

'If Tom says "Yes,"' she replied resolutely.

He knew she was too fond of him to withstand his offer very long. He must marry her before her brother or father got any idea of the affair or he felt sure she would never be his wife at all. He must use diplomacy in the matter at once or he would lose the chance within his grasp.

'So you won't trust me,' he replied sternly, getting up from his seat. 'If you loved me as I love you no one in the world would stand between us. I am terribly hurt, Leila. All the joy has gone out of my life.'

'Don't say that, Emilio, please don't,' and she rose and stood by his side. 'Don't be vexed with me, but I love Tom so much.'

'Better than you do me, that is plain enough. Under those conditions we had better say good-bye.'

He turned and faced her. She saw how white and stern he looked, and she already repented of her words.

'Is it to be good-bye?' he repeated somewhat gently. 'Is it, Leila?'

'No,' she added sadly, 'no, not good-bye. I could not bear that; it would kill me. Don't go. Emilio, forgive me.'

He kissed her again and again, and in the first flush of her youthful love she promised to keep Tom and her father in ignorance of her engagement.

She was so inexperienced, so afraid of losing the only man who had ever loved her, and there was no loving motherly hand to guide her, no one to bid her beware.

'We will make this spot a rendezvous for the next few days, Leila. I do not think it would be wise for me to go to Green's Cottages to see you, but my man can bring you messages and my letters to you; the replies you can return by him. It is best to arrange that, then there will be no curiosity at the post office. For the present our arrangements must be kept dark, for your sake, do you understand me?'

'Yes,' she replied hesitatingly; 'but why cannot you call on me? My cousin's *fiancé* always came to dinner and tea, and spent long evenings with her, and, anyhow, your man will know me if he comes to the house.'

'Your cousin did not live alone, darling, as you do, and as for my man, well, he will be sworn to secrecy. He will have full directions to ask for you and come straight up into your sitting-room. Do not fear him, he is safe enough; but do not offer him beer or wine on any account, for Whanks is too fond of his glass.'

'Whanks! what a name!'

He told her the story of the name 'Whanks,' and she sighed and determined to be his friend even before she had seen him.

'Well, Leila, the time goes on, I must be off. There's an afternoon performance, and I am due at the circus at half-past two. Good-bye, my darling, my pet! Kiss me Leila; you are mine for ever.'

What a glorious light came into his dark eyes! What rapture was there as he spoke so tenderly and kindly! How happy she was! She forgot the deception, the vile secrecy imposed upon her. Was not his love all the world to her? What was there she would not have done to win his smile?

'Good-bye, Emilio. Will you take this rose and wear it for my sake?' She pulled the only white one she had from among the crimson. 'I love white roses, they are my favourite flowers. I will give or send you one every day. Will you wear it, dear?'

'Always darling. Every night when I go into the ring I will wear your love token. The pure rose, Leila, shall remind me of your promise to-day. I will use this one to-night; it is but a bud, so it will not fade so quickly as would the open flower, and to-morrow you will send me another—is that so?'

'Yes, every day until the months of roses are over.'

'By that time I hope I shall have claimed my own white rose,' and he kissed her most affectionately.

He took the flower and went his way.

Her love was in the beauty of its prime, her joy ecstatic. The present and the future were crowned with glorious hopes, and pictured with fond delight.

But hopes are sometimes like butterflies, that rise on the breath of fancy whenever the sunbeams lure them.

Signor Emilio Castelli was happy in his love for Leila Gurney. He had been engaged to her nearly a fortnight, during which time he and Whanks had paid many visits to Sandcliffe. It wanted nearly half-an-hour before the evening performance, but Castelli had gone to the circus early to see one of his valuable horses which was a little out of condition. He was sitting in a small office, which he shared with two other showmen, thinking of Leila. Outside there was heard horses' feet, and a general running to and fro, then an angry voice was raised and oaths fell plentifully, a crack of a whip and boy's cry of pain. Castelli was used to such things, and they did not dispel his thoughts; he was in no hurry, he was already dressed for the ring, with a white rosebud in his coat.

Whilst he was thinking of Leila, 'Cleo,' the celebrated tight-rope artiste, was wondering why

Castelli had changed so much towards her, and to-night she had determined to find out. She sat on the bare wooden table in a dressing-room allotted to her and a female acrobat. Her partner's 'turn' did not come on till late, so Cleo had the room to herself. She was a fine, handsome woman, about twenty-five years of age; and her beauty had rendered her popular wherever she appeared. In figure and face she was considered perfection, whilst her wit and repartee had made her a great favourite in the circus.

Bayhaven was partial to equestrian performances, and the circus proprietor had put up a temporary building for the season, and to it flocked both residents and visitors.

Cleo had attracted a great deal of attention and her 'show' had been one of the successes of the season. Three years before, she had met Castelli in a circus in Liverpool. She fell desperately in love with him, and for a time he seemed to return it, as she thought, for he humoured her fancies and spent much time in her company. But when the circus closed for the season, and they each went to new engagements, she was bitterly disappointed that he did not ask her to be his wife. Castelli had never dreamt of marrying the 'greatest tight-rope walker in Europe.' She was beautiful, it was true, but vulgar, coarse, and passionate, and his dreams were of a lady gentle and refined.

Cleo threw a long black cloak, lined with fur, over her bespangled tights, and then crossed the sawdust spread passage to Castelli's room. In answer to his response she opened the door.

'Halloa, Castelli, all alone? Did you ever feel such infernal draughts as there are in this place?

Matchbox partitions, nothing but matchbox,' and she closed the door behind her. 'My gracious! what *is* that?' she exclaimed. 'Why, if it ain't a dog tied to the leg of the table! Is that for *me*, Castelli? What a little sight to be sure! Oh, I suppose it is one of Zaro's performing dogs, is it?'

'No, it's mine,' replied Castelli, not too well pleased at being disturbed.

'*Yours*, that fluffy white thing—where's Athol then?'

'At home,' he replied curtly.

'I say, Castelli, guess what I have got for you.'

'I can't guess. What a damned fool you are, Cleo!'

'Oh, that's the tone, is it? You want to be off with the old love, do you, for the new?' and she laughed impudently.

She had been sure there was somebody else held in preference to her, for Castelli had worn the same kind of flower in his buttonhole every night. She knew some lady must be the donor.

'Be quiet,' he exclaimed angrily; 'you're not the old love, anyhow, and I'm hanged if you are the new!'

'Oh, so there *is* a new, is there? That's the game! Who's the girl?'

Her eyes had become more brilliant as she spoke, and Castelli tried to turn the subject off with a joke.

'Well, we won't quarrel,' she said, assuming her natural tone, 'will we, dear? Now, will you wear this to please me to-night?' and she took from under her cloak a buttonhole of exotic flowers. 'They will suit you better than that white rose.'

She held it towards him, but he refused to take it from her.

'I shall wear the one I have, and none other,' he said.

In a moment, like a flash of fire, her passion and indignation burst forth.

'Will you, I vow you sha'n't,' and she stepped close up to him, quivering in every limb with violent excitement. Before he was aware she had caught hold of his coat in her eager desire to snatch the flower from its place. In an instant he resisted her with all his great physical power and flung her from him.

'What she-cat gave you those roses?' she screamed. 'You've been glad enough to wear my flowers before to-night. I've the right to know who gave you the white rose—tell me, do you hear, you treacherous man?' Her breath came fast and strong as she gasped: 'Answer me, do you understand me, Castelli?'

Her face was distorted, defiant, and maddened with rage; it seemed as if the very devil was before him. The flowers she had brought had fallen to the ground. He saw them lying there in all their delicate beauty, but ruthlessly he put out his foot and crushed the petals into a shapeless mass.

'There are your flowers, and if you don't get out of this room I'll thrash you as I would a hound. Get out, or by heaven I'll keep my word.'

'You villain! You hypocrite! You—'

But further conversation was put a stop to by the bell ringing for the first 'turn.' He put her out of his way as if she were a dog, and taking up his long whip from the table, went into the ring, smiling as he did so.

Cleo, left alone, foiled, baffled, and exhausted, devoured and pained by jealousy, was convinced that her doubts were right, and that Castelli, the only man she loved, had passed her by for another. But how could she prove it? That was the difficulty. Sauntering to her room, she saw Whanks standing helping the grooms to get ready Castelli's performing horses. In a moment an idea struck her. If she could only get Whanks on her side the rest would be easy enough. Her passion was gone now, but her eyes still retained their bright steely look, as if a hidden revenge was lurking behind her artificial smile.

She went up to Whanks softly and asked,—

'Whanks, shall you be busy to-morrow?'

'Depends on the master, miss. I might have a minute or so to spare. I ain't sure.'

'I wish you would come round to my place. I want a job done to some rope. Can you come, do you think?'

'I'll do my best, miss, and leastways I can ask the master, when he comes out of the ring after the horses has performed, and let you know what time he can best spare me, miss.'

Whanks had often been allowed by Castelli to do odd jobs for Cleo, and so the request did not astonish him.

'Don't trouble to ask your master, Whanks. I'd rather you did not. Just run round to me after morning rehearsal if you can.'

'Right you are, miss. I'll try and come as nigh to one o'clock as I can,' and the man touched his hat respectfully.

Castelli passed her as he left the ring, but he never glanced at her, and the white rose was still in his coat.

'To-morrow, wait until to-morrow,' she murmured, 'and I'll find out his game. Trust me for that. I'm not quite the fool he takes me for.'

She had planned her revenge.

## CHAPTER V

### ENVY AND HATRED.

A WEEK had passed. Cleo had been very cautious in all her plans. Whanks had been enticed to her rooms under various pretexts. She had given him sufficient to drink, but not enough to make him intoxicated, for had that occurred she knew that his master would question him, and that would ill suit her purpose.

To Castelli she was particularly attentive, meeting him with a smile, and being more gracious than usual; neither by tone nor manner did she betray that he had offended her.

But the time was passing, and every day her chances of seeing Whanks alone grew less, as Castelli might find out his visits, then the game would be up.

One afternoon she sent for Whanks, and determined it should be a final visit. She gave him small quantities of whisky and water, not much at a time, but little by little, which had the effect of making him muddled, yet he was sufficiently sober to understand her questions and to give coherent replies.

When he was off his guard she began with great dexterity to find out all the particulars she wished to know regarding Castelli.

'You're away a good deal from the rehearsals lately, Whanks, I suppose you are engaged in the stables more?'

'Yes, I has more business out of the circus altogether now, very particular, for the master. I haven't time to go into the stables neither,' added the man, with an air of grandeur.

'It's nice to be trusted with particular "bis" for the master; it shows he relies on you,' she replied cunningly.

'Ay, he trusts me fast enough. Ah, I know a thing or two, bless your heart, I know a thing or two!' and he laughed stupidly.

'I daresay you know a good many things, Whanks,' she responded gently.

She tried to appear unconcerned, in case her curiosity should become too pointed.

'I rather think I do, Miss Cleo. Ay, the master is a funny one,' he continued, half drowsy, 'very funny. He's on with one, and then another, and I've enough to do going his errints.'

'You have to go a long way for him, I suppose?' she asked with skilful indifference.

'Well, I do now and again.'

Although his comprehension was somewhat dulled, he retained sufficient control over himself to be a little on his guard.

Cleo saw this, and she refilled his glass. Another drink would bring him up to the point. As she anticipated, he became more talkative after the last and stronger glass of whisky.

'Yes, I has to go to Sandcliffe most days when the master don't go hisself. First there's a dog to be took, then a hoss for an hour or two, then a book, or hosses and letters and messages.' He paused after so long a speech, looking dazed, and quite unconscious that he had betrayed his master's secret.

'Who do you take these things to, Whanks? I suppose some gentleman friend? I know Castelli *has* friends in the neighbourhood.'

The latter part of her sentence was purely a make up, but it answered her purpose to draw the man out to say more.

'Ah, that's telling who it is; there ain't much of

the gentleman in the business; but I sha'n't split. I promised master I would not, and I won't.'

He rose to go, standing with his hand on the back of the chair to steady himself.

'I must be off, Miss Cleo. I've got the hosses to see about. If I'd only my aunt's money I'd never look after another blessed hoss.'

Cleo smiled. She had gained all the information she needed, and she did not press him to remain; indeed it was best that he should get clear out of her rooms without delay.

Partially satisfied with her interview with Whanks, there was still much more to find out, and she resolved to go over to Sandcliffe to see if she could discover anything for herself.

Accordingly the next day she set off by the morning coach, and after partaking of some refreshment at the inn, she started up the village. As she passed a small shop she saw a fisherman standing at the door with a kibsey full of fresh shrimps.

'Good morning,' she said kindly, and the man looked round with astonishment to see such a handsome woman in the remote village. Her attire was elegant, she must be someone very grand, he thought, so he touched his hat respectfully and replied,—

'Good morning, my lady; beautiful weather we are having now.'

'Beautiful,' she added, 'and this place looks so lovely I cannot think why more people don't come to see it.'

'Are you staying here, lady?' asked the man with interest.

'No, unfortunately, I am not. I came over this morning in the coach just to see the place. I have been staying in Bayhaven. You don't often get visitors here, I suppose?' she said unaffectedly.

'Not often, lady; it's agin us, having no trains. Folks don't care about coming in the coach. It's ackard when there's children and luggage. No, we sha'n't hope to do much till we gits the rail. They've talked of that a long time, but there it ends. Let me see,' added the man, taking off his hat and putting it on again dubiously, 'we has one visitor here, of course, a young lady lodging up at Green's Cottages—a very pretty lass she is too, quite a lady, so they says. I takes shrimps up there most days.'

'Oh, well I hope you will soon get the line here, and then plenty of people will come.'

As she spoke she pressed a shilling into his hand.

He thanked her profoundly, and she turned to go, but suddenly she inquired carelessly,—

'Where are Green's Cottages? Far from here?'

'There they lies, lady. Them there white ones on the slope of the hill. The prettiest houses in the place to my thinking.'

'Thank you. Good-day.'

The man watched her up the hill, and then he went into the back parlour behind the shop and informed his wife of the bit of news.

'She was grand enough dressed, Marier Ann,' he said, 'but I can't help thinking as she was after somebody or something. Maybe I'm wrong, but methinks I'm on the right track. I wonder if she's aught to do with the young lady up at the Cottages. There's summit going on.'

As his faithful spouse could not enlighten him, he started off with his shrimps, telling the story of the lady at every house he called.

Cleo turned down a narrow path which was cut out of the side of the cliffs, and walked on to see if anyone was on the beach in the vicinity of the Cottages. She went on for some way, when a horse in the distance arrested her attention. She stopped suddenly, and putting up one hand to shade her eyes, she scanned it closely.

'That's "Fleetfoot,"' she said to herself, 'and the man on him is none other than Castelli. It's he, sure enough,' she argued. 'Now I will watch the farce out at a safe distance.'

She returned up the narrow path and regained the road. He must not see her, whatever came to pass. From there she could observe without being seen. She sat down and waited.

She heard the horse gallop past on the sand beneath. She heard Castelli's voice urging the animal on. When they had passed she rose up quickly to be sure it was he. One glance sufficed to tell her that her suspicions were confirmed.

For a moment she felt inclined to call out loudly after him, but she refrained. She would not be rash or indiscreet, but abide her time. Later she went towards the Cottages, and when close to them she saw a tall, delicate looking girl coming in the opposite direction. No doubt this was the lady come from her meeting with Castelli. Probably she had reached the road by another path up the cliffs.

As Cleo passed her she noticed how beautiful the girl was, with her simple gown of pink cotton, relieved with bunches of white roses at her throat and waist. She knew now where the flowers came from each evening for Castelli. Under one arm she carried a small dog, the silver bells on his collar tinkling as they passed; she was sure it was the same animal that Castelli had tied to the leg of his table.

Cleo turned back after the girl. She must know which cottage was the home of Castelli's sweetheart.

'Oh, it's the house with the white roses, is it?' she said to herself. 'Ah, my lady, you won't go on in your fool's paradise, if I can help it, very long. So, you think Castelli an angel, no doubt; I think he is a devil—yes, a devil,' she repeated loudly

On her way home she decided to let Castelli know she had found him out; at the same time she would see what persuasion would effect before speaking her mind to him.

On the evening of the day on which she had visited Sandcliffe she walked unceremoniously to his room.

'What do *you* want?' he said somewhat curtly. 'I'm really very busy to-night.'

'Have you not time to speak to me?' she asked quickly; 'you used to like a chat with me. You're strangely altered, Emilio. I don't believe you care for me one little bit now, do you?'

Her voice was gentle and tender. She wanted to hear from his own lips whether he loved her or not, and now was her opportunity.

'I always liked you,' he answered evasively, 'but we can't always be chatting; it is quite absurd to expect it.'

'I believe you love someone else,' she remarked, going to the point at once.

'There is no reason why I should not,' he answered drily. 'I suppose I am free to do that if I like?'

'No, you're not free, after making a fool of me,' she answered hotly. 'You've always led me on to suppose I should be your wife, and now you chuck me off. If you're in love with anyone else, you are a liar and a hypocrite!'

She was losing her temper, for she saw that her sweetness had no effect upon him.

Castelli was anxious for Cleo to leave him, and he moved up and down the room restlessly. At last he said,—

'It's no use you standing there calling me foul

names. If I am in love it's nothing to you, and as to your ever being my wife, I would not marry you if there wasn't another woman in the world. I never intended to do so, I never shall, and once more I tell you I am busy.'

'Oh, you weren't too busy to go to Sandcliffe this morning, were you?' she replied angrily. 'You didn't know I saw you, did you? But you see I did, and a nice fool you're making of the girl,' she added with scorn.

His face grew white with suppressed passion as he answered,—

'How dare you spy upon my actions? How dare you address me? It's nothing to you where I go. I suppose I can ride to Sandcliffe if I choose?'

'So can I, and I mean to go again, and just as often as I like, without your permission.'

'Go to blazes if you like, but hold your vicious tongue or I will make you.'

'Oh, you want to shut me up, do you? You're afraid I've found out too much. Anyway, I've seen the lady and the roses and the dog, and she lives in a cottage on the hill. By Jove! it's quite a romance for the circus. Fancy a girl like that marrying a ringmaster! I wonder if she knows how you have led other women on, and how you swear and curse. It's a pity such a little innocent should marry you,' she added mockingly.

Castelli's passion was terrible to behold. For a moment he could not speak.

'You devil!' he hissed, 'you tell me I've led other women on. You lie, you scurrilous wretch! Unsay what you have said or by heaven I'll shake your life out of you!'

'You daren't. You coward, to threaten a woman! I wish the dear young lady was here,' she replied tauntingly. 'I wonder what she would think of you. It's a pity you don't show yourself in your true colours.'

In a moment, before she was aware, he grasped her roughly by the arm and shook her fiercely several times.

'Now, then, I'll stand no more of your nonsense. I've had a devilish sight too much of it already.'

He turned in his anger and glanced hurriedly round as if in search for his whip.

All the fury of her nature was aroused. She did not plead for mercy, but stood her ground bravely. He held her so tightly that she could not escape from his grasp, but with her disengaged hand she fought him with all her strength.

'I'll teach you to shake me!' she panted. 'You brute, you devil!' and she struggled violently to free herself.

But that was impossible. He dragged her easily across the room, resistance was useless, nearer and nearer to the chair where the thin riding-whip was lying. He had it within his grasp, when the door opened suddenly and a voice called,—

'Ten minutes to nine, sir. The horses are ready for the ring, sir.'

Whanks could say nothing else. He was fairly frightened out of his few senses.

'Don't stand there, you fool, gaping at me,' said Castelli, as he flung down the whip. 'I daresay you're in this confounded business. I shall find it out, and then we'll see who is master.'

He flung Cleo into a chair, and hastened into the ring, followed by Whanks. A roar of applause greeted Castelli's appearance.

His smile was as fascinating as usual. He looked just as dignified, just as calm as ever. The scene with Cleo had not in the least disturbed his serenity before the public.

Cleo was faint and exhausted with her struggle. Castelli's fingers had left an ugly bruise on her arm, which was swelling and looking purple and blue. It was a good thing her 'show' had been one of the first. She could never have faced the people with those hideous dark contused spots, growing more painful every moment.

She went to her dressing-room and divested herself of her stage attire, and then sat down almost too weary to think. She heard the applause as Castelli left the ring. She heard the horses gallop past to their stalls, and a wild gleam came into her eyes. She was recovering her spirits, and with them her thirst for revenge. She must tip Whanks to hold his tongue. It would be the most cruel degradation to her should the recital of her treatment become the topic of conversation amongst the grooms and artistes in the circus. This being accomplished to her satisfaction, she hastened to her apartments, but on her way thither she called to order a carriage and pair to drive her over to Sandcliffe at ten o'clock the next morning.

She had planned to rob Castelli of his bride.

The following morning Leila Gurney was standing watching the scudding, restless clouds. The night had been stormy, but the morning was balmy, with fitful gleams of sunshine. Truly the world was in a joyful mood. Leila shared this great natural happiness, for was not her life like the summer, full of a thousand tender hopes, since the man she loved had sought and won her heart? Had he not charmed away despondency and misery from her life, and given in its stead promised joy and peace? With what keen delight she looked forward to his coming again on the morrow. She would soon listen to his voice, that voice she loved, almost to her as tender as the ringdove's cooing, and as soothing as lute to the wearied ear at eventide.

She turned from the window and spoke to her dog—*his* gift. Marcus, shall we go down to the sea? Marcus, your master will be here to-morrow to see us, and we are going driving, doggie,' and she picked him up and kissed him passionately.

A wag of the fluffy tail and a few licks was the dog's mute answer.

'Let me put on your collar, Marcus, with the pretty bells,' and she jingled the collar in the air.

'A lady to see you, miss,' announced the landlady somewhat curiously.

'To see *me?* There must be some mistake, I have no friends here.'

'It's no mistake, Miss Gurney,' answered a kindly voice; 'I have called upon particular business.'

For a moment Leila thought it was some messenger from her mother, and her face flushed painfully. Leila asked her to be seated, meanwhile admiring the handsome, elegantly dressed woman, so different in appearance and manner to the ladies she had ever known.

'I wonder who she can be?' was her mental rejoinder. Poor lonely Leila had no friends to come dropping in for a cup of tea, and the advent of a stranger caused her to be painfully nervous. She could not speak for the throbbing of her heart.

'I must apologise for calling,' began the lady, 'but I happened to hear by chance that you are here alone and without your friends, and as you are, I find, slipping without knowing it into a great danger, I have come to warn you, to speak to you as one lady should to another. If what I hear is correct, I believe you are engaged to be married to Signor Emilio Castelli, the equestrian manager of the circus now in Bayhaven. Is it so?'

She paused, and Leila sank down on the sofa, clutching the dog against her as if to still the beating of her heart.

'Yes, it is quite true; I am engaged to him, I am proud to say. But I do not wish to discuss the matter with a stranger; thank you all the same,' she added more gently, as if ashamed of her brusqueness.

'Now, listen to me, my dear.' Leila winced at the familiarity. 'You're going to marry this man, and you don't know a thing about him. He is very handsome, and you are smitten, but if you knew as much as I do about him you'd thank me to the last day of your life for coming here. If you value your happiness, have nothing to do with Emilio Castelli. There, I have at least done my duty in warning you—no Christian could do more. Let me tell you that I know his character perhaps the best of anyone in the world.'

'I don't want to hear anything about him,' Leila replied hotly. 'I love him, and intend to marry him, whatever *you* may say against him.'

'You'd rather not hear what I have to say. For love of this man you'd rather risk all your future—you'll repent of your choice when it is too late. I tell you Castelli has been engaged to heaps of women, that his character doesn't stand too high, and he has had a sweetheart in every town the circus has ever visited. He is a liar, a hypocrite, and unprincipled! And yet, rather than listen to me, you'd trust your life to his keeping!'

'I would,' answered Leila determinedly. 'I don't suppose you are in a position to judge much about him?'

'Oh, you mistrust me, do you? But you see I happen to be Cleo, "the only Cleo, Equilibrist," and Castelli and I have met constantly these three years. And who should know him better than I do? I was actually engaged to him, until a few weeks ago, when he threw me off like a hound'—she paused—'and you're the new love.'

'I do not believe a word you've said,' replied Leila gravely.

She was terribly astonished, but her infatuation was so intense that she never for one moment believed the speaker.

'You doubt me, do you, Miss Gurney?' said Cleo, losing her temper. 'This is all I get for troubling myself on your behalf. I'd rather die than let any woman I know marry that man with my consent.'

'I haven't asked your consent,' said Leila quietly, although she could hardly speak for agitation. 'I love him with all my heart—nothing can part us now.'

'Oh, couldn't it?' replied Cleo scornfully. 'Suppose I tell you that *I* love him, and have done so for years. To me he has been the one joy of my life. Will you take another woman's lover? Is that square and honest?'

'You say *you* love him, and yet you warn me against the same privilege,' said Leila. 'If you love him, surely I may do the same. If he is good for you, he is for me.'

Cleo saw she had let the ground go from under her argument, that the girl was as sharp as she was, but she still held tenaciously to her purpose.

'Oh, I thought *you* were a lady. I never profess to be one,' she added, with a sneer. 'I did not know the racehorse would eat with the sow.'

'I am satisfied,' said Leila, 'with my choice. He does *not* love you, for now I remember he did speak of you, and I have heard all about the "disagreement between you."'

Cleo turned white. Her fury rose. She was almost mad with passion. She jumped up from her chair and exclaimed excitedly,—

'You dare to sit there and insult me! He has told you all about me, has he? Well, it's my turn now. I daresay a ch't of a girl like you don't know much of circus life. To you, I suppose, it's all gilt, music, clowns, horses, and applause. Fun for such as you, that's what the paying public see. None of you would like to see things as they are. It would distress your fine nerves too much, and disturb your comfort. It's such men as Castelli that make the circus a hell. He—'

'I won't hear any more about him,' replied Leila, now angry. 'I trust him thoroughly. Say no more, if you please.'

'I won't be silent,' said Cleo, interrupting her. 'I came here to have my say, have it I will. Emilio Castelli,' she continued, 'is a cruel brute. It's a bad day for horse or girl when they fall into his way. Ah, you don't know the secrets behind the scenes, how horses are thrashed until they drop exhausted in the ring, and your lover Castelli is more pitiless than the rest. Ask Mdlle. Donis, whom he trained, what he's like. She'll tell you how he made her life a curse, a burden. How one day in Leeds, in my presence, he lashed her with his whip for bad "trick riding," and for two long hours kept her at it, bruised, bleeding, and sobbing, and then when she dismounted, kicked her in the ring—yes, kicked her. That's how he treats women. That's how he'll treat you. He knows no mercy. He's fierce and cruel. You'll get more of the whip than love, more curses than blessings, and more kicks than kisses,' she added with intense passion.

'You are telling me untruths,' said Leila curtly. 'Why should he be so cruel?'

'It's the way with some in our profession. Castelli is the biggest brute I have ever come across. I wish you luck with him.'

'Be good enough to leave this room. I have no wish to hear more. Go at once,' exclaimed Leila, standing up, facing her visitor steadily. 'Be good enough to leave me. I shall marry whom I choose. Your visit to me has not influenced me in the least.'

She went to the door and held it open.

Cleo saw it would be fruitless to remain, but she intended to play another scene before the curtain dropped upon her expedition.

'I'll go out of your room, never fear, but the day will come when you will repent of your bargain, when you'll wish you had listened to me, and I hope it will,' she added, with a fiendish smile. 'It will jolly well serve you right,' and with this she bounced out of the room.

Leila was half inclined to cry now the interview was over, and for a moment she sat as if in a stupor. Suddenly loud voices were heard proceeding from the kitchen, at the rear of the house. She opened the door again and listened. A woman's voice was saying,—

'You'd better let her friends know before it's too late. Tell them how things stand, and do warn them that marriage isn't much in his way. He'll never make her a wife.'

Then the landlady replied,—

'I guessed there was something up by the dog coming and the groom bringing books and a horse most days for her to ride. And the master hisself comes pretty often. There's always somebody coming to and fro. But still it's not my place to interfere with my lodgers. If she gets married, she must. I'm not in charge of her. The doctor sent her here. I was in his service before I married. It's nought to do with me.'

'Well, my good woman, you'll get yourself into nice trouble if she does go off with him. Be advised and write to her friends. He's a regular bad lot. It would be her ruin. It must be stopped before it is too late.'

'Oh, I'll just get my husband to write a line to the doctor. He'll be home to-night. It can do no harm. Leastways, I hope not, for the doctor lets my rooms for me most seasons.'

There was a scuffling of feet, the voices grew nearer, and Leila guessed the woman was coming past to the front door and closed hers gently.

She had heard enough to make her miserable. She determined to write off to Castelli at once, and hear from his lips whether the cruel statements were true.

She was just as faithful to him. Her heart was unshaken, and his love was still her most cherished hope. Yet somehow the summer did not seem so bright, for the rankling wounds of remembrance would remain despite the wish to forget.

A few teardrops marked the day.

## CHAPTER VI.

### NO JOY COMES UNMIXED.

LEILA looked very pale and tired when she went to meet Castelli at the old trysting place under the tall grey cliffs.

The long restless hours of the night had robbed her of her charms. The brightness of her glorious eyes had grown dim, and in its place there was an anxious, eager look, and dark circles had formed underneath them, giving a very ill effect to the lovely face.

Ah, it does not take much to rob the lilies of their bloom. One cruel storm and the fairness is destroyed.

Leila smiled faintly as Castelli approached her. He was prepared to see her look worried. Her urgent letter calling him to her side had shown him how distressed she was, but he was horrified at the change in her appearance.

He kissed her warmly and then remarked,—

'My darling, what ails you? Are you ill? I came over as quickly as I could after having your note. Now tell me all the worries and just what has happened.'

'I am frightened, Emilio, dreadfully frightened,' and she hid her face on his arm. 'I'm almost afraid to tell you all I have heard; it is so dreadful.'

'Don't be afraid,' answered Castelli in a kind voice fraught with sympathy. 'Have I not the right to help you, Leila? Now, sit down and let me understand what has happened.'

She sat down, with her thin white hand in his, and then she told him all the story of Cleo. At times she was so agitated that she could hardly continue the conversation, and when she had finished she burst into tears.

Castelli looked very grave, and said firmly but gently,—

'Don't cry, Leila, but listen to me. All this woman has told you is untrue, utterly false. She has lied for her own mean ends. She hopes still to triumph over you by her tyranny, to make you quail before her threats, to prevent us from becoming man and wife. My love for you has roused her anger. She hates me, and for revenge tries to corrupt your thoughts, and tells you I am false and base. Leila,' and he pressed her hands tenderly, 'do *you* doubt me?'

His tone inspired her with a sense of awe. She had never heard him speak in this strange and eloquent style, and it awoke in her a certain shame and regret that he should have to ask her if she believed the woman who had tried to throw such a ban on his name.

'I could never doubt you, Emilio, you must know that. I was certain you would not marry her. But is *all*, quite *all*, she said untrue? Have you had sweethearts in every town you have visited?'

'One I've had, Leila, and that is you,' he replied soothingly. 'No one else has been dear to me. I have never whispered love to another, never pictured with fond delight the pleasures of a home except with you and for you.'

He breathed a sigh as he finished speaking, and to Leila it seemed like an anguished heart. In a moment all her tender sympathies were aroused, and she replied in soft tones,—

'I believe you, Emilio, dear Emilio; but why did that woman say such very dreadful things? I can't bear to think of them.'

'Because she hates us, Leila, and if she can mar our happiness her joy would be complete. But that can never be, my Leila, for are not our hearts fortified with a great love too deep to be put asunder?'

'Yes, oh, yes,' she answered, with just a little hesitation, whilst a flush overspread her pale face.

Something in her manner implied she was not

quite satisfied. The woman's words had given her some fears, some feelings of impending shadows rising in the future, and she could not as yet quite shake off the forebodings, transient as they were.

The tenor of her tone struck him at once, and he continued,—

'There is something still, Leila, that is troubling you. Won't you tell me what it is, dearest?'

Ignoring his direct question, she asked very meekly,—

'Are all circus people cruel to women and horses?'

There was an affectionate hope in her voice that he would deny this also, still there was a pleading, a yearning to know the truth from his lips.

'None of us, Leila; it would not pay us to be cruel. Of course we are firm, and have to train with a masterly hand or there would be no circus for the people; and to avert danger and to save our lives we must be stern. Sometimes there is a dreadful struggle between a horse and his rider, and we have to make ourselves the master once and for all.'

'But what about Mdlle. Donis?' asked Leila, with sudden curiosity.

His face grew stern, the softness died from his eyes. His temper was ruffled when he found how much Leila had been told, but his tact and skill came to his rescue, and he threw a lustre over his deeds which he knew the inexperienced girl could not gainsay.

'I did train Imra Donis. The woman told you the truth for once,' he said with withering scorn, 'but I never ill-used her. She was light and pretty, and we were all fond of her and proud of her riding. Her grace and suppleness was perfection, and it was to my advantage to treat her kindly. Talent and dexterity are absolute necessities in the ring, and cruelty would not develop either, so put away such ideas, Leila, my pet, or I shall think you don't love me.'

'I have but one love, Emilio, and that is you,' she replied with fervour.

Her inquiries were beginning to be rather difficult to answer satisfactorily, and he saw that the matter must be brought to a climax before she had time to reflect longer on all that Cleo had told her.

He was cunning—she so trusting.

'Leila,' he spoke her name so gently, 'do you love me well enough to do anything I ask you?'

'Anything,' she replied. 'Anything in the wide world.'

He stooped and kissed her.

'We must be married at once, Leila, or we must part for ever. The landlady is sure to keep her word—your father may be here to-morrow, and we should never meet again.'

Leila was thinking how dreary that going home with her father would be, and she shuddered as she thought of the loss of her handsome, kindly lover. Her life was so happy basking in his love— a love which had taken possession of her heart and soul.

'Must we?' she asked vaguely, as one in a dream.

'Or say good-bye. You must decide, Leila, which it is to be?'

Her passion for him was like a giant wave—it rushed madly over both mind and body, it overwhelmed her with its depth, and left her resistless, susceptible only to her dream of delight. It had dulled her for the time to the realities of life. She was stupefied with the cup in which the sweet poison had been so temptingly and insidiously held to her lips. Hope, youth's prophet, had said: 'Drink to the dregs, and so chase away anxious care. Love to you will be the balm to all ills, and the cure of sorrow. Why tread a lonely way when his love is shining for you like the morning star.'

She was entranced. Her love was almost divine. Castelli saw her wavering in her decision for one moment, and then she spoke.

'It can never be good-bye again,' she said faintly. 'I will do what you think best.'

'You are brave and true, Leila; now listen to me. If the landlady wrote last night, your father will probably be here by to-morrow morning, perhaps to-night.'

'Oh, no, he won't,' replied Leila, interrupting him quickly. 'He never does anything in a hurry.'

'Well, then, we'll give him until to-morrow. He or the doctor is sure to be here by train to-morrow. You must leave quite early in the morning, about six o'clock, before anyone is about, and don't bring anything with you or it may arouse suspicion if you meet any of the fishermen coming from their boats in the bay.'

'I must bring Marcus,' she replied. 'I couldn't leave him behind.'

'Yes, Marcus can come, and you might carry a towel in your hand. It would seem then as if you were going to take an early bath. Whatever you do, avoid calling people's attention to you. When you have left the house, walk by the beach as far as Dread Point. It is about two miles, not more, straight ahead towards Bayhaven.'

'I have been there,' she replied quickly. 'I know the spot well.'

'That's good,' he replied. 'When you get to Dread's Point, Whanks and a carriage will be waiting for you on the road which runs along the

Downs. He will drive you at once to the fishing village of Thorpe. It is thirteen miles from here, and seven on the other side of Bayhaven. I shall drive over there and find you some apartments, and in them you must stay until I can join you with a special licence. You must remain in the house, answer no questions as to who you are, or where you come from. Understand me, Leila, that is most important.'

'But the landlady will wonder who I am, and where my luggage is. I shall have nothing with me. I couldn't go like that.'

'Then you must give up the enterprise at once, unless you like to make out a list of a few necessaries, which Whanks can bring you, and after we are man and wife, Leila, I will come over here and demand your belongings. Two days at the most you will have to wait.'

'But the landlady will think it so funny to see me there alone. There will be no excuse.'

'*I* will see her, Leila, when I take the rooms. I shall ask her to care for you until I come with the licence. When all is ready for the marriage I shall tell her the truth. Leave it to me, Leila; I will manage her. Only do as I tell you the rest will be easy.'

Leila was not sufficiently worldly wise to understand that money can do everything. She did not comprehend that Castelli's management of the landlady meant a goodly bribe of gold.

She was satisfied. She would do what he bade her, trusting in his love and his guidance.

They parted for the last time as lovers. Her depression had passed away. A joyousness shone again in her eyes, and her voice was full of gladness as she said good-bye until the dawn of another day.

'Good-bye, Leila. To-morrow, sweetheart, you must come away.'

'I will,' she replied with determination, 'I will be there.'

On his way home Castelli wondered if she would be afraid when the last decisive step must be taken, whether natural timidity would usurp its sway and he should lose his prize for ever.

He loved her dearly, and longed for the time when he could call her wife. He had made up his mind to keep his pearl at Thorpe, even after the wedding was over. She must be aloof from the circus entirely.

In the meantime there was much for him to do, for the hours speed on, and the morrow comes almost before the sunset dies away.

When the early day dawned, when the happy birds had begun to fill the silent air with song, when the soft breezes were wakening the sleeping flowers, and the sea murmuring sweetly on the shore, Leila Gurney, with restless haste, set out upon her journey—a journey which would bring her one step nearer to the goal of bliss, that haven of rest for which she had so ardently longed during her sad and shadowed life.

Five hours later Charles Gurney and Dr Burton sat in the little parlour in Green's Cottages. The landlady was propounding her theories loudly as to the whereabouts of her lodger.

'When I came down this morning, sir,' she said, turning to the doctor, 'she was gone, clean as a whistle. I never heard her go out, yet I was awake at five o'clock. Her bed has been slept in, so she can't have gone far. She couldn't walk to Bayhaven surely, and the coach hasn't gone yet. She's got the start of you, but you're bound to find her.'

Charles Gurney replied before the doctor had time to speak.

'You wrote to warn me, Mrs Thomas, for which I am deeply obliged, but as the bird has flown there is no reason for us to detain you longer.'

'Don't hurry, Gurney. I should like to be sure of one or two things before we leave. I was instrumental in placing your daughter here, and I mean to get every scrap of information possible.'

'Do you know for certain that she has gone with this man connected with the circus at Bayhaven, Mrs Thomas?' he asked.

'As far as we can be sure of anything in this world, sir. The lady as called here told me she was engaged to him; my husband saw them together yesterday under the cliffs, and to-day she has gone.'

'Are all her things here?'

'Just as she left them, sir, except the dog. She took him with her, I suppose, for he ain't here.'

'Where does this unscrupulous villain perform, did you say?' asked Gurney.

'At Duval's Royal Circus, Bayhaven, sir, a good seven miles from here.'

'Oh, I'm not going after her. I don't care whether it is seven miles or seventy,' said Gurney hastily, with a sullen look on his face. 'But I should like the brute's name and address.'

'I know it's Castelli,' said the landlady, 'but there was two other names before that, so the lady said. It began with *E*, one of them did, but it beats me to think what she called him—sounded like a name *I* never heard before, fureign I should say. Why, let me see,' she exclaimed suddenly, 'I believe the lady wrote it down on the baker's book, as I had in my hand when she came to the kitchen door. I'll go and see, sir.'

She left the room, and both the men seemed too

full of thought to say much. At length the doctor spoke.

'Gurney, we must find her—fancy her at the mercy of this man alone—we had better go to Bayhaven at once.'

'I sha'n't. You can go a fool's errand if you like. She has gone somewhere, and there she can remain.'

'Gurney, she is your only girl, the one—'

Before he could complete the sentence the landlady appeared.

'Here it is, sir, wrote down under the quartern of flour. S-i-g-n-o-r,' she spelt out persistently; 'but there, perhaps one of you gentlemen had better read it. I'm a good scholar, so my husband says, but I can't manage names that hasn't got any Christianity in them.'

'"Signor Emilio Castelli, Duval's Royal Circus, Bayhaven,"' read out Gurney. 'I'll take the name down, if you don't object, madam.'

'Well, I hope I sha'n't get into any trouble over the affair, as my husband says I can't be expected to look after the lodgers.'

'I shall make no trouble, madam,' said Charles Gurney, rising to leave. 'I had hoped to have saved her from the degradation of a marriage far beneath her, but as I am too late I don't intend to trouble more about her.'

'You'll think better of that, Gurney, by-and-by,' replied the doctor, almost ashamed of the father's callous bearing and loveless tone; 'she must be found without delay.'

'Not by *me*,' answered Charles Gurney, 'not by me,' he repeated severely and coldly.

'Well, sir,' said Mrs Thompson, as she reached the front door, turning to face Dr Burton, 'I hope you'll send me some more lodgers; it's no fault of

E

mine. I believe this scandal will be pounds out of my pocket; my husband says it will. I'd give anything if it had happened in someone else's house and not in mine.'

'I shall always do the best I can for you, Mrs Thompson, but I won't send you any more unprotected girls. There must be a father or mother in the business next time.'

He shook hands with her, but Charles Gurney did not even speak. He nodded slightly towards her, and with this scant courtesy Mrs Thompson had to be satisfied.

After they left the house Dr Burton insisted upon taking lunch at the hotel. The train did not leave for another three hours, and he was in hopes that Gurney, in the meantime, would look at the matter in a different light, and seek his child whilst there was the chance.

When they were seated in the little stuffy bar parlour, waiting for the eggs and bacon being duly prepared for them, Dr Burton made another effort on behalf of the young girl he had tried to befriend and which had so far ended with such disastrous results.

'Don't you think, Gurney, instead of taking the trap back to Wellston Junction, we had better go home by way of Bayhaven and see what has become of the girl? At least we can ask for this man Castelli and learn the truth. We could pay the driver and send him off at once. It is our duty, Gurney; your daughter has been led away. Don't be too hard, but save her if you can.'

'I shall go back the way I came, as I said before. You can please yourself, but I think you're making a confounded fuss over a girl that never belonged to you. If I choose to disclaim her, I suppose I can.'

'No fuss, Gurney. The girl is to blame; but I do

think humanity should make you more kindly, more anxious to rescue your child from perhaps sin and shame.'

The lunch coming in interrupted the conversation for a while, and the doctor did not allude to the subject again until they were strolling afterwards on the cliffs.

'We shall lose this train anyhow, Gurney. See how clear the water looks. Shall we go down to the beach?'

Down to the beach they went, the beach which had been the trysting place of Gurney's daughter and Castelli, and where their troth had been plighted and their marriage arranged; but neither of the men knew this.

And the sand and stones around them were dumb.

'Gurney, what are you going to do?'

The doctor's persistency angered Gurney, and he turned to him defiantly.

'Look here, sir, she has gone, and I forbid you to speak her name to me again—a girl that goes off and marries a man no better than a groom, or doesn't marry her, that's more like it,' he cried passionately. 'It's the cursed mother in the child; the same treachery over again, the same heartless ingratitude, the same bad passions, and yet you bid me seek her, the daughter of the sinful, wretched mother—a woman no better than one who haunts the streets.'

'Hush, hush, Gurney. She was your wife,' said the doctor gently.

'Wife!' he hissed. 'A wife without honour, a wife without shame, a woman who rushed to her ruin. Let her perish, as she deserves, and the girl too. She shall live her wretched, honour-stained life alone. Those who have the prize can keep it. I renounce her for ever. She deserves her fate, the daughter of an accursed mother. I shall never deplore their loss. And now we had better drop the subject for ever. It's nothing to you, and if I choose to adopt measures you don't like, be good enough to keep your own counsel.'

'Certainly,' replied the doctor stiffly. 'But the day will come, Mr Gurney, when you will repent your decision.'

'That, too, is my concern.'

The two men travelled home together, scarcely addressing a word to each other on the journey. When they arrived at the village station the doctor put out his hand towards Charles Gurney.

'Good-night, sir. I don't think we need meet again, unless I am required in my professional capacity.'

'Please yourself,' replied Charles Gurney curtly, as he turned away without taking the proffered hand.

'What a cruel, wretched man he is,' murmured the doctor on his way home. 'No feeling for those he should have loved, no heart. Brutal, that's what he is, perfectly brutal. I'll have no more to say to him. I wish I'd never seen the girl. But perhaps, after all, she is happier away from her unnatural father. I hope she is.'

He was glad to be at home again, and whilst he enjoyed his tea with his wife and little chattering daughter, Charles Gurney walked up and down his small sitting-room. The defiant, scornful look had died from his face, and one of anguish had taken its place.

Away from curious gaze, the strong man gave way to feelings which he thought long since gone. The conduct of his daughter had brought back, in some extraordinary manner, softer thoughts of his wife, and as he paced the room he spoke aloud.

'No one can heal a bruised and broken heart,

and I loved her so dearly. Heaven has doomed me. I have had to part with all I cherished. All have forsaken me. First, my wife went, then the boy—but God speed *him*—and now, to-day, the last has gone. Men talk of affection. What is it? But the blossom on the spray for a time. Then some rude hand dashes it to the ground, and there it lies and withers, with none to heed its pain. I can never forget her—wife—mother. She left me, and unheard, unpitied I complain. If she lives, she smiles perchance, but not for me. I don't know her destiny, whether she is dead or not, but thoughts of her come to me with the loss of other and happier days.'

His face suddenly changed, and it was terrible to see. It grew white and passionate. His eyes were sullen, and the old fixed, leaden expression came round his mouth. The tender feelings were gone. They were but a remembrance come back to make the present more miserable by comparison.

Forgive them—never—never. Let the broken vows of the adulterous wife be accursed. Let the sinning daughter fall into the shades of hell as the mother had. They were best there—forgotten—hated—despised.

Pity or compassion he had none.

## CHAPTER VII.

### 'TACTA EST ALEA.'

Two days after Leila Gurney had left Sandcliffe she became, by special licence, Mrs Emilio Castelli. On the morning of her bridal day she had felt very lonely and ill at ease, and it took a great deal of gentleness and kindness on Castelli's part to reassure her and bring the smile back to her face.

The early day had been stormy and wild. The great trooping masses of clouds muttered in angry thunder tones, and flashes of lightning gleamed across the sky. The sea's trembling waves rose with wilder swell, and the wind sighed gently and moaned as if in anguish. It seemed to be chanting a dirge for the dead.

All this had tended to depress her. She took the storm to be an ill-omen, the voice of prophecy destined by Nature to warn her of the dark shadows which lay before her in the years to come.

Castelli laughed when she told him her fears, and said kindly,—

'The storm cannot last for ever, Leila; the sun must come out again. Don't fret, my darling. I hope your life will be all happiness despite the tempest.'

'Perhaps it will be like the rainbow when the storm has passed, all colours, all brightness.'

He kissed her, and she was once more satisfied.

Another hour and the wedding was over. There had been no one present but Whanks and the clerk as witnesses. The clergyman, an old man, hurried carelessly over the service, scarcely evincing any interest in the contracting parties. He never altered the monotone in his voice excepting twice, when two awful crashes of thunder seemed to burst right over the tiny church. When they had signed their names in the vestry he bid them 'God speed,' and that was all. He had done his share of the duty, the rest never troubled him.

Leila looked up at him once, just before she left the vestry, hoping he would smile at her. She longed for one congratulation, one kindly word of encouragement, one benison on her marriage day. But he offered her none. He began to disrobe in a most offhand and practical manner, and the newly married pair left the church as quietly as they had entered. Outside the porch they found Whanks, who held out his hand to the bride.

'Every blessing shine on you, Miss Leila; oh, I beg pardon, madam. You see it's rather hard to change your name all of a sudden like. I wish I had my aunt's money, then I should get spliced too. I hope you'll both be happy, sir,' he added, turning to his master, 'that I do.'

Leila shook hands with him, and her husband did the same. She could not thank him, for she was choking down the sobs which his kind words had called forth.

'You're a good fellow, Whanks,' said his master, 'and we are both grateful for your kind wishes.'

They walked back to the apartments quietly, arm-in-arm, with Whanks in the rear. The thunder had ceased, the clouds were breaking, showing bright blue beyond, the wind had dropped, and the heat was quite oppressive.

After luncheon Leila decided to write to her father at once. He would have to be told, and the sooner the better. She dispatched her letter, and then she and Castelli started for a drive.

How beautiful looked the summer afternoon. All traces of the storm had gone. There was joy and life all around. The birds sang with all their might, as if keeping high revel and exulting in gladness as they flitted amongst the hedges or darted into the bushes, too happy to do aught but clap their wings and proclaim their welcome to the smiling earth.

The softness of the day gave Leila a feeling of languor and repose, and the calm, placid sky shed a halo over her mind, and for the time entranced her senses, like the sweetest music stealing over a restless spirit.

As she drove it seemed as if the air kissed her with a breath of love. In the distance the sea murmured soothingly, and the cliffs and the fields breathed out visions of radiant joy and enduring love.

She was so happy in her dream of youth. There were no sombre clouds with angry rugged edges seen on the horizon as yet. All was light and hope.

After her marriage she was somewhat disappointed to learn that she was not to reside in Bayhaven as long as the circus was there, and upon this point her husband was gently firm.

'It's no place for you, my darling,' he had said kindly. 'In another month we shall have to go to Manchester, and then you shall go with me now and then to the circus; but we have rather a rough lot here just now, and you would not like to meet Cleo again, would you?'

'No,' she replied, 'I should not. Where is she now?'

'Down at the show.'

But he did not add that he had made her so uncomfortable that she had been glad to arrange to leave at the end of the week and take a Continental engagement.

The fact was, however, that he did not wish his wife to be too rudely introduced to the life. He dreaded her learning the truth all at once. Some day she must know all the secrets and the cruelties, but at present it pleased him to keep her innocent of all guile.

'I shall be so dull here all day alone,' she said to him.

'Oh, no, my darling. You will have your dog and Athol, also a horse to ride, and books, and I might get some of the fishermen to give you a row for an hour each day.'

'But you will have to go so early every morning, and won't be back until late at night.'

Her voice fell, her eyes filled with tears at the thought.

Most men would have given way when they saw the upturned, anxious face, but Castelli only put back the golden curls and kissed her tenderly.

'What, tears! and only married two days? Come, come, I must have my sunbeam all smiles, and she must remember that if Bayhaven was the best place for her she should go. But, believe me, darling, I am doing what is kindest for you. And there is Manchester in view next month, and then you won't be dull.'

Kind as he was, she felt she could not contradict him. He possessed some power which held her completely under his control, and she replied,—

'I'm sure you do the best you can for me, and I won't grumble any more. I wish father would answer my letter. Do you think he will?' she asked him anxiously.

'Not just yet, perhaps, my darling. He will wait a little while. You see he must feel rather riled to find his daughter fled and married; and fathers don't always forgive in a hurry.' Observing her disappointed look, he added: 'There is very little time gone by. It will all come right if you don't worry.'

The next day Castelli's holiday came to an end, and he went back to his duties. When he arrived at the circus he found several letters awaiting him. They were all on business save one, and that came from Leila's father, and its contents ran:—

> 'HEATH COTTAGE,
> BRIARHILL.

'SIR,—I am told you have married my daughter. If it is so, which I doubt, I wish you joy of her. The child who leaves home and friends, and bolts with a groom, will surely make a good wife. She inherits sufficient of her mother's good qualities to make her turn out a devil by-and-by. The girl is the offspring of a wicked woman, who left me and her children. This, I hope, will be a strong recommendation for her.

'When you have tired of her I have no doubt her excellent mother will undertake the rest of her education, and cultivate her mind, soul, and body in order that she may follow in her footsteps.

> 'CHARLES GURNEY.'

After Castelli had read this scurrilous and sarcastic letter he pondered in his own mind whether he should show it to Leila or consign it to destruction at once. He picked up the envelope and found it contained another letter, addressed to his wife, but securely sealed. Then he decided to let her see his letter.

When he arrived home he gave the sealed missive to Leila, who changed colour rapidly as she opened and read it:—

'Child of your miserable, unhappy mother, so you have found your level—the level made for you by that woman, my wife. You could not be pure as others are. Your blood is tainted; nothing can purify it.

'Married, are you? Well, that is no business of

mine. I don't care what you are, but remember, when the scoundrel you are with has cast you off, don't come to me for mercy. As you have made your bed, so you must lie on it. I would not give you, a castaway, shelter even if you lay in the gutter at my door. This is all I shall ever write to you.
'CHARLES GURNEY.'

Leila had never loved her father very dearly, but his letter was a terrible blow to her. She turned so white that Castelli hurried to her side.

'It is bad news, my darling, isn't it?'

'Yes, read it,' she answered faintly.

He perused the cruel lines, and hard and stern as he was, his sorrow and sympathy for his young wife was deep and sincere.

'Never fear, my pet, he'll forgive you some day. That letter has been written on the spur of the moment. I also have had one from him. I think you had better read it—there should be no secrets between husband and wife.'

She laid both letters down on the table with a sigh. For the time her happiness was gone. A cloud had cast its gloom over the shining star; its brilliancy had declined.

'Leila,' said Castelli quietly, 'before we were married you led me to suppose your mother was dead; is it true she ran away from your father?'

He waited for her reply.

The crimson blood rushed to the fair cheeks. She put her hands to her face, as if to conceal her shame from his gaze.

'Yes, yes, it is true—all true.'

'Never mind, darling, I think no worse of you for your mother's faults. But why did you not tell me before? I thought you had lost her by death.'

'Why did I not tell you?' she said, now roused

to excitement. 'Why should I spread my mother's shame abroad? Was it not hard enough to bear without that? Was all my happiness to be ruined for her sin? I tried to forget she ever lived, tried to forget all the misery she brought to us, and the loss of our home. Oh, how happy we were,' she continued, 'father, mother, Tom and I, all together at home! Her sin will always cling to me; I must bear the burden—it is cruel, cruel!'

She sobbed aloud, and Castelli was really distressed.

'I don't visit the sins of a mother upon the child if others do,' he replied kindly. 'You are just as precious to me. Whatever your mother is has nothing to do with me.'

She kissed him, and he put his arms round her and did his best to comfort her.

'Come, now, what have you been doing to-day?' he asked, anxious to turn the conversation.

'Reading Pope's *Homer*, and of the high esteem horses were held in when they first came into Greece. I was so amused, because in the fifteenth Iliad they speak of an extraordinary feat of activity where one man manages four horses at once, and leaps from the back of one to another when going at full speed. Why, I saw that done in a circus years ago by quite a boy.'

She laughed gaily at the idea, and Castelli, taking up the cue, related anecdote after anecdote about his horses.

And so the smiles returned, as the sun shines after the April shower.

## CHAPTER VIII.

### HORROX.

Six happy months had glided on. Leila was as joyous as on the day Castelli had made her his bride. She had been treated with the greatest kindness and consideration, and in each place they visited her comfort had been her husband's chief thought and care.

Of the actual circus life she had seen very little. Two or three times she had occupied a stall to see the performance, but she had never been behind the scenes.

Some of the company had for fun now and then twitted Castelli upon his marriage, and asked him to 'show up the lady.' 'What on earth do you keep her shut in for?' one of them would ask; and another would say, 'She's too good for us, I suppose, a kind of angel all to herself.'

To all these taunts Castelli turned a deaf ear. If they pleased them it pleased him equally well to keep his wife to himself.

Sometimes, when Leila was alone, she would wonder why the horses in the ring looked so scared at the trainer, and why their eyes were fixed upon the thin small whip he held before them. Castelli had told her, in answer to her questions, that all horses did the same, and she believed him implicitly.

One evening, when she came home from a performance, she spoke to her husband again on the subject, which had lately filled her mind and given her a certain amount of uneasiness. She had witnessed the performance of a troupe of acrobats, and one little sad-faced boy of very tender years had aroused her sympathy.

As usual Castelli had put her off with explanations which seemed to be truth, but she had no means of going into the rights and wrongs of the case, and her husband had no intention of going into details. But still the white face haunted her, and the thin arms and heavy breathing were present in her mind; she could not forget him, and was only partially satisfied that all was well.

For some time after this Castelli kept her from the circus, under one pretext or another, but he was beginning to tire of the constant vigilance necessary to keep his wife in ignorance, and when they arrived in Leeds he took her to professional apartments, in which another member of the circus with his troupe lodged, and here it was that Leila first learnt the horrors daily practised on some of those who are trained by an atrocious system.

'The Guarez Family' occupied the ground floor of the house and also the top rooms, whilst Leila and her husband had the drawing-room floor. This arrangement led to the troupe constantly passing her doors on their way to the higher story. She soon discovered that there were six of them, the eldest girl being about fourteen years of age. There was only one boy, by name Willie, a sickly, wan child of seven summers. In these children her curiosity was soon aroused. When they passed her they never spoke, only giving her a frightened glance. She never had seen children behave so before, and this set her wondering. At last she questioned Castelli, as they sat at supper one evening.

'I should like to see those children who live downstairs perform. How miserable they do look. Is Horrox their father? and where is their mother?' asked Leila.

Her husband frowned a little, but he was too

wise to lose his temper over her perpetual questioning.

'No, he is not their father, Leila. Probably there are six different mothers. They are not related; they are children he has taken and trained. He allows each mother so much a week and takes all they earn for himself,' replied Castelli quietly.

'Why do they call themselves "The Guarez Family" if they are not one family? And they call Horrox father. I cannot understand what it means,' said Leila, somewhat vexed at the deception around her.

'Look here, my dear,' said Castelli, with just a little tone of irritation in his voice, 'it is the custom for children who perform together to be called "a family," and the trainer is always the father; it's more convenient altogether. In the bills "The Guarez Family" sounds more complete than calling them all by separate names; it could not be done. Sometimes it is troupe, not family.'

'It is not true at anyrate,' said Leila.

'Quite, as the profession accept the term,' replied Castelli. 'It's no use your worrying, my dear, about things that cannot be helped.'

'I must,' said Leila somewhat hotly, 'when I see things and hear, too, what I do not like or understand. I am firmly convinced Horrox is a cruel man, and I shall find out if he is. In the morning, when you are away at the circus, I hear moans and faint screams, and loud voices and awful language. There must be some reason. Why will you not tell me the truth, Emilio?'

'You are mistaken, Leila. The children practise in the top room, and perhaps you hear a scream when they fall and get frightened. And as to your finding out whether or not Horrox is cruel, take my advice and leave him alone. You would not like him to come up here and inquire about me, and he in his place will not like to find my wife asking impertinent questions.'

As he finished speaking he pushed his plate on one side and took up a paper, as if further conversation on the subject would not be agreeable to him.

Leila sighed. She felt somewhat hurt by his manner. Why should he always avoid speaking to her about the children engaged in the circus?

He heard her sigh, and he turned to her kindly.

'Don't fret, my pet. It's no use talking over disagreeable topics. I am quite willing to own that Horrox has to be very strict with his troupe, and in saying that I have said all I know about him,' and he kissed her tenderly.

But Leila was not satisfied. A terrible sense of uneasiness had come over her. She felt almost certain that some hardship, some wrong was going on.

She was fully determined to sift the matter for herself. She believed honestly that her husband was as ignorant as she was on the subject, therefore she would be quite sure before she spoke to him that cruelty *did* exist. If she found the children were ill-treated she would ask his help and assistance.

The determination and courage which had made her Castelli's wife now stood her in good stead, and all her energy was devoted to finding out what the strange cries and occasional screams could mean.

One morning, some days after her conversation with her husband, she was sitting thinking, and watching the busy street beneath. 'Marcus' was asleep upon her lap, and her work lay untouched on a table by her side. Suddenly her reverie was broken by a bitter cry, a cry so full of pain and distress that Leila jumped up hastily and opened the door. She listened attentively for a few moments, and then the sound of a child's voice reached her distinctly. Without pausing to consider, she shut the dog in and then carefully made her way towards the top staircase, for the sounds proceeded from that direction. The children were at practice in the attic room, and thither she determined to ascend. Very cautiously she crept up, waiting now and again, as every step she took made a creaking sound, and she was afraid it would attract attention to her presence.

When she reached the top the door was ajar. She peeped through the small aperture, scarcely daring to breathe. She could just see from where she stood the little boy attired in tights. He was deathly pale, whilst the perspiration rolled down his face. He seemed to be trembling from head to foot.

'Are you going to do it or won't you?' asked the angry voice of a man. 'I'll take the skin off your back in a moment if you don't. Go on.'

'I can't, sir, indeed I can't. I would if I could,' replied a plaintive little voice.

'You shall. Once more, will you do what I tell you?'

The child did not speak, he only stood there, a sad, quivering little creature, with none to help him in his awful ordeal.

Leila saw Horrox step up to where the child was standing. She heard the thin stick he held in his hand whistle through the air as it fell on the defenceless boy, accompanied by a curse.

'Stop that, do you hear?' cried Leila, flinging open the door and stepping hastily into the room.

The man for a moment was so astonished at the intrusion that he was fairly taken aback, and the child ran to her for protection, calling as he did so:

'Oh, save me, save me! He beats me dreadfully, and I can't do what he wants. The bar's too high,' and he hid his face in her dress.

Before her she saw the tall, dark, angry man, with a cruel leering face and cold fierce eyes, but this did not daunt her. She was unaware of the desperate nature of his character.

'What brings you here?' he asked roughly, advancing one step nearer to her. 'Be off, out of this room, or I'll put you out.'

'The cries of pain from this wretched child brought me here,' replied Leila angrily. 'I've heard him many times, and to-day I resolved to come and see for myself. I saw you strike him, poor child, but you sha'n't do it again now I'm here.'

She spoke as if her presence and strength were sufficient to keep the enemy at bay. As yet she did not realise how powerful he was or of what cruelty he was capable.

'Oh, sha'n't I,' he replied tauntingly. 'As you are fond of listening at other people's doors, and coming where you are not invited, you can stay here until I choose to let you go.'

And before she was aware of his intention he stepped behind her and locked the door. For a moment this disconcerted her, and a vision of her husband rose before her.

'Keep close to me, Willie,' she said as the child began to tremble again. 'He shall not hurt you,' and she put her delicate white hands round the boy as if to protect him.

With a terrible oath Horrox called the boy to come to him.

Leila felt the child move, as if to free himself from her grasp, to obey the master's call.

'Don't go to him. I'll take care of you, dear,' she added soothingly.

Another awful oath fell from the man's lips, and then Leila felt the boy torn from her grasp.

'You see *I* happen to be master here, and the boy is mine.'

'He is not,' replied Leila stoutly, although her heart began to beat with apprehension. 'My husband said none of the children were yours, and you shall not ill-treat Willie—if you do, there's the law to protect him.'

'I'll show you what *my* law is,' he said, with a cruel leer upon his face, as he rapped his cane on the floor.

'You see that, don't you?' he said, clutching the boy by the arm, and pointing to the two horizontal bars placed in the centre of the room, with their steel wire guys screwed into the floor. As he spoke he thrust the child on to the thin woollen mattress which stretched between and beyond them. 'Now then, one, two, three, jump and catch the bar or I'll make you, by ——.'

But the feat was beyond the boy's power to accomplish, and he missed the bar by several inches.

Down came the cane upon the thinly clad limbs, until the child screamed out in his agony.

'Oh, don't, don't!' wailed Leila. 'How can you be so cruel?'

But Horrox did not heed her entreaties.

She watched his face growing more cruel, more fiendish every moment.

'Catch that bar, you young fool,' he roared, 'or I'll do for you.'

'I can't, indeed, I can't,' sobbed the frightened child.

'Do it! do it! Do you hear?'

The child made one more desperate attempt to fulfil his master's bidding, but alas! the tiny form had not the physical strength. It was beyond his powers to perform such a feat.

'He cannot do it. Why do you ask him?' cried Leila, almost in despair.

'He shall do what I tell him or I'll show you how I punish him,' cried Horrox in a passion. 'You've come to see the training, and see it you shall.'

Again the child tried and failed, falling with a thud to the mattress.

In a moment, before Leila could even guess his intentions, Horrox made a dash at the boy, and seizing his hands, beat them until the blood fell upon the tiny tights in bright and hideous spots.

With a scream of intense anguish the child sank down to the ground, holding his bleeding hands tightly together, as if to lull the pain.

'There, you young devil, if you can't do the work for me you sha'n't do it for anyone else.'

As he spoke he kicked the boy savagely. Leila leant for support against the door. She was beginning to feel sick and ill, she gasped with difficulty.

'You cruel brute! I will tell my husband.'

She could not say more, her heart was beating so fast. She was becoming afraid of the tyrant before her.

'Your husband, faugh! He's a nice one, he is. Look here, madam,' he continued in a voice of suppressed passion, 'your husband is as cruel as I am—more so, he's a brute, if you like, and it's only because you're such a silly doll, such a half-baked fool, that he daren't tell you what he is. You've never seen him train his horses, have you, my lady innocent?' he added, with a sneer. 'Before you come spying here again suppose you try your luck with him. Just take a peep in the ring some fine morning when he's rehearsing; you'll see another show equal to this, perhaps a little more spiced.'

The child moaned and sobbed under his breath, and this again roused the man's anger.

'Hold that infernal row or I'll thrash you again.'

There was almost silence in the room. Leila was breathing hard, and the boy hushed his sobs. Horrox, thinking a fainting woman would be a nuisance, and rather fearing Castelli's wrath, moved towards the door.

'Stop!' said Leila suddenly, as if gaining courage from his action.

'My husband has never been guilty of cruelty. You lie! He's the kindest, the best man that even lived; but you—but you—you're a cruel devil.' And then she turned to the child, who sat shivering with fear and deadly white. 'I'll help you, Willie dear; wait until to-night and you shall be saved from *that* brute,' and she pointed towards Horrox, with horror and disgust written upon the handsome face.

'Ha, ha, ha!' he laughed rudely, unlocking the door, 'it has given me much pleasure to introduce you to the "profession," and it has saved your dear, good—oh, kind, isn't it?—husband a disagreeable job.'

He pushed her out of the room as he spoke.

Dizzy, faint, and sick as she was she pleaded once more for the child.

'Don't hurt him again, he is so small; promise me you won't, before I go.'

'You be damned! You won't get over me with your pretty face and cunning ways. Leave the boy to me; I'll square him directly.'

'Then I shall appeal to a police officer, and take

out a summons against you directly my husband comes in.'

'Oh, I would if I were you. Your husband will tell you how to go about it. He's so good and *kind*, you know,' he added, with a sneer.

She went to her room and wept.

The sadness of the child's face and his faint pathetic cry for mercy had entered her soul like a knife, poisoning her fresh young life. In that hour she had grown years older. Youth had suddenly withdrawn its magic wand.

Time went on and she still sat thinking, until a telegram was handed her by the landlady's daughter. It was from her husband, to save her anxiety respecting his non-return to dinner. Ever since they were married he had never neglected to send her a word if business detained him. She knew it would be late before she saw him, and so she determined to act upon her own judgment with regard to the ill-treated child.

She hurried down to the police court, and after having seen the superintendent of police, she laid a formal charge against Horrox. She was promised that a summons should be served upon him and the child duly examined at the court.

Having completed the arrangements she felt happier, but her anxiety to hear more of the children induced her to seek the landlady, to whom she was determined to relate the whole circumstances.

That evening, seated in the old-fashioned sitting-room, she told her story of what she had seen, expecting the landlady to be surprised and horrified as was she herself, but to her astonishment she received the intelligence very quietly.

'He's the wust trainer I've ever had here,' she began. 'There's been nothing but bothers since he came. Some of them is very respectable, but this Horrox is a regular brute to them youngsters. Anyhow, he won't stay here. Ah, you don't know as much as I do as to how them children suffer.'

'They won't suffer much more,' added Leila. 'I have been after a summons. It will be served upon him to-morrow, and that will end it.'

She spoke quietly, as if she had done no uncommon thing.

'What—what!' exclaimed the astonished landlady. 'You've done what?'

'Been to the police court and told them how the child is treated. Surely that was the right course to pursue?'

'Oh, my dear, what *ever* will your husband say when he hears of it? One professional never does that to another. I'm afraid there'll be a terrible shine, that I do. But still if I can help you I will, for I've seen enough to make me sick of circus folk for many a long day. I shall try actors next, I think. My house ain't bad, is it?' she asked, looking round with an admiring gaze.

'It's a very nice house; anything would be better than tolerating cruelty, and even if my husband *is* vexed at the step I have taken, I shall still feel I have done my duty.'

'Well, I'm glad I'm not in your shoes anyway. As you have done the deed, I don't mind backing you up,' replied the woman emphatically.

'You must tell the truth if you are questioned,' said Leila gravely. 'But tell me what do you know of this "Guarez Family?"'

'Oh! I'll tell you all I know,' said the woman willingly. 'They came to lodge with me some months ago; there's six of them—five girls and one boy. That eldest girl, Alice as they call her, was taken very ill after they came here with low fever. Horrox got tired after a time of looking after her, and one night the girl was made to perform on the trapeze, ill and weak as she was. Later on in the same evening she did acrobat work, flip-flaps and other tricks, such as supporting four of the other children on her shoulders and holding them out by her hands. When she came home he abused her awfully. I was that sorry for her that the next day I made a point of watching for her to see if I could speak to her alone, but I got no chance. The children are never allowed to receive letters; and once when one came for Alice I managed to smuggle it to her on the stairs, but he beat her later when he found it out; indeed he works them all day and thrashes them cruelly. I caught him once beating Alice with a broom handle. I interfered several times, but having no husband, I am really afraid to go near him. To-day the boy came down for some hot water. I asked him what ailed his hands, for they were bandaged. He said he had burnt them. You see he dared not tell me. But I knew they hadn't a fire upstairs. I took him into my room and gave him an orange, and then the little man told me the truth. Bless his heart! I could have cried, that I could. I made up my mind then and there that Horrox should pack up his traps and go, and so he shall.'

'Why don't they run away?' asked Leila, who had grown pale and troubled during the narrative.

'They're all apprenticed to him, my dear. He pays the parents perhaps as much as thirty shillings a week for the use of the elder children. And those kind of parents don't care as long as the man sends the money. And where are they going to run, with no one to take them in? No clothes, no money, although Alice did tell me she'd run away at the first opportunity.'

'Why don't they tell someone—a policeman—in the street?' asked Leila innocently.

'Why, bless you, they never go out alone. He's too sharp for that,' said the woman knowingly; 'and several times, when the children have by some means reached the police, the trainers get them off to the Continent. That's what Horrox will do long before the summons comes on for hearing. You'll have your trouble for nothing I believe.'

'Surely the law will protect the children,' said Leila somewhat sadly. 'I must try to do what I can.'

She was determined to strike at the root of the evil, to expose rudely the horrors she had witnessed, to prevent, if possible, the children being shut out from protection and being forgotten by the world's thoughtless, forgetting throng.

Leila went to her room that night a saddened woman. She was stricken with a terrible dread. She has just begun to know, feel, and see the care and pain which children bear for the people's pleasure. Death, she thought, would be mercy compared with the daily toil and anguish suffered so patiently, so uncomplainingly.

She yearned to set the captives free. Hush! there was a footstep. It was her husband's. 'He will help me to save the little thin, wan boy from sufferings. He will prevent the cruelty, for my sake. He loves me so much.'

There was a great sorrow before her. The clouds were drawing nearer to the bright star, but she did not see them.

## CHAPTER IX.

### UNPROFESSIONAL.

The charmed spell, the sunlight, and the glory were passing away.

Sorrow and anxious care were very near.

Life's warfare was beginning. The gloom was about to rest on the flower, blighting it for ever.

Leila saw a terrible change come over her husband's face when she told him of all she had seen and the information she had given the police respecting Horrox.

She had expected he would give her sympathy, and offer prompt assistance, instead of which he turned upon her angrily.

'You have done this thing, Leila, without even asking me first. Do you forget I am your husband?'

He moved impatiently as he spoke. His face grew very white and stern.

'If you are my husband, surely you cannot blame me for putting an end to such cruelty. It shall not continue in any house where I am living,' replied Leila, with determination.

'And your interference will not be permitted,' said Castelli coldly.

'Perhaps not mine, but there are the police to interfere, and I'll take care they shall. Poor little boy!' she said with deep sympathy.

'*You* will take the thing in hand, will you?' replied Castelli, with suppressed passion. 'I'll take care you shall not.'

Leila looked at her husband in astonishment. He had never, till now, spoken an unkind word to her. He had been so gentle, so kind, so glad to listen to her various schemes and ideas. Suddenly he seemed transformed, his eyes had lost their kindliness, and he flashed a very angry look at her when he spoke.

'Emilio, do you mean it? Do you really mean what you are saying?'

'All, and a great deal more. Sit down,' he added sharply, 'I have something to say to you.'

Leila had been standing by the table, and his command aggravated her intensely.

'I prefer to stand,' she replied curtly.

'And I prefer that you should sit down. Leila, do as I tell you.'

Once again the old authoritative tone made her feel his power, and she moved towards the chair. He was silent until she had obeyed him, and then he continued,—

'You are *my* wife, and you must make up your mind to act as I wish. You have done a most foolish thing. I never heard of such a case excepting once, when two circus men appealed to a British Consul in Spain, saying that some English child was ill-treated by his master,* and a pretty upset there was over the brat. It is not usual for one person to split of another in our profession; we leave that job to those who are meddlesome and ignorant.'

She flushed scarlet, annoyed at his words, which seemed to imply that he thought her guilty and ignorant.

'It's ignorant people who *dare* not speak; it's not meddling to protect tiny children from brutal men—you know it is not,' she added with passion.

'I know it's not *your* place to interfere. There'll be a fine row to-morrow when Horrox finds out what you have done.'

* This is founded on the case of William Gregory, sent home from a circus by the British Consul at Barcelona in the *Alberio*, 1889.

'It will serve him right. I do not care in the least,' she added calmly.

'But I do; it may cause both Horrox and me to lose our engagements here. Proprietors do not care for a police court advertisement. Leila, you have behaved like a fool.'

'The man Horrox is the fool, I think,' replied Leila angrily, 'and don't apply that epithet to me. It's not kind or polite, and I should be glad if you will tell me if the proprietors of circuses are unaware of these horrible cruelties. I gather that is so, or why should you be afraid of the result of my action?'

Leila, by being constantly with her husband, had developed a very determined spirit. Naturally there was much of her mother's indomitable perseverance and courage, even if the cause was on the wrong lines, and her marriage with Castelli had fostered it largely, and added to her more experienced life. She was quite capable of standing her ground firmly on behalf of the little tortured child.

'Of course the proprietors don't know how the training is done,' replied Castelli hastily. 'They advertise for a "show," performing horses, acrobats, gymnasts. Do you think they are going to question *how* and by what method they are trained? The "show" is perfect. It will "draw" into the treasury plenty of gold. What else do they care for? It's not their place to ask questions. Perhaps some of the circus proprietors would make the devil of a fuss if they knew *how* the training is done, but you see they do not.'

'Then there *is* cruelty in the training, and you knew it all the time,' said Leila in a grieved tone.

Castelli smiled, not one of those gracious smiles which had fascinated her in the early days of their courtship.

'Of course I have known it all along, but it was no use to worry you with a lot of details.'

'Then you have grossly deceived me,' said Leila. 'You have lied to me, put me off with any story, but I have found you out at last.'

'Hold your tongue, Leila. You are forgetting yourself.'

'I will not.'

'Listen to me or leave the room,' said Castelli, now fast losing his temper. 'I'm not afraid to own my opinions before my wife, and now I will tell you straight off that force and cruelty are and must be employed to teach children their difficult and dangerous feats. If the brats won't work, and turn obstinate, there's nothing for it but the whip, and I approve of the method if success is to be won; how else is such perfection to be obtained?'

'You approve of it,' gasped Leila, 'you who pretended cruelty did not pay! I know now why you kept me so carefully from going to the circus. You were afraid I should hate you if I knew the truth. How could you deceive me?'

Her voice was soft and pathetic, and its tone struck Castelli painfully. Yet he was determined to put a stop to Leila taking proceedings against members of his profession. She must see that he was quite determined or mischief would come of it.

'Yes, I approve of discipline and severe measures when necessary, and in our line it *is* necessary.'

'Then I am sorry I ever came amongst you,' said Leila sadly. All her anger was gone. She was so bitterly disappointed that her heart sank within her, and she murmured faintly: 'All Horrox said was true then—all—all—'

'Go to bed, Leila, it is nearly one o'clock. For heaven's sake don't do the tragedy business. It does not suit you.

She never moved from her chair. His cruelty of words had shattered her nerves, overstrained her excitable and loving disposition.

'Do you hear me? Go to your room. We've said all there is to say at present. Drop the subject until I choose to speak to you again.'

She rose mechanically to do his bidding. As she passed him she hesitated one moment, and then, as if breathing out the most tender love, she said,—

'Emilio, will you kiss me?' She laid her little hand on his coat sleeve, as if to draw him nearer to her.

He stood looking at her, stern, austere, and unbending—a giant in his strength compared to the fragile figure before him.

'No, Leila, not to-night. I am very vexed with you—very.'

She turned away, choking down a sob as she did so. The anguish of that moment was supreme.

She went to her room, exhausted, weary, bereaved of her husband's love and kindness. Dispirited, and a little frightened at what she had done, she opened the window, as if hoping to gain some comfort from the clear, still air. She saw the moon was flooding the dark, grim-looking houses with a pale glimmer, making the great town look almost ghastly; and the bright cold stars made the scene very impressive, strange, and solemn.

But she was too crushed to notice the beauty of the early hours, the best and brightest before the dawn. She could only remember that the mask had fallen, and that the plain unvarnished truth was before her, to be borne as best she could. She had awakened to stern reality, and the waking robbed her of her joyous daydreams. Her happiness was like a delicate rosebud, born, but destroyed before the time to flower, or like the frail, tender blossom that would never turn to fruit.

She had trusted him implicitly. A doubt had never crossed her mind that he told her aught but truth, and now her faith was bruised and she could not heal it.

But she loved him still.

When the morning came, Castelli went down to the circus early. He had been coldly polite to Leila, indeed almost kind, but he had not kissed her or treated her in any way as usual.

All because she tried to wipe away childish tears, and to soothe a little broken heart.

'I say, Castelli, your fine lady wife has made a nice muddle down here. Horrox tells me that she had a summons served upon him this morning for beating one of the troupe. Is that so?' asked the manager.

'Yes,' said Castelli, 'it's quite true, I am ashamed to say.'

'Well, he's going off to the Continent this afternoon, so he declares, the whole "family" too, but I think he should remain at his post; it will make us short for the performance.'

'Oh, he'll be here right enough,' said Castelli. He was anxious that the manager should be appeased or awkward questions might be asked, although he knew that even then Horrox was on his way to Paris.

'I hope so; he has another month to run here. But did he really beat one of his apprentices?'

'According to a woman's point of view, yes; from ours, most decidedly not. My wife is a lady, refined, educated—well, a thorough lady, with a tender heart —and knows no more of circus life than the unborn babe. I suppose the child cried out before he was hurt, and my wife went up to the top room where the Guarez Family practised, and she saw Horrox strike the child with a cane—no more than a schoolmaster might do.'

'Oh, she's one of the modern women faddists, is she?' said the manager; 'one of these intolerant, interfering persons who belong to half-a-dozen ranting societies. Take my advice, Castelli, and put her to some work—a lady wife is no use to any man in our profession. I suppose you leave her to spend the day as best she can; no wonder she gets into mischief. You must employ her mind; but for heaven's sake keep her from making fools of us all in this style.'

'It will be the last time she will ever do it I can promise you,' said Castelli, who began to feel very uncomfortable and angry.

'Don't keep her at home doing nothing; that's the mischief,' repeated the manager, as he walked off without waiting for Castelli to reply.

Castelli was enraged to think that his wife had put him into such a degrading position in the circus. To have her talked over, and his management of her, drove him to think some hard things of the girl to whom a few short months before he had pledged such loving vows.

He turned to go towards the stables, when Hans, the vaulter and clown, came up to him.

'Is it true, Castelli, that your wife has run a summons on Horrox? My, she must be a good 'un, and no mistake! I'm glad she don't belong to me if she has.'

'It is not for you to question what my wife has done,' said Castelli loftily.

'Well, I suppose it is not, now I come to think of it,' replied the man, who kept the fun going in the ring for the children, and grown-up folks too.

'Pity you did not *think* before you spoke,' said Castelli.

'So I did. I thought what a fool she must be to do it, and what a fool you are to let her. So I thinked a think, didn't I?' he added, putting on a tone of voice he used in the ring and winking his eye at a groom standing near.

'No one wants to hear your jokes,' said Castelli, now furious. 'Keep them to yourself.'

'Couldn't, couldn't oblige you anyhow. You see I am a "quibber" by profession—bred in it, born in it, paid for it, and shall die in it,' and a good-natured smile overspread the man's face. 'I really only asked you the question for fun, because, when I heard of the summons, I was thinking what a stunning joke it would be if she tried the same game with you and your "gee-gees,"' and his face brightened at the mere idea of such an event.

'It will be time to think of that when it occurs,' said Castelli sullenly

'I should *think* it would indeed,' replied the clown with emphasis. 'But forewarned is forearmed, and I'm blowed if I'd trust her not to get you into some scrape.'

He hummed a popular air as he turned away, and Castelli went to the stables.

Whanks was there, busy with the horses. He came up to his master.

'Excuse me, sir, but be it true that Madam has summoned Horrox for cruelty to the children? You see, sir, I serves you, and all the circus keep asking *me* if it is true, and I don't like to be kept in the dark. It looks darned queer, in my position.'

'Yes,' replied Castelli, 'it is correct. As all these confounded busybodies seem to have heard it, you may as well know the truth. Don't ask me any more questions. You've got your answer, once and for all.'

'God bless Miss Leila!'

'She is my wife, Whanks, not Miss Leila at all,' broke in Castelli quickly.

'Beg pardon, sir. Well, heaven bless her, her heart's in the right place! I wish there was more like her, that I do—a dear good creature! I only wish my aunt's money would come and I'd help Miss Leila—bless my soul, I should have said Madam —to protect the children, that I would.'

'Be off to your work,' was Castelli's reply.

The man touched his dirty greasy cap as a token of respect, and shuffled off to the horses, and then Castelli wended his way home to his disconsolate wife.

He had determined upon the punishment he should inflict on Leila for her indiscretion. He would take her away from her quiet home life, from her books and dogs, and make her work as other women work.

But he did not count the cost of that labour for Leila. He forgot she was like a piece of delicate china which needed very careful handling.

Others went through the toil, and she should do the same. She would have no time then to find fault with the training of children.

But he was too wise to keep up the feud which had arisen between his wife and himself. She must look her best, and do him credit, and for this end he would meet her kindly.

She was sitting in a low chair as he entered, and he was really sorry to see her looking so wan and ill. She flushed slightly as he called her name.

'Leila, have you a kiss for me?' he asked her gently, as he put his face close to hers.

She did not reply, but burst into a flood of passionate tears. The reaction was almost too much for her to bear.

'Don't cry, Leila, my girl. The best of friends fall out sometimes. I daresay I was a little too rough with you, but I was dreadfully put out about that confounded summons. You see, Horrox has gone off to avoid the hearing, and down at our "show" they are not too well pleased.'

'He has gone, and the children too?' asked Leila between her sobs.

'Yes, gone off to the Continent,' said Castelli.

'Poor little Willie, and I *promised* to help him, and now he has gone.'

This thought brought the tears again in abundance.

'Don't fret like this, Leila, for heaven's sake. Be a brave girl. You will be quite ill,' said Castelli kindly. 'Besides, I have something cheerful to tell you. What do you think it is?'

She shook her head sadly, as if nothing could bring back either her happiness or her smiles.

'Well, I have been thinking you must be very dull here alone all day. I ought to have thought of that before. What do you think of coming down to the circus and learning professional riding—the *haut ecole*, of course, I mean? You ride so well now that you would soon become an expert, and come mounted into the ring with me. It would be nice to ride together, Leila, and make a really pretty "show." Will you try?'

She brightened at the idea. A little of the sunshine came back to the sad girlish face at the thought of the lonely days, now at an end, to be replaced by happy hours spent with her husband.

'I should like it very much, very much indeed. It has been lonely here sometimes. The days seem as if they would never pass. The change will be delightful.'

She almost looked herself again, and he was

truly glad to see the gloom dispersing and the old happy joyousness take its place.

'Well, by next week I daresay we can get your habit and skirt made, and then I'll mount you on "Mayflower." She's a splendid mare, and carries a lady to perfection. She has no vice—a baby could ride her—one of the finest in my stud,' said Castelli proudly.

'How kind you are, to think of me when you are so busy,' said Leila gratefully.

'Well, my precious little wifie must not sit here and mope any longer. Come, will you kiss me?'

She put her arms lovingly round his neck, and he stooped and kissed her many times.

'Now we are good friends again, eh?'

'Yes, oh yes,' she answered gladly, looking up at him with such a glad smile.

She was happy once more, yet her love had received a rude shock, and she could not forget all he had told her, and the deception practised upon her. She forgave him, but still the white page of her married life had a blot marring its fairness.

She could never feel quite the same, her heart had been so deeply wrung, and there was one slight wound which would never heal—the canker of a first quarrel, the remembrance of the first harsh words, the first wane in the brightness of their gladdened life.

'It shall be the last unhappiness,' Leila said to herself, as she lay down to rest that night, 'the very last.'

But the future was veiled.

## CHAPTER X.

### JOINING THE PROFESSION.

A KNOT of grooms and loungers were standing near the ring, gazing with admiring eyes at the dexterity of Castelli's young wife.

The trained horse knew its work better than its rider, but she was quick to take the cues, and they both seemed to yield, as if to assist each other.

Leila possessed a natural talent for riding. She had no fear. During her childhood she had been several times chidden by her riding-master for sheer recklessness. Most days since her marriage she had mounted a horse placed at her disposal by her husband, and had gone miles into the country with faithful old Whanks as guide and protector; but riding quietly just where she pleased was very different to displaying the talents of a celebrated 'trick horse.' But she was an apt pupil, and soon won the admiration of the artistes engaged in the circus.

On this particular morning the rehearsal had been a great success, and Castelli felt very proud of Leila's equestrian feats. Even the grooms and attendants were excited to plaudits. She held her seat firmly whilst the horse knelt down, and performed other difficult tricks.

Castelli saw money in his beautiful wife, and he determined to lose no time in bringing her before the public.

'You must try her again in the waltz, Leila,' said Castelli, 'but you had better rest her for a moment or two.'

Leila did as her husband directed, but the beautiful, impatient creature was difficult to hold in. Castelli saw her trouble, and went up to the horse, putting up his finger before it. In a moment it ceased his restless pawing of the sawdust and became subdued. Leila was astonished at the docility of the animal. She did not realise that his training had been forced by the whip for resistance and a carrot for obedience.

Whilst she was resting she caught sight of a woman amongst a group of men who had just strolled into the circus. She had seen the face before, but not since the dear courting days at Sandcliffe. It was Cleo. There was no mistaking the handsome face which looked at her with such scorn and pride.

To Leila it seemed as if she said, 'Oh, you're come to this, are you?' and she felt almost ashamed that she should be seen there in the ring as one of them, for had not Castelli boasted everywhere that she was a lady, and not to be connected with the circus at all. Of course he had led everyone to believe that the choice had been his wife's, and that he had consented to please her, and to this arrangement Leila had given a tacit consent.

In a moment she realised that this woman had been meeting her husband since their marriage, and had now probably taken an engagement at the same circus. The very idea of this brought the blood to her face in an angry flush. All her interest in her work was gone for that day, and she signalled to her husband, who was chatting with another trainer in the middle of the ring, to come to her.

'I should like to dismount; I don't think I shall ride any more to-day'

'Are you ill, Leila, that you make such a strange request? You must remember it is business here, not a place for me to indulge you in absurd fancies,' said Castelli sternly.

'I'm not ill, but I will *not* ride with that dreadful woman Cleo standing there; I will *not* be in the same place with her. I am going home,' replied Leila, with great determination.

'You are *not*,' said Castelli quietly. 'The woman has as much right here as you have. She begins an engagement here this week, so you must meet sometimes. Don't be foolish, Leila, or you will make me angry.'

'I shall call one of the grooms, for I mean to go,' said Leila, 'I'm not bound to work here.'

'What you have undertaken *I* will see you carry out, and as ringmaster I command you remain here until I consider your rehearsal at an end.'

His face grew very stern and hard. The group of which Cleo was one wondered at the change, and surmised that the conversation between the couple had not a very pleasant purport.

Castelli saw that wondering eyes were upon them, and to avoid further observation he ordered in a loud voice the grooms to bring in the five-barred gate for Leila to take her leap. He approached the horse, and examined bit and bridle carefully.

'If you expect me to take the gate safely to-day let me tell you I have not the courage to do so,' said Leila, trembling with passion.

She had only gone over the gate a few times, and Castelli always took every precaution to ensure her safety. He was anxious now to steady her before the leap.

'Leila, do be brave,' he added kindly. 'Let them all see what you can do. Would you fail because an enemy is here? Rather show her how clever you are, and how proud I am of you.'

His words were sufficient to give her back all her courage, all her determination. He could not have fired her ambition better than by uttering those few sentences.

The men placed the gate in position, and Castelli called to Leila,—

'Are you ready? Sit back, quite back, and you'll be safe. She'll take you over in good style.'

And she did. Without the shadow of a mistake she cleared the gate, and landed with ease on the other side.

'Take care of the door frame, Madam,' said one of the grooms. 'You're apt to catch your 'ead if she makes for the stables sudden like.'

'Thank you, that would be a terrible death,' said Leila, grateful for the man's warning.

Her husband came up to her and rewarded her with a smile, and Leila was gratified with her success.

But there was one there who could have cursed the groom for his timely warning, one whose cruel wrath against an innocent woman knew no softening: in her breast was buried undying hate, she would have slain the fair rider had she dared. Passion, jealousy, and unconquered love ruled her still.

Leila was happy in her work, and as yet she had witnessed no cruelty in the ring during the short time she was at the circus.

One morning she strolled down earlier than usual. She passed the horses in their stalls, and spoke a kindly word to the three boarhounds, which were playing in an unused stall, and then she made her way into the circus. She began to feel at home now in the great, bare, cold building, and her husband allowed her to go in and out pretty much as she liked, as long as he was about; but business had taken him from the circus this one day, and Signor Pandini was delegated to act as riding-master for the occasion.

Suddenly a dull, continuous sound of horses' hoofs reached Leila's ear, and at intervals the crack of a whip—someone was rehearsing—she would go and see who it was, for she was young enough in her profession not to have lost any of the charm of the life, and her curiosity was as keen as ever. An infamous oath, followed by the crack of a whip and a shrill cry of physical pain, smote her with apprehension. She hastily put aside the heavy curtains which hung over the great doors, and the horrors of the ring burst upon her.

The daylight was streaming in through the high windows, making the circus look cold and cheerless with its hundreds of vacant seats; there was no one to be seen excepting an angry man in the ring, and a mere girl, dressed in a wide grey skirt and knickerbockers, loose at the knees. She had made several 'slips,' and had just received a severe cut or two from her master. She was very pale, and her face was stamped with an expression of the greatest fear and suffering. Leila stepped back into the shade of the curtains—she would not retreat farther, and she dare not let her presence be found out.

Again and again the hoop was held by the trainer, but from want of courage the girl failed to spring at the last moment.

Leila saw her taken from the horse, and such punishment bestowed on her with a thin white-thonged whip, that she withdrew with a shudder.

Her cries for mercy, and the degradation of the girl's position, made Leila grow very faint. She was rooted to the spot by the terrible spectacle, but she dare not move. There had been a time when she would have called for assistance, and led the way herself, but somehow she had grown strangely afraid of Castelli; and she did not wish to incur his anger if it were possible to avoid it.

When the man had expended his wrath, he kicked her several times, and then her awful lesson came to an end.

Leila escaped from her hiding-place, and betook herself to the office used by her husband and Signor Pandini. She felt ill and sick at heart. And had it not been for incurring Castelli's displeasure she would have begged Pandini to dispense with her lesson.

He was waiting, however, and he remarked as she entered,—

'I wonder if Dutasti is out of the ring yet? He keeps his pupil such a darned long time.'

'I think the lesson is over,' said Leila faintly, 'for I met him a moment ago.'

'Then we'll proceed to business at once,' said Pandini, and together they went into the ring. The horse was brought out, and Leila went through her duties mechanically, as if her thoughts were far away from the circus. Once or twice Pandini noticed her inattention, and fearing she might loose control over her horse, he called her to order rather sharply. 'I think you might do your best, Madam, even if your husband is away; it's rather ungracious to ride your worst,' he said in a vexed tone.

Leila felt the man spoke the truth, and she threw off her distress for the time, and gave all her energy to her work.

'That's good, Madam, very good,' said Pandini from time to time. And when her lesson was over she was still more gratified to hear his warm approval of her efforts.

Then she went in search of the wretched ill-treated girl, whose name she heard was Louie Paran. But a week passed before she was able to have any conversation with her. After that she had one or two secret meetings with her.

Leila was horrified to hear of her constant sufferings.

'I am kept practising morning, noon, and night, for if it is not horses it's "bending," which is contortion, you know. There is no rest for me,' said the girl sadly, 'and I am covered with bruises; sometimes I ache in all my limbs so that I cannot sleep at night. My life is a misery to me.'

'Well, it cannot last for ever,' said Leila with great compassion; 'the day shall come when you will be free, as others are.'

The girl sighed, the hope of that seemed so far away.

'I am only sixteen,' she replied; 'I have five years yet to serve my master.'

'Is there no appeal against such cruel treatment?' asked Leila; 'have you ever made an attempt to get protected?'

'Never. One of our girls managed somehow or other to summons her master, but the magistrate dismissed it, and she got the worst of it. The summonses are always set on one side, the girl gets no chance against her master. There are lots of dodges, heaps of means to get out of the scrape. The girl is told she must tell the magistrate she is very happy, and the parents are paid to declare how much better in health the girl is since she was apprenticed, and in due course the master has the pull. I wouldn't try,' she added; 'I'd rather suffer to my death than take the risk of losing the day. Ah! you don't know what the existence is. Sometimes I think I shall put an end to my life; death cannot be worse to bear—it can only come once, and then the pain is over.'

'Be brave, dear girl; I will see what I can do. Don't do anything rash, promise me you will not,' said Leila in distress.

'I shall not have the chance, I am afraid,' replied the girl wearily. 'I only wish I could see a lady who was the wife of the proprietor of a big Continental circus. She was English herself. She was very kind to me, and saved me a terrible beating one day when I was giddy and kept falling. You see, my master did not mind her, knowing she belonged to the circus and up to all the secrets, but she begged him to leave off, so he did, after abusing her for interfering. I heard she is coming here on business, but even if she does I may not get a word with her.'

'Yes, you shall; what is her name, Louie? I will look out for her and mention you to her,' said Leila in a glad tone of voice.

'Madame Meurice,' replied the girl; 'but I am afraid the chances of her coming are very small,' she added desperately.

'Shall I write to her?' asked Leila.

'No, no, pray don't do that, it might all be found out,' said the girl hastily, all the while fear of her master's anger rising before her.

'You can trust me, my dear,' said Leila gently. 'I shall never mention a word of this conversation. You must believe me, I am so sorry for you,' and she pressed a kiss on the girl's thin cheeks.

The little act of kindness touched Louie Paran's heart, and a few silent tears coursed down her face.

Poor child, she so rarely heard loving words, and had forgotten who had kissed her last; it was so many years ago, it seemed like a dream.

'Good-bye,' said Leila; 'I will do the best I can to find your friend, and one of these days I shall come and chat with you again.'

'If you get the chance,' replied the girl sadly, as she turned away, but happier for the tenderness which had gladdened the gloom.

When Leila and her husband were sitting together that evening she never mentioned the incident of the day. It had become usual for her now to keep her troubles and vexations to herself.

Castelli stood lighting his cigar at the candle, and then, after settling himself comfortably in the arm-chair, said,—

'That Canadian skating show has got the sack from the manager down at our place. Rather hard considering they've only been married eight months.'

Leila's sympathy was aroused at once, and she asked,—

'Why have they left?'

'Oh, because the wife is ill,' replied Castelli carelessly, 'and she will not put on a smile to the public, and lets every fool know she is unhappy. Her husband told me that she had been crying all day before she went on the rink, and now they have both to turn out. The managers do not want people who *show* when they are ill—you can't expect it.'

Castelli spoke in an offhand, curt manner, and betrayed no sympathy with the suffering woman.

'What a shame!' said Leila; 'she cannot help being ill.'

'No one said she could, but she *can* help showing it. The people pay to be amused, not to be depressed and made sad,' replied her husband in a cold tone.

'It seems to me,' said Leila, 'that amusement must be procured for those who can pay for it whether others suffer or not.'

'Just so; as long as the people clap down their money we must provide them with what they pay for.'

'And they require the performance of feats at

the expense of cruelty and hardships,' replied Leila with disgust.

'The public don't care a curse as long as they get their shilling's-worth,' said Castelli quietly.

'I believe they would if they knew the truth. It's want of knowledge not want of heart which makes them applaud the very things which have cost the artiste the greatest suffering, the sharpest pain. Dare you or any master of apprentices train in public? You would not like all the world to know that the whip has so prominent a place; but some day the truth will out, and then shall come the remedy.'

'Rubbish!' said Castelli angrily. 'What a pity you are not a Methodist preacher. You'd better hold your tongue. I daresay I shall live to hear that you have joined some confounded society which gets big subscriptions from the weak-minded rich to enable them to poke their noses where they are not wanted. It's time to put a stop to your interference. At anyrate, I don't intend you to pose as a philanthropist, so make your mind up to that. A woman's place is to do as she is told, and not go gadding about talking like a fool. Philanthropy be hanged.'

'I wish there were more philanthropists,' said Leila gravely, 'and more protection for the children.'

'Philanthropists be hanged!' replied Castelli with rising passion.

She rose and left the room. She was so hurt when he spoke to her thus. It was a very common occurrence now, yet she could not accustom herself to it, and the tears always came, battle against them as she would.

It takes time for unkindness to pierce the anguished heart. The way is through grief, sorrow, and disappointment. Kind words must have die and love taken its flight before it can reach the soul.

Some weeks after Leila's chat with Louie Paran she heard that the girl had run away, and all efforts to trace her had utterly failed. After her 'turn' in the ring at an evening performance she was never seen again.

Only Whanks knew that Madame Meurice had driven past the circus, muffled up most carefully so that no one could recognise her. He alone had seen a sign which had been agreed upon, and in a moment Louie was in the cab and off; and the next day, when all the circus was in confusion over the loss of Louie Paran the great 'trick rider,' Whanks could have told them that she was on board a steamer bound for the East.

But he held his tongue, and only murmured to himself, 'If I had my aunt's money I would have gone too, be hanged if I would not.'

Whanks had seen the girl go—for Leila had made the way easy. She did not forget her promise. The white slave had escaped the tyrant's cruel hand, and Leila was happier for the risk she had run in taking part in the girl's abduction.

But she kept her own counsel.

## CHAPTER XI.

### IN THE TRANSVAAL.

BETWEEN Leila and her brother there was—space, that great undefined yet limitable division which separates one half of a wondering world from the other.

There was the sea, girding the earth like heaven, the same for ever, stamped with the great impress of the Unchangeable.

There were only memories left for either of them. Like a dream came back the sound of a beloved voice, the grasp of a familiar hand, and the unity of profound love, the dearest thing which wealth can never buy.

Away from the glare and heat of the cities, away from the civilised world, away from home and friends and all that the young hold dear, was Tom Gurney. Yet he was very happy, and grateful to those who had given him the opportunity of starting in life in a new country.

The splendid climate had given him renewed health and spirits, which influenced his physical nature and the tendencies of his mind, rendering him less hopeless, and making him forget much of his shame.

The roadside store which had been Tom's home for the last two years belonged to his friend's father, Mr Webb, and was known as Malan store. It was situated near the Vaal River, which forms the boundary between the Orange Free State and the South African Republic.

The store itself was a commodious one-storied building. In appearance it was of somewhat rude make; sand and sun-dried bricks being the only commodities at hand. It was used for articles of sale alone, and the accommodation was hardly sufficient for the demand made upon it. Three hundred yards apart from the store was the house occupied by Mr Bates, the manager, two clerks, and Tom Gurney. Both buildings stood by the side of the track which served as a 'waggon road' across the undulating veldt, over which travellers often had very disagreeable experiences.

Tom had frequently known an ox-waggon to arrive at the store the occupants of which could tell him of blinding storms of dust swirling and sweeping all that lay before them, of fearful paroxysms in the storm, the fury of the wind, the terrible darkness, the dazzling flashes of lurid lightning followed by deafening peals of thunder. But as suddenly as the storm arose came the lull, and the sun would shine over the veldt with renewed lustre and beauty.

From the store little could be seen but short stunted grass, and there were no trees to spread forth great arms of bushy leaves to give a grateful shade from the scorching heat of the midday sun—bare, intolerably hot, the air often heavy with dust, it tried the patience of the four Englishmen at times beyond endurance.

When no clouds of dust were rising from the ox-waggons there could be seen in the far distance a collective circle of huts—Kaffir kraals—just distinguishable against the clear blue sky, where the stalwart forms of the Zulus reposed during the heat of the day.

Tom would sigh sometimes when he gazed upon the little piece of enclosed land which surrounded the store and dwelling-house, where nothing grew but a field of mealies and a few common vegetables, and he would long for just one sight of an English garden, with its roses and budding carnations, its freshness and its summer beauty.

But with the thoughts of the flowers came the remembrance of his mother, and his sigh would turn to a happy smile of contentment because no shame arose from the mealie field or from the great tract of land which lay beyond.

Tom's life was a busy one despite the lack of genial companionship and the fact that the nearest neighbours were four weary miles away and all the farms just as far apart.

The Boers were continually riding their pack-horses up to the store, or driving in their ox-waggons, for the purpose of bartering for goods and drink. They would bring skins or wool, and sometimes garden stuff, tied up in rags of such disgusting appearance that they were speedily dispensed with. When Tom had been at the store only a few weeks, he refused on several occasions to receive these exchanges; and then Mr Bates explained to him the nature of the people with whom they had to deal.

'You must always take something in exchange,' he told Tom kindly. 'It does not matter whether it is worthless to us or not. The Boers are our customers. They are terribly cute, and prefer to barter rather than pay money, in the hope of getting the best of the bargain. If once you refuse to take their offer all the farmers round would hear of it, and we should get a bad name and lose custom. So, when you see a Boer coming to the store, you must use your eyes and your tact or he will impose on your ignorance and we may be considerable losers.'

Tom did not forget this friendly warning, and for the future he kept very strict guard over all the transactions of the Boers.

But there was another class of customers who were very welcome to all at the store, and those were the travellers who were 'on the road' from Durban to Pretoria. These people often 'outspanned' for a few hours, and then was the opportunity of learning news of the world and the old country. It was a source of great delight to Tom to watch for the little dim shadow, which in the far distance looked like a tiny cloud, gathering larger and still more large as it came towards him. He knew it was the herald of the approach of travellers, and that the mass was but the dust, the result of the team of oxen drawing the great heavy lumbering waggon towards the store. Their progress was always slow, and Tom would watch with interest the slow pace of the oxen coming across the veldt, with their freight of human beings and cases of goods and furniture. But sometimes, as the waggon came nearer, much to Tom's chagrin, it was found to be nothing more than the waggon of the travelling 'smouse,' making for the store to buy clothes and other things suitable for emigrants coming into the country that he might have run short of. With these articles the smouse traded, visiting the distant farms and homesteads, but he rarely had much news to convey to the store, and he, like the riders of transport, was never very welcome.

Through the kindness of Mr Bates, Tom Gurney had seen a great deal of the vast country around him. He had been allowed to spend a short holiday at Barkly West, the small colonial town on the bank of the Vaal River. This gave him the opportunity of wandering in many picturesque spots by the broad, winding stream, and enjoying the beauties of the scene, which to him had all the pleasure of novelty, besides being a relief after the dry, barren surroundings of the store. On one occasion he had been sent to Peniel on business for the manager, and Tom was delighted to make acquaintance with the first mining town. From there his work took him to Warrenton, a low-lying district, but rich in luxurious gardens, fields, and fruit, nourished as it was by the irrigation of the cool waters of the Vaal River. There was much to impress him, and on his return to the store he wrote to his father, giving him a varied description of all he had seen, recounting graphically the fort at Barkley West—or Klipdrift as it was once called—and which had no other significance than implying that the 'drift' or ford situated close to the town, for the accommodation of the huge ox-waggons to cross the Vaal, was very stony when the waters were not too high to render it dangerous. He described how he had stumbled and slipped over the immense number of loose stones which were lying about on all sides, telling their silent tale of how eager, trembling hands had turned them over when Barkly West had been the site of the old diamond 'diggings.'

Whenever he wrote these long letters home a longing to have his father and sister with him always arose in his mind. Yet he knew his father would never settle down to the new life and his sister become the wife of a colonist. So, after all, they were best in the old country. But sometimes he felt he would give much to meet one gentle English girl, someone with whom he could exchange a few tender, refined words. But though he loved to linger over the thought, he quickly banished it. Was it likely that the barren veldt, the heavy ox-waggon, could furnish him with such a treasure?

But there is a fate even in the desert land.

One hot afternoon, as there were no customers in sight, the manager locked the door of the store, and he and his clerks went forth to indulge in a game of cricket. The ground was hot, dried, and cracked, and it was some time before Tom could arrange the wickets satisfactorily. At length the game began. The spectators consisted of a little band of Kaffirs and Swazi labourers from the store, who sat at a safe distance, watching with silent, scornful wonder the 'white man's' eccentricities.

So eager was the play that a cloud of dust gradually developing in the distance was unheeded, and the tent waggon, drawn by fourteen slow-going oxen, came towards them.

Suddenly Tom called to his companions,—

'Look out, old fellows, customers are on the way.'

At this bats, balls, and wickets disappeared, and they all turned to the store to be ready to supply the necessities required by the advancing party.

When the waggon drew up it was seen to contain a middle-aged man, George Herepath, a young girl, a little younger than Tom, and three small boys.

A couple of Swazis were in charge of the oxen, and all seemed very fatigued after their dusty and heated journey. Mr Herepath alighted, and Tom, who had lingered near the door of the store to satisfy his curiosity as to who had arrived, was the first to be addressed.

Tom saw with one rapid glance that the man standing before him was a gentleman and an Englishman, two virtues highly appreciated at the store. Yet there was something strikingly sad about the stranger's face; it was so grave, so devoid of happiness, that it gave Tom the impression that he was either ill or disappointed with his prospects in the new country, and a pity arose in his heart for him even before he spoke.

The voice of the stranger was subdued and almost weary in its monotone as he said,—

'Good day, sir; can you tell us where we can out-span for the night? We must rest a few hours, replenish our stock of provisions, and look to the beasts. We have kept close to the waggon road, and there have been several long reaches without surface water. The cattle must be both hungry and thirsty.'

'Certainly,' replied Tom. 'Look here,' he called

to the two Swazis, 'you can draw the waggon near to the enclosure by the house, and the oxen can feed a little lower down. The grass is the best we have about, and there is plenty of water.'

Before there was time for the stranger to utter his thanks Mr Bates came out to the waggon.

'They are an English party,' said Tom, 'and they will out-span here for the night. I have told the men where to take the oxen. Is that right, sir?'

'Quite,' replied Mr Bates with satisfaction. 'And so you have come from Durban I suppose?' he said, turning to the stranger.

'Yes, we are on our way to Pretoria,' remarked the man in a hopeless voice. 'Sometimes I wish I had never brought the chicks so far; but here we are, so I suppose I may as well make up my mind to put up with it.'

'How many are there of you?' asked Mr Bates, ignoring the man's discontented mood.

'My daughter and three little boys,' said the man sadly. 'Five of us altogether. There were six when we started from England, but my wife died on the voyage out, and we buried her at sea,' he added in a tone of deep distress.

'Well, suppose the Swazis take the waggon to the out-span and you bring your little family in to supper,' said Mr Bates kindly, really sorry for the man's trouble in a lone land.

The offer was gladly accepted, and soon the matter of introductions was over and the party sat down to a very hospitable board. Mr Bates and Mr Herepath kept up a lengthy conversation about the country in general, touching on the administration and the different settlements and the local irritation in some of the outlying districts; the three younger boys made merry with the clerks; and Tom Hasketh—the name he had always been known by in the country he had adopted as his home—was left to entertain Fanny Herepath.

She was a finely developed girl, with dark eyes and hair, and her whole appearance was one of the greatest intelligence. Honesty of purpose, an outspoken manner, a determination to make the best of the journey at once won Tom's admiration, and his sympathy was aroused when she told him with faltering voice of the death of her mother.

'I shall have father and the boys to see after now. It's a good thing I'm strong, for with health I can be the right hand and do for them as mother would have wished.'

'It will be a dreadful toil for you, in a new country too. I am awfully sorry for you.'

'I hope I have a brave heart,' she replied stoutly. 'It is no use to be thinking of the work before me. It is best to meet it as it comes.'

'You are brave,' said Tom with genuine admiration, 'and I am sure your father and brothers will find you a treasure.'

'I must help them all I can. The children must not miss *her* care,' she added softly. 'And as to father, I can make him comfortable and get a home around him. Happy he will never be now mother is dead. Poor father, he has lost his money and his wife all in a year. This time twelvemonths death and ruin seemed very far away. It does seem years since then.'

Something like tears glistened in her big brown eyes, and Tom offered all the consolation he could.

'Brighter days are in store for you at Pretoria,' he said cheerfully. 'Your father will grow strong and rich, the boys will be giants in their strength and health, and you will marry a rich colonist.'

'Marry, and leave the children!' she repeated with contempt, as if the suggestion had been almost an insult when her duties lay in the little family circle. 'Never; I shall never leave them—never,' she added with emphasis.

'But they will not be children always,' said Tom apologetically. 'Of course I meant when they were big boys.'

'That will be a long time. Let me see, Percy is only ten, and Willie eight, and Georgy seven. They are all babies,' she added sadly, 'and—motherless.'

Suddenly, as if wishing to break the line of conversation and change the subject to one more pleasant, she exclaimed,—

'The journey here was most enjoyable. If novelty could be said to give pleasure, we had several adventures which interested me. Do *you* care to hear, or does it bore you? I daresay my experiences will be only the old stories over again.'

'I shall be a most delighted listener,' replied Tom. 'Any news is appreciated I can tell you. In this region, charming as it is, the isolation from the outer world is trying at times and makes us greedy for incident of any kind. Please go on.'

She smiled and continued,—

'Coming across the veldt our trek of oxen had a "scrick" and bolted. We were afraid we should be upset, but our Swazi driver handled them splendidly. They ran a long distance. The boys enjoyed it, but I knew the danger.'

'What scared them?' asked Tom.

'The smell of the lion skin at the back of the waggon; it is strange that oxen should be so afraid of even the smell of a lion,' said Fanny Herepath thoughtfully.

'It is,' replied Tom; 'but they must possess some wonderful instinct, for it is a fact that calves born in the colony and grown up here, and who have never seen a lion, will bolt at the smell of the skin.'

'When they stopped they were very restless, and our "voorlooper" had to lead the two front oxen even when there were no dangerous places for him to guide them over ; but he advised us to out-span for a time. So we did, or we should have arrived here a day earlier. After that we came along splendidly, until we came across a waggon which had broken down on the road, and we waited to help the Boer and his vrouw and children out of their difficulties.'

'Did you come across any of the Zulus asking for tobacco, or what they call *gwi* ?'

'Not any,' said Fanny ; 'are they fond of it ?'

'Very. Sometimes the whole of a Zulu kraal will surround a waggon and demand with the greatest persistence *gwi*, and nothing will satisfy them until their demands are attended to ; and it is a funny sight to watch both men and women sitting smoking with their bone pipes, made out of the leg bone of blesbok. It's a pity you did not come across them.'

'What are blesbok ?' asked Fanny. 'You see, she continued, 'I know very little of the country at present, and the name is quite unfamiliar to me.'

'Blesbok, springbok, koodoo, and elands are large game, and fine sport for those who have time to go out gun in hand. A Kaffir brought me a slice once, and showed me how to prepare it— the flavour was delicious.'

'Have you many flowers here ?' asked Fanny Herepath ; 'it all looks so bare, so dry and dusty.'

'Well, you see, you are rather too late, and not early enough for what few there are. The stony roads between the low hills are covered by a plant called the Vaal bush ; the perfume is sweet, the leaves are often boiled and used as tea, and very pleasant in flavour; and I have seen lilies quite equal to any met with in English greenhouses growing among the rocks in the kloofs near to the springs. But, of course, to my mind there can be no flowers so beautiful as those which grow in the dear old country.'

Somehow, flowers always reminded Tom of his home. The blooms on the veldt spoke silently of the sweet-scented roses in the cottage homes of England.

'Ah! I must not think of England,' said the girl, rising from the table; 'where the thoughts are the wish will be sure to follow, and I must be content where I am for the sake of the others.'

Tom knew then that the girlish heart was very sore, that the craving for home was very keen, and what an effort it was to speak so bravely for the sake of those she held so dear.

Surely no soldier went to the battlefield with more heart, more courage to fight for Queen and Country.

Mr Bates and Mr Herepath had finished their lengthy chat, and the clerks had done their best to amuse the little boys. Altogether the evening had been very happily spent. Tom was more struck with his charming companion than he would like to have owned.

And they all retired to their out-span more cheerful for the hospitality offered them and the genial companionship.

Fanny Herepath and her little brothers retired to rest in the waggon, upon a thick mattress and plenty of rugs, but her father occupied a tent attached to the waggon, while the Swazi drivers made themselves comfortable beneath it.

But Tom did not repose so peacefully. His

thoughts were upon Fanny Herepath, and when he did fall asleep it was but to dream of her trouble and her bravery, and to wish she was not going to Pretoria, so far away.

When the morning at last dawned, Tom and Fanny Herepath met again. This time they stood outside the store, Tom helping the native labourers to put tea, coffee, sugar, mealies, and flour into the waggon, whilst Mr Herepath was hearing from Mr Bates a description of the road, and where water was to be met with between the store and Pretoria.

After the necessaries were loaded, Tom stayed by Fanny's side, watching a group of Zulu girls, who had brought maize and vegetables to the store to exchange for some beads and brass wire, which they used as ornaments.

'They are very handsome girls,' said Fanny with admiration,

'Yes, some of the Kaffir tribes are very handsome,' said Tom. 'They are so tall, so erect. I never saw a Kaffir woman stoop.'

'How is that?' asked Fanny with curiosity.

'The constant habit of carrying heavy Kaffir pots of water on their heads. This, of course, can only be done by walking very upright,' replied Tom.

'Are you ready, Fanny, my girl?' broke in her father. 'We shall start directly.'

'Dear me! I nearly forgot that I want some needles,' replied the girl. 'You have some here, of course?'

She went into the store with Tom. He was a minute or so before he returned to her, and when he did so he carried a small box in his hand.

'Will you accept this, Miss Herepath, as a little remembrance of our pleasant meeting? It contains needles, pins, and cotton sufficient for six months. It will give me much pleasure if you will take it.'

'Thank you, Mr Hasketh,' added the girl gratefully, whilst her flushed face betrayed how great was her pleasure at the gift. 'It is my first present in the new country. I wonder who will give me the next?'

'Perhaps I may,' said Tom. 'I fancy we shall meet again some day. I hope so, indeed I do.'

She looked up, somewhat astonished at his earnest tone.

Without thinking, she answered,—

'I hope so too. It would be delightful.'

All the odds and ends were in the waggon, the Swazi drivers had taken their places on the waggon box, the voorlooper was standing by the trek of oxen, all was ready for the start.

'Good-bye,' said Fanny kindly to Tom, as he placed her in the waggon, 'and thank you very much.'

'Good-bye,' replied Tom quietly, as he squeezed her hand in his. 'We shall meet again, Miss Herepath, some day. Remember me till then.'

'I will,' she said, as the waggon moved off. 'Good-bye.'

Tom stood watching it growing less and less across the veldt. He saw the distant hills, one blaze of golden light, the clear atmosphere casting lovely and varied reflection around him. Above was the bright, glowing sky, a brilliant landscape almost too grand to be appreciated by mankind.

But the waggon had gone. It was hidden altogether behind a rise in the land, and as Tom turned towards the store it seemed as if some of the tints in the rosy sky had faded and some of the loveliness of the morning had departed.

They would meet again some day. He was sure of that.

And so was she.

## CHAPTER XII.

### 'MOTHER!'—'LEILA!'

FIVE years had passed, and to Leila they had been very weary years. Never very strong in health, the life had told upon her delicate constitution. Performing as she was obliged, at the circus with Castelli every day, sometimes twice, and the constant moving from place to place, either on the Continent or in England, fatigued her dreadfully. However, worn out and tired, she must move on when her duties called her. There had been no home life, nothing but exchanging one set of apartments for another, one town for the next. Added to this she had the heavy responsibilities of motherhood. Two children, a little fair girl of four and a delicate boy of three years, claimed her love and her care. To them Leila was devoted. It was for their sakes that she struggled so bravely against the hardships of her life. It was for them that she faced her husband's anger and toiled as the slave at the galley.

Had it not been for the kindness of some of the wives of the riders, and other artistes, Leila would have had a much harder time of it than she had, for some of them were always willing to 'mind' the children whilst the mother was at her rehearsals, and in the evening they would offer to let one of their children go up and sit with them until they fell asleep. These acts of genuine kindness touched Leila to the heart, and bound her with a debt of gratitude and love to those so far beneath her.

It had been a terrible time for Leila when she had awakened to the true character of her much loved husband, when she found how hard and cruel he was. At first the dawning of the truth stupefied her, she could not grasp the situation. But the consciousness came all too soon, and she knew then the awfulness of her position.

Discarded by her father, and as she thought by her brother also, for she had not heard from Tom since her marriage, the wife of a man who had forgotten the love he had promised her when he first sought and won her girlish heart—was it any wonder that she looked back on the past, sometimes revelling in the visions which memory raised in moments when she was free from care? These feelings of the bygone days were the only joy, the only light piercing through the gloom, and she welcomed them with an unhealthy yearning.

Poor Lelia, was it not a shame that a husband's harshness, a husband's cruelty should dispel the promised love and joy, and that grief and fear should break the dream once so fraught with bliss?

But alas, it was so!

Five years of dark shadows had not tended to improve Leila's character. A great deal of the gentleness and sweetness of disposition was changed. She had grown cold, unbending, doing her duty, and suffering in silence, asking neither for praise nor sympathy. It was only when Castelli was displeased with her that any of the old and more kindly nature showed itself. His power over her was as strong as in the earlier days. Sometimes she would plead with him not to speak such cruel words, to kiss her just once.

But he refused the transient pleasure that love demanded, and Leila would turn away and try to crush the pain and still her throbbing heart.

Once when she was rehearsing, too weary and depressed to take much interest in her work, a sharp cut from his whip and a fearful oath from his lips caused her to faint from actual physical pain and fear. It was the first time he had ever struck her, and like a crushed flower she bent her head and dared not look up for very shame.

She would have left him after that, but the motherhood within her bade her stay. Must she not guard the little ones, and shield them, and be the bright star to shine over them through all the miseries of their roving life? to be near to comfort them, to dry the tears from the baby faces, to win back the smiles to rosy lips? Yes, that was her duty.

Fear, shame, and despair must be endured for their sweet sakes—the tender, the young, from whose lips the divine word 'mother' gave Leila such intense happiness. For them she would have sacrificed her life if the need arose, and yet their father was the man from whom she had received the greatest insults.

But she was their mother.

The circus had been in Paris some time, and Castelli and Leila had done much by their performances to draw large audiences to the cirque in the Champs Elysées, and the weeks had passed more quietly than usual. Her apartments off the Faubourg St Honorè were comfortable, and if the street was small at least it was quiet, and this Leila enjoyed after the wear and tear of constant travelling.

The Lenten gloom was over, and Eastertide, with its joys and pleasure, had begun. The streets were so full that it was hard to get along; the cafés were crammed with men, women, and children; some of the visitants were sitting sipping their coffee and cognac at the small round marble tables outside and enjoying the passing and repassing of the mighty throng.

There was life and pleasure everywhere.

Leila, carrying her baby boy and guiding Vanda as best she could, hurried through the crowded streets. She looked so pale and weary that the people at the tables gave her glances of sympathy as she passed, and murmured words of pity, and ceased their chattering to watch her on her way.

'Keep close to me, Vanda, darling, or mother will lose you.'

'How far is it now, mother?'

'Not far, darling.'

Leila was getting exhausted, the weight of her boy was considerable; but she hurried on, looking neither to the right nor left, and never paused until she reached the 'Bodega' in the Rue Rivoli. She was about to enter, when a short, dark man of about thirty years of age stepped up to her.

'You are here first, then, Ringens,' said Leila calling him by the name he adopted for the ring. Everybody called the clown Ringens, and so the custom had grown until his real name was nearly lost.

'Your husband told me you would be here at five, it is now nearly half-past.'

'The boy was so heavy,' panted Leila, 'and the crowd so great, I had difficulty in getting Vanda along.'

'Let me take the child,' said the man kindly. 'He's much too heavy for you. You must have some cognac before we start.'

Leila was exhausted by her efforts, and she drank the brandy eagerly. How gladly would she have rested at home that one evening of freedom. She had ridden twice that afternoon, and during the *fête* week the evening performance was more varied, and Leila for once was free.

She had decided to take her children for a treat

to the *fête* to give them a holiday; but almost at the last moment her husband had forbidden her to go unaccompanied. If she could find one of the artistes to go with her, well and good, if not, she must remain with the children at home.

By mere chance she learned that Ringens was not to appear in the evening, and she begged him to assist her in carrying out her plan.

If her husband were willing, Ringens was, and so the children spent their holiday at the *fête*.

Dick Wynscote, known in the ring as Ringens, was much respected by his fellow-artistes and those connected with the different circuses he visited. His character was beyond suspicion. He never thought it necessary to use profane oaths, or in any way to disgrace his name as husband and father. He had married a country lassie whom he had loved since boyish days; and much as he liked to have her with him, he never allowed her to undergo the fatigues of a Continental tour.

'My wife and the babies are best in London,' he would say when inquiries were made about Mrs Wynscote.

And Leila wished sometimes that Castelli would be as thoughful for her, but then she earned good salaries, and Mrs Wynscote had nothing to do but care for her home and her children.

At one great circus Dick Wynscote had been christened in derision 'Saint Ringens,' because on Sunday morning he regularly attended the service at the cathedral. 'It is better to be a saint than a sinner,' he would reply, 'and I intend to serve my God as well as I serve my master.'

Upon this point he was always firm, and Leila would sometimes gain much comfort when he spoke to her of a higher life where the toil and misery would end for ever. Indeed he had been her one friend during the long Continental tour, and Castelli had made no objection to their chats and strolls; and this was a great pleasure to Leila.

So it was, as it will be for ever, the power of good asserted itself, and was felt even by those whose ways are ill and whose deeds are dark.

Relieved of the child, she managed to get along better, and they were soon in the great public gardens. They wandered about for some time showing the children all likely to interest them, and then Ringens suggested they should take some seats within a *café chantant* and listen to the concert about to begin. A magnificent band had already commenced a lively waltz, the gardens were one blaze of lamps and light, the people were preparing with a graceful yet matter of course air for the coming cheap amusement. Leila was glad enough to rest.

The first artiste to appear was quite a young girl, who in a bespangled dress flaunted her coarse, bold manners to the immense delight of the audience. With apparent relish she sang a song which caused Leila to flush deeply She was ashamed of her sex, but the people applauded and would have an encore, and the girl grew more forward with her successful reception, more vulgar, more loose in her songs. At last she left the stage with a knowing wink and a nod, much to everyone's amusement, but Leila felt nothing but disgust and annoyance.

Her natural refinement rebelled against anything which tended to pander to low tastes, and she had frequently desisted from visiting many of the *café chantants* in the towns in which they had been resident, because the amusements provided had been distasteful to her.

She was true to her instincts through all.

Vanda began to fidget, and Leila said gently,—

'Sit still, dear. What is the matter?'

'I am so tired, mother,' said Vanda wearily. 'Can't we go home?'

'Yes, darling, soon.' And then she leant forward to speak to Ringens, who sat in a chair before her nursing Adrian, who had fallen asleep. 'I think I must go soon,' she said in a tone of half apology, 'the children are *so* tired.'

'Do you mind hearing one more song, and then we will go? Coloris is going to sing. I heard her six years ago in Brussels at the Casino. She was a fine woman, really beautiful, with a good voice.'

'Coloris, what a funny name,' said Leila somewhat interested.

'Yes, but it means colouring, a tint on a picture, and it was very applicable to her, her face was so brilliant and her complexion rich and dark. She is English, too, and must be getting on now. I thought she had left the Casino business long ago.'

'Has she any children?' inquired Leila.

'I really do not know. I am afraid there has been some scandal attached to her name. I heard so, but do not let that bias you against her, because it may not be true.'

Leila had no time to respond, for the curtain went up and a tall, elegant woman stepped to the front of the stage. She was dressed in a white silk robe which had seen its best days. The lace and the ribbons had been evidently added, but with all she was beautiful. The contour of her limbs could be seen as the clinging silk fell in scanty folds. Her face was thin, but the glow of colour was there in the shape of two brilliant patches on either cheek. So strange, so weird did she look in the blaze of the footlights that most of the audience instantly fixed their eyes upon her in comparative silence, wondering whether her quick, hurried breathing was nervousness or illness. Thinking to encourage her, they stamped with their feet and clapped their hands lustily.

It was during this tumult that Leila, white as death, rose from her seat and left the café hurriedly. Ringens, who had seen her leave, followed her hastily. When they had reached the quiet gardens he asked her if she were ill.

'No, not ill,' she gasped faintly, 'but I have had a great shock. 'Coloris is'—she paused—'is my mother!'

'Your mother, Madame Castelli!' replied Dick Wynscote in amazement, 'it cannot be.'

'It is—it is she.' She trembled so violently that he feared she would fall to the ground.

'Shall I fetch someone to you? Shall I go for your husband?' said Ringeus, now deeply concerned.

'My husband!' The word seemed to make her realise the situation at once, and in a distressed tone she cried: 'Leave me alone for one minute, I shall soon be all right; but don't send for Emilio whatever you *do*; don't tell him I have seen her, will you?' she asked pleadingly.

'Certainly not, if you don't wish it,' replied Ringens, wondering what all the mystery meant.

She recovered soon, however, and said quickly,—

'Give me Adrian. Get me a carriage; I will go back to my rooms. And you, I want you to go at *once* and find out my mother's position and what she needs before I see her. Break it to her gently, but tell her I will come and see her to-morrow. She is dying, I am sure of that!' exclaimed Leila with great excitement. 'Please don't delay or I may lose her again for ever.'

Ringens placed her in a cab, and after seeing that she and her children were comfortable, he hurried back to the *café chantant*, but the wearied singer was gone. After some difficulty he found her address, and thither he proceeded at once.

In a small and frowsy room on the top floor of an old, wretched house on the other side of the river, he saw the broken-down woman. She was sitting in a faded dressing-gown when he entered, leaning with her head back on a heap of soiled cushions.

He explained his business, and gave her Leila's message. She listened attentively, not breaking the silence once. There was only the deepening of the crimson flush to show how strongly she was battling with her feelings.

She heard that her daughter was the wife of Emilio Castelli, that Leila was the mother of two little children, and that she wished to come to see her on the morrow.

Then it was that some of the vigour of olden days came back, and she paced the room with hurried steps. Suddenly she exclaimed,—

'You've come here to tell me of my daughter. You tell me she is married to a man who belongs to a circus. They let her come to that, did they? Anything was good enough for the child of the erring mother, the runaway wife. Perhaps you do not know the story, do you?' she asked wildly.

'Certainly not,' replied Ringens. 'I never knew until to-night that Madame Castelli had a mother.'

'Mother, mother,' she repeated, 'can I call myself a mother? *I* who left her years ago, *I* who brought shame on her name and ruin to her home. I'm not fit to see her, not fit to stand in the same room or breathe the same air that she does. What greater curse can rest upon me than that? And yet,' and her voice became more gentle, 'I yearn to tell her that I repent of all my sin, that I am contrite, and implore her forgiveness. Oh, if but for one short hour I could feel happy, if I could clasp my children in my arms, if I could'—her voice fell—'if I could hear my husband say "I forgive you." If I could feel his lips touch mine I should die happy; but he would hurl curses at me who wrought his ruin, and his fury would fall upon me now for the awful past. I am deserted, despised, corrupted, and lost.' She grew more excited as she continued. 'Would it not have been kinder to have plunged myself into the sea? The record of my life would have gone then, and my child could not have seen me as I am—degraded and shunned by all. But let her come if she will, let her see my doom, let her hear me curse my destroyer before I die. She shall see how he left me to exist, without money, without friends, like a dog in the street; how he spurned me as an evil thing, and hurled me to destruction. Curses, curses on Herbert Clifford!'

She sank down exhausted, and then Dick Wynscote saw how dreadfully ill she really was. He thought it best to ignore her terrible story, and inquired if she needed anything to ease her panting, laboured breath.

'Want anything?' she repeated. 'Do you know I spent my last franc yesterday? To-day I have only eaten from that loaf,' pointing to a small piece on a plate, 'and that is all I have had. I have been long without an engagement. I cannot earn much now. My voice has no strength and my heart is broken—and I am dying, I know it,' she added sorrowfully.

Dick Wynscote took a handful of francs from his pocket and laid them on the table.

'I am sure your daughter would like you to send for what you need. Please do so, and to-morrow, please God, you shall see her.'

He rose to go. There was nothing he could say to the poor half-frenzied mother. He was horrified at all he had heard, and had no desire to prolong the interview.

He put out his hand and grasped hers kindly, and bid her good-night.

He went home and wondered how men could ruin homes, and bring those they tempted to sin to such degradation and misery.

He forgot it was vice, not love.

The next day Ringens related to Leila his experience of the night before, and he urged her to tell her husband and get his consent to remove the unhappy woman to more congenial surroundings; but to this Leila was strongly opposed. She would do all she could for her mother, and supply her with money, but Emilio should be none the wiser; for had he not thrust the mother's sin at the daughter and taunted her with the shame? But she could not tell that to Ringens, so she ignored his advice.

'She is so hopeless, so desponding, she will need all your care and kindness,' he said, just before she started on her sad errand.

'She shall have it,' replied Leila gravely.

. . . .

'Mother!'—'Leila!' They had met in one fond embrace. 'Leila, my Leila!' What torturing retribution, what wild remorse that name called forth.

'Mother, dear mother.'

The angels of mercy and forgiveness were hovering around, therefore break not the hallowed spell. Hush! Hush!

## CHAPTER XIII.

### 'MY AUNT'S MONEY.'

DEATH had come—sorrows and sickness were over—the earthly pilgrimage finished. Whanks' aunt was dead at last.

But the letter telling him the news, and requesting his presence in York to wind up her affairs and prove the will, did not reach him until she had been buried some weeks. It had followed him about to several Continental towns, but it was not until the circus had anchored for a time in Liverpool that the important missive caught him up.

At last, after much patient waiting, he had come in to his property, and in future he would be the master of his own actions.

He read and re-read the letter from the solicitors, as if afraid there was some mistake. Then he turned the enclosed cheque for ten pounds over and over, as if the more readily to understand its value. It had been sent him to meet his immediate expenses and to defray his journey to York.

He decided that he must ask Castelli's permission to go at once, then he would write to the solicitors and tell them he would arrive in York the next day.

But, unluckily for Whanks, before he could carry out these practical arrangements, his craving to have 'a drink to his luck' overcame his discretion, and after asking a few of his 'chums' to join him, he retired to the 'Three Arms' public-house, where several hours were passed in discussing his prospects and good fortune, while his glass had been refilled many times.

At last, drunk and excited, he presented himself before his master at the circus.

Castelli, who had no idea of his groom's good luck, lost his temper, so the inebriated servant and the angry master engaged in a quarrel which did credit to neither of them.

Oath after oath fell from Castelli's lips as Whanks, contrary to custom, answered him with equal warmth, and when he refused to leave his presence before he had told him 'what he thought of him' Castelli's rage knew no bounds, and he struck him a heavy blow. This maddened Whanks, who blurted out in a thick voice some home truths respecting his treatment of Leila. 'Everyone shall know you've broken her heart,' he cried out passionately. 'But I've got my aunt's money now, and—' But further conversation was arrested, for Castelli took Whanks by the collar of his coat, and after shaking him vigorously and telling him never to show his face again at the circus, he hurled him into the passage leading to the stables.

Leila was standing in her riding-habit, ready for a rehearsal, when Whanks was thus summarily dismissed. He almost fell against her as she was leaving her dressing-room.

'What is the matter, Emilio?' she exclaimed, looking at the prostrate groom and her irate husband.

'Cannot you see for yourself that the beast is drunk! Out he goes this time, once and for all.'

'You need not be so rough even if he is intoxicated,' replied Leila with spirit. 'He is kind and good to us when he is sober.'

All the indifferent treatment she had received from her husband had not crushed the loving heart, it was just as tender for those in trouble; and to anyone in need of sympathy and protection she always strove to give her support and assistance. She would speak out, even at the risk of incurring her husband's terrible anger. She had suffered so acutely herself that the pain of seeing others suffer was in itself renewed agony; and her sympathy for Whanks was intense. He had been her friend on so many occasions, surely she must plead for him now.

'How dare you question my actions, Leila?' said Castelli angrily. 'He's dead drunk, and needs a good thrashing to bring him round. Come to your work, and leave me to manage for myself. I don't need your advice,' he added severely.

Whanks in the meantime had picked himself up from his lowly position, and leaning against the wall for support, looked at Leila in a helpless, stupid fashion, which angered Castelli more than ever.

Ignoring his remark, Leila addressed Whanks kindly.

'Go home, there's a good fellow. I cannot talk to you now. Go and get some food and sleep and you will be all right to-night,' pleaded Leila.

'You hold your tongue at once!' replied her husband. 'Once more let me tell you I am waiting for you,' he added impatiently.

She went towards him quietly and calmly, but there was a subdued defiance in her eyes and manner which did not escape her husband's notice.

He knew she was chafing against the restraints he imposed upon her, and that her duties in the ring fretted her continually, but so long as her defiance did not openly betray itself he was satisfied; for her inward sufferings he cared little. Once or twice, when they were on the Continent, his attention had been called by Ringens and others to his wife's delicate health; her pale, careworn face, with its brilliant hectic flush, her large eyes, looking like those of a hunted fawn, had drawn very honest sympathy from those engaged at the circus. But this commiseration had not the slightest effect upon Castelli. He was considerably annoyed that his wife should be under their discussion at all, and he frankly told them that it was no business of theirs, and that his wife was well enough and he did not mean to have her made into an invalid; perhaps they would look after their own wives and leave him to do the same.

They never interfered again. But Ringens and Whanks watched her grow more fragile every day. They saw the flush deepen upon the slightest exertion, and at times her eyes grew bright as stars and she would seem nervous and restless as her time came to go into the ring.

Once, in Brussels, when she seemed unusually tired, Whanks had ventured to advise that she should rest a little, he was so fond of the young girl who had come among them, and her husband's neglect and severity had been a source of great trouble to the faithful servant, and Leila, grateful for any small kindness, returned his devotion ungrudgingly.

'No, I cannot rest, Whanks,' she replied, amused at his tender thought for her health. Your master would not approve of that; he would think I was lazy.'

She smiled, but there was such a sad look on her face as she did so that Whanks felt, as he afterwards described it to a fellow-groom, 'as if he could have cried like a baby.'

'The master is as hard as a brick, and terribly cruel at times, and if I was in your place I'd—'

'Hush,' interposed Leila firmly, 'you must not speak so; he is my husband.'

'More's the pity, that's what I says,' replied Whanks, unabashed at the reproof; 'more's the pity,' he repeated.

There were others who thought the same, but Leila did not know it. She was unaware of all the kindly feeling bestowed upon her by those around simply because she was Castelli's wife and the mother of his children.

But so it was.

The next day when Castelli went down to the circus, expecting to find Whanks as usual, for his notice to quit had so far been a mere form, he was surprised at his non-appearance.

In answer to his inquiries, he was told that Whanks had come into some money and had started or was going to start to York that day. Castelli could hardly believe that the man was gone, he had been so accustomed to scold him for his faults, to use horrible oaths, to give him notice to quit his service and then retain him, that he supposed naturally this occasion would not in any way differ from the others; but to his dismay he found the faithful retainer gone at last. The day wore on, but still no Whanks appeared, and as the evening approached he sent a messenger to the man's apartments. He had gone away by train that morning, that was all they knew about him. He had told them he was not going to the circus again as business called him to York. This put Castelli to the greatest inconvenience in the ring, having to find a substitute at so short a notice, and Leila passed a very uncomfortable hour with her husband previous to the evening 'show.' He abused Whanks heartily, and used such terrible expletives that she felt almost afraid to be in his presence; yet she dared not interrupt him or suggest that he had dismissed the man himself, and therefore could not blame him. She only sat and listened, sighing now and again.

Whanks, unconscious of all the trouble his absence

had caused in the circus, had spent a few very busy hours in York. He had seen the solicitors, and was satisfied with the interview, and as he sauntered down to his apartments, through Bootham Bar, he was meditating what his best plans for the future would be. Leave the circus profession he was most determined. He knew he had no strength to withstand the temptations of his old surroundings. He would break with them once and for all; and when he entered Gillygate he had made up his mind that his only chance to get on would be to go away, as soon as his arrangements were completed in York, and not to put himself in the touch of his old comrades again.

He felt happier after making this resolve, and it was not until he was standing at the window of his sitting-room, looking out on the short garden backed by the crumbling city walls—for it was not in the days of restoration, which enables us to walk round the city ramparts—that his thoughts became centred upon Leila and her children. In his excitement he had forgotten that he must part with them also, that giving up the circus meant that Leila would be left without a friend. And then there would be the good-bye to be said, and perhaps he should never see her again. Why should he not go back to the circus and keep sober, and he could be a friend still to the pale, weary wife? Then his thoughts rambled on to his condition. The very last time he had seen her had he not disgraced himself, and stood before her besotted and incapable of protecting himself from Castelli's wrath? Like a hound she had seen him flung at her feet. No, he would not go back. He would write to her one last letter and tell her his plans and his hopes.

He called for paper and ink, and sat down to

his self-imposed task as if fearful of altering his decision.

'GILLYGATE,
'YORK.

'DEAR MISS LEILA,—It is right that kindness should never be forgotten. To remember it is the fruit of friendship. Poor outcast as I am you were never too proud to befriend me, although I took more to drink than I should. I trusted too much to the beer before I knew the effect of the habit, and I shall repent all the carousing until I die. I hope you will believe that, Miss Leila—God forgive me for calling you Miss Leila. The old proverb says, "What is well begun is half ended." I began to call you Miss Leila years ago, and somehow the old name rises on my lips, and I should like to end with it, so you must forgive me. They say everyone has two ways of thinking, and I think it would have been best if you had been Miss Leila to the last. But you think differently I suppose.

'I am not coming back again to the circus. Tell my master that the worm he trod on has turned at last—that the grain of my patience has run out. But I am writing to wish you good-bye and good luck, and to tell you that I have my aunt's money, so I am going away to some other country—where, I don't quite know yet. If I stay in England all my money will soon be spent, and then it will be too late, and all will be done for. I shall try and get some work in the new place—because I could not live and do nothing—and it's "better to play a small game than stand out." That's a motto my poor aunt was fond of saying to me years ago, poor dear.

'I have been thinking what keepsake I could send you, but on second thoughts I think the master might not like *me* to send you a gift, so

I shall send you a promise instead, which is, that for your *sake* I shall *keep* out of the public-house. That is a keepsake turned the wrong way about, but I think it will be one that will please you.

'I was going to give a "foy" to some of my chums before I leave the old country, but I have made up my mind not to do it, in case I am a fool again and don't resist the drink. They may expect me to treat them, but when I think of you, Miss Leila, I determine to be steady.

'Miss Leila, will you say good-bye to the children for me. Tell them Whanks sends his love, and he will never forget them. I am a bit troubled about the master's horses. I loved them all, they all knew me, and "Spanishfly" would neigh every time I went to her stall; and now they are left to other hands. Perhaps there is no one to stroke them and soothe them after the whip. I think they must look for me sometimes and wonder where I am. I wish you could tell them all about it, and set their hearts at rest. I would have come and seen them myself, but I couldn't face the farewell, I'm such a mortal coward. My aunt left me four hundred pounds. No more news. So once more I bid you good-bye, Miss Leila,—And remain your devoted servant,   WHANKS.'

'*P.S.*—God bless you, the children, and the horses. I never mean to get drunk again.'

When Leila received this characteristic letter from Whanks she was filled with grief at the loss of her old friend—for such she had learnt to regard him. As her husband's treatment of her became worse she had relied more on the faithful servant, and he had always been specially kind to her and devoted to her children.

In the mother's heart regret at Whanks' departure was very sincere, but the loss of him for her little ones touched her more deeply. Whanks to them had been everything. What time he had he devoted to them for little walks. How many pence he had spent to please their childish fancies, how tender and gentle he had been to them, and often, when Leila was heart-broken and weary, he had fetched the children for a bit that she might rest.

At the rehearsals, too, he had, as he expressed it, 'kept an eye on Miss Leila if the master was in one of his tantrums,' and it had been his special pride to keep her mare well groomed and to send her into the ring the smartest horse in the stables. And now there would be no one to do all these kindly offices for her and the children, no one to whom they could look for uniform kindness and attention. Somehow Leila had felt a sort of safety and protection in Whanks, an undefined feeling that nothing very terrible could happen to her or the little ones as long as he was near to them. She could hardly realise all this was at an end, that the old familiar face would never cheer her again with its welcome smile, that happiness was gone now, the pleasure past. The future must be faced, but it would be more lonely, more weary now he was gone.

There was a void in her life because the true-hearted friend and servant was gone.

'Friend and servant.' The world will sneer at the affinity. Let it scoff and express doubt with ludicrous scorn that such a thing can exist. It matters not, for the association lives despite contempt and disdain. That is well.

Whanks had been the soul of loyalty to his mistress, and a very pattern true-blue to his master. Leila knew this, and appreciated him deeply, consequently his loss seemed to her most serious. But her husband viewed the matter much more coolly, and when she expressed in strong terms her sorrow at the man's departure, he replied,—

'Don't be a fool. I can get a groom before this time to-morrow better than Whanks fifty times over. He was a drunken beast. I'm glad he's gone.'

'He was so kind to me and the children,' said Leila. 'I shall miss him dreadfully. The place won't seem the same,' she added wearily.

'Pity you did not go with him if that's how the matter stands,' replied Castelli with a sneer.

Leila was silent, but a flush of shame overspread her face at his despicable words. Why did he impute sinful thoughts to her when she had remained faithful and true through all his cruelty, all his harshness, without a murmur or wifely retaliation?

But his words made another wound in her heart. No wonder she felt alone and grieved when another friend was gone.

She never spoke to Castelli of Whanks after that day, and she hushed the children in his presence when they spoke together of 'dear old Whankie.'

The gulf between husband and wife was growing deeper and wider. The bridge of unity and confidence had long since been destroyed.

It was impossible to reunite the structure.

A week after Leila had received her letter from Whanks a ship was moving slowly out of the Mersey docks in Liverpool. Very stately she looked as she glided towards the open sea, bound for foreign lands. Many of her passengers stood on the deck, waving their hands and handkerchiefs to the loved ones left behind. One man stood a little apart from the rest. He never glanced at the group of distressed friends on the quay. He never heeded a young girl by his side, weeping for the mother left behind. He only turned his face seaward and cried, 'God bless Miss Leila—God bless her,' he said solemnly, and something like tears made their way down his rugged cheeks. 'My heart is with you to the last, Miss Leila, to the last, though you may never know it.'

The *Southern Cross* sped on her way, carrying her freight of gladdened hearts and sorrow-laden lives—some going to those who had waited patiently for years for their outcoming, others had left home, wife, and children to seek fortune in a far-off country.

Whanks had gone to begin a new life, to avoid the temptations he could not resist.

Leila was left behind to mourn a faithful friend gone for ever.

Such is life.

## CHAPTER XIV

### 'THE WAGES OF SIN'

THERE is a tenderness born in the soul which breathes out memories that can never die—a sweetness sown at birth and cherished lovingly until hoary age.

That is a mother's love.

What a mystery lies in that tenderness. Surely there is magic in the sound of the golden strings which strain the tune of a mother's love; surely the sweet voice comes back, bringing with it visions of beauty and rapture for ever the same—like a meteor's flash they brighten the darkest night, and light the shadows when the world is full of woe, and hopes lie dead.

How divine a thing it is!

But when the coils of sin wind themselves round

the bonds of love so that its beauties are hidden, its fragrance gone, its exaltation defiled, how terrible is the curse.

Leila, more or less, had felt her mother's shame since the day she became Castelli's wife. Some slight, some word brought to her the taint of a mother's depravity, and she had constantly to bear the burden of another's wrong.

It was nearly six months since Leila had seen her mother on the stage of the *café chantant* in Paris. During that time the dying woman had wanted for nothing that love and money could procure. At first she seemed to rally, and Leila began to hope that she would regain her health as time went on. But how vain was such a hope. The runaway wife, the discarded mistress, the broken-hearted mother was fast fading away, and death was hovering near.

Unknown to her husband, Leila had gladdened her mother's last days on earth ; and it was not until an act of carelessness on her part betrayed the secret that Castelli had the slightest idea of the clandestine meetings between Leila and her mother. Inadvertently she had left a letter directed to her on the table whilst she went into another room to dress, preparatory to going to the post office. Castelli returned somewhat unexpectedly from the circus and found the missive. An angry flush passed over his face as he read the address, Mrs Gurney, Scotland Road, Liverpool.

'So her wretched mother has come on the scene, has she?' he murmured, and without the slightest scruple he tore the letter open. He read the few loving lines, which sent a postal order for rent and food, and then, with an imprecation, he hastily put it in his pocket.

Leila entered the room at this moment, and seeing her letter was gone, she divined the truth at once.

The worst was at hand—her secret was out at last, there was no need to confess it. Her letter had told him all. There were only the consequences of her deceit to bear, and the sooner the explanation was over the better. Outwardly she was very calm, but her heart throbbed loudly, and it was with difficulty she restrained her voice from showing how much she dreaded the ordeal.

For a moment she stood confronting him, and then she spoke.

'You have taken a letter of mine from the table I believe,' she added quietly. 'It is a private affair of my own, please give it to me.'

She looked at him. He stood silently before her, pale, firm, and resolute, like a man who had determined upon a resolution and intended to carry it out without flinching.

At last he broke the terrible silence.

'There is nothing private from your husband. I have read your charming letter, it does you credit as a dutiful daughter—and a lying wife,' he added with a sneer.

'I can write to my mother if I choose,' replied Leila angrily. 'It has nothing to do with you.'

'Well, I intend to make it a great deal to do with me for the future,' he replied firmly. 'But before we go on further with this nice little comedy, may I inquire how this correspondence came about and how long it has been going on?'

Leila knew that to prevaricate would be useless before so stern a judge—it would be better to try and win his favour rather than arouse him to further anger; and so in a few words she described the meeting in Paris, and Ringens' kindness in calling upon her mother, and the awful poverty to which she was reduced. Eloquently she pleaded for the deserted mother.

He had listened attentively throughout the painful recital, and when she paused he said calmly,—

'Indeed, and what is all this to do with you? You and that Bible reading Ringens thought best to keep me in the dark. If your mother has come to want, it is just what she deserves, and I shall permit no further help to go from this house. By-the-bye, how came she to Liverpool? What other sneaky trick was played upon me? Speak out; I will have nothing but the truth.'

'I asked Ringens to bring her over when he left our circus; she was here a week before we were. I could not leave her there to die,' pleaded Leila with much feeling. 'Emilio, she is my mother.'

'Your mother—a fine mother! I wonder you care to own the relationship,' he answered with a sneer. 'So all this pretty arrangement was carried out for you by Ringens, was it? Is he your lover,' he asked coldly, 'that you should persuade him to deceive me and to make your life a fraud, a lie?

For a moment Leila was aghast at his terrible question, and then she replied with a voice trembling with rage,—

'Do you dare to impute such a name to him! He was good, and true, and kind; he saved my mother, and I will thank him for it till I die. You—you have no heart. It was worse than useless to appeal to you. She might have died for all you would have done, I knew that, but I *will* give her all the help I can, for *all* you may say, for *all* you may do,' she added passionately.

'You will not,' he replied firmly; 'and as to imputing such wickedness to you, I don't know why I should not. A woman who lets another man, rather than her husband, carry out secret plans and plots can't be over straight—that's plain enough. You can't make me believe chalk is black, or that you are too white. Ringens is a church-going hypocrite, and the next time that gentleman comes across my path I shall have a nice lot to say to him.'

'You are lying—putting others down to be measured by your own bushel. It was humanity—humanity,' she repeated with force, 'which made me deceive you in order to save my mother.'

'Let those save her who took her from her home. I will not allow *you* to support a woman of that class, mother or no mother. I'm not going to slave to keep such a woman, neither shall you. She has a husband and a protector. It's a pity one of the gentlemen cannot support her,' he added with a sneer.

'Are you so *very* moral that you can speak of my mother in those terms? Are you not one of the class that tempt women and leave them when your passion has died? I have heard of you, Emilio, before to-day. I know your life has not been all plain sailing. Why condemn my mother? She is what a man has made her,' she added sadly.

'What you have heard about me I don't care the least,' replied Castelli calmly. 'But, once and for all, I forbid you sending letters and money to your mother. It shall not be done again.'

'It shall,' replied Leila with great determination.

'Do you intend to disobey me, Leila?' asked her husband severely.

'In this case, most certainly. I do not intend to forget my duties as a daughter,' replied Leila with great determination. 'Your insults will not hurt me, but to neglect my mother in her extremity would be wicked indeed. I shall not risk the responsibility.'

'I shall,' answered Castelli firmly; 'and as my wife you shall obey my orders.'

'I will not,' said Leila with all the firmness she could command.

'Then I shall take steps to make you. You are quite resolved to follow your own way, and I am just as determined that you shall follow my way. There is no more to be said.'

Leila's face changed as her husband finished speaking. The eyes grew less fixed and determined, a gentler look came over her. She would plead now for the erring mother; she would try to melt the merciless heart of her husband. She went closer to him, and putting up her hands, laid them timidly on his shoulders, and spoke with great effort on behalf of the sinning woman.

'Emilio, for the sake of the dear old days, for the sake of the love you once bore me, *won't* you let me do this one thing for my mother? It would make me so happy. Do listen to me this once,' she pleaded.

'I cannot,' he replied more quietly than he had yet spoken. 'You've deceived me throughout. It is useless to expect me to meet you on your own terms now. My decision is irrevocable. You should have told me honestly the first time you met her in Paris. It is too late to beg the favour now,' he added decisively

'Surely, surely it is not,' she replied pathetically, the tears welling to her eyes, her white, sad face looking more hopeless than ever in the intense anguish she was suffering.

He put her away from him forcibly, but not roughly. She looked up into his face, but there was no sign of relenting, no tender smile to assure her it was all right. As he did not speak, she continued,—

'Will you think it over and not refuse me yet?'

'No, Leila, I shall be firm to what I have said. There is no chance of my relenting—none.'

His tone of positive refusal aroused her temper in a moment. Supplication turned to anger, her entreaties gave place to acute pain, caused by his heartless and persistent cruelty.

'You can be firm, and so shall I,' she replied angrily. 'I work hard enough for what I earn, and I shall spend it as I choose.'

'Will you?' He smiled meaningly. 'I think I can settle that question.'

And settle it he did. From that day henceforth he withdrew from Leila the usual sum for the household expenditure. All bills he paid himself; he knew exactly how much every item cost. The money they earned together for their 'show' he kept towards the general expenses. At the same time he was careful that his wife should not actually want for anything to which he had accustomed her; she might order necessities both in food or dress, but he would settle the payment. By this means no money passed through her hands; practically the means of assisting her mother were gone.

Castelli had said no more on the subject, but quietly he adopted these measures, and rigidly enforced them. His conduct gave Leila the greatest worry and anxiety. What could she do in her dilemma? She dare not apply to Ringens for money; her husband was obdurate, there seemed no mercy, no help at hand, and Leila began to grow very much paler and more languid.

What little love had remained for her husband faded out of her heart and life during this period of intense suffering. She would have been so grateful to him if only he would have helped her to soothe the last days of her mother. They would not be many; the doctor had told her that the disease was making terrible headway, and Leila knew that was true. Some days she seemed better and brighter, almost herself again, then came awful days of suffering for the consumptive patient.

One morning Leila, in spite of her husband's wishes, visited her mother in Scotland Road. She knew money had run out, and that the invalid must be in need of actual necessities. She deemed it wise to tell her mother at once that she could supply her no longer with funds to provide for her daily expenses.

Mrs Gurney listened to every word her daughter uttered, and then she startled Leila by exclaiming,—

'Your husband is quite right. Why should he help to keep me? me, a profligate woman, a dissolute creature,' she added excitedly. 'I will go to those who should help me. I will go once more to my seducer, and show him my pitiable condition. He cannot refuse me now, surely. I must have food, and he shall find it.'

Leila begged her mother not to appeal to the man who had been the direct cause of all her misery; but she held firmly to her purpose in spite of her daughter's remonstrances.

'Why not write to my father?' asked Leila gently. She did not like to use the word husband. 'Surely he should know how ill you are and how great is your need. I have brought you a little money,' she added sadly, 'but it is not much—two pounds in all. I have parted with the last gold ornaments I have, so this will be all I can give you. Something must be done.'

'Something shall!' replied her mother wildly. 'I've made up my mind to go to Southport and see Herbert Clifford—go I will, this very day—but write to my husband—never, never!' she screamed. 'Are you mad to propose such a thing? Ask him for money, when he would gloat over my death, and tell me how just was my punishment—never, no, never!' she added with passion.

Leila saw at once that her mother's condition

was not such as to warrant continual contradiction, therefore she decided to go home and write to her father in her mother's name, telling him of her remorse, and begging his forgiveness. This done, she felt as if she had done all that remained to her. If only Tom had remained her friend she would have turned to him now to help their mother, and half the burden and care would have been removed. But Leila had written to him after her marriage and received no reply, and she never wrote again. Poor Leila, she did not know that the vessel carrying out her letter had been cast away and all the mail lost. She put his silence down to anger at her marriage. She was ignorant, too, of a pile of letters which had come to her at the old home, to be sent on, but which had been given as food for the flames by the unforgiving father. So to Tom she never dreamt of applying. He, like her other friends, had gone out of her life.

Bitter, bitter were her thoughts of the past, with all its happy unshaded hours, the whispered love, the joys of home.

But these delights were lost to both for ever now.

Herbert Clifford was lounging in his library, smoking and reading to while away the time. Through luck, not quite apart from swindling, he had risen from a comparatively poor man to a very wealthy one, and with his riches his character had become more loose, more dishonourable than ever. His face and form had lost none of their beauty and grace since the day he had tempted Alice Gurney from her home, but he had used his radiant eyes, his fascinating face to lead others into the great vortex of the lost. And they in turn were left to their depths of despair and misery, cursing the day when the handsome Herbert Clifford had crossed the threshold of their lives.

But their griefs did not trouble him, unbridled passion knows no mercy, and morally he had sunk so low that to stamp a deeper dye on his blackened heart would have been impossible. His corruption and iniquity were complete. No hell-hound could boast of blacker sins or grosser vice.

Was it likely, then, that the dying woman, the wreck of his sin, should hope for mercy from him in her direst agony?

The door opened, she was announced, and Herbert Clifford saw before him the woman he had once professed to love. There she stood facing her deserter, all the glow of beauty decayed, all the magic charm gone, with nothing but despair to take its place. Her quick, hurried breathing could be heard in the silent room. She put her hand on the back of a chair for support, and with one desperate impulse she cried,—

'Herbert Clifford, have you forgotten me? You must remember me?'

She put out her arms towards him, but he drew back and repulsed her roughly, and exclaimed with fury,—

'How dare you come here? You are nothing to me. What do you mean by coming to *my* house? Are you not ashamed to show your face?'

'Not to you,' she replied wearily. 'To *all* else, but not to you. I have dared to come because I am ill—dying, and almost starving for bread. I have come to you because you promised once to care for me till death. You have made me what I am. You have brought me to guilt and misery. It is to you I come for help—can you refuse it?'

Her imploring tone, her agony and despair were nothing to him, and he replied, with a cruel smile,—

'Did I promise to care for you till death? If I did I was drunk when I said it. If you are ill and dying it's nothing to me, and your parish will give you bread. You have no right to come to me for help. I am not going to undertake to look after every woman who chooses to run after me. You left your home for a passing fancy, and now you repent, that is no business of mine.'

'Left my home for a passing fancy?' she wailed; 'oh, Herbert, Herbert, I left it for you, and you alone. I was vain in those days, and you whispered to me of love and hopes. You bid me fly. You roused my passions, and, maddened, I obeyed. Apostate, liar, coward, you mock me now, do you? You would thrust me from your presence, to die in yonder street, and scoff at me as you passed?'

'I daresay I should,' replied Herbert Clifford carelessly as he lit another cigar. 'You see,' he continued, 'you grew tired of your husband and home. I, like a fool, took you in, and there's the end of it. If you choose to change your life, no one is to blame but yourself,' he added cruelly.

'You say that to me when you led me astray— you who have made my life a misery, a curse too heavy to be borne; you who tempted me from plenty, to cast me off without enough to buy a loaf. Shame, shame! Herbert Clifford, shame be on you to the grave!'

She cast her eyes about wildly as she spoke, and her breathing became more laboured.

'Thanks for the good wishes,' he replied with sarcasm. 'You see the devil was very busy the day I was born; and as for the casting off business, I never asked you to come with me. There's the workhouse for such as you,' he said with a fiendish laugh.

She sank down upon a low couch as he spoke and hid her face with her white hands, upon which the wedding ring still glistened. It seemed as if she wished to hide her eyes from the hate and loathing of the man before her. Suddenly she arose. A sullen, hopeless wrath had come over her face, as if she had remembered that love, honour, pride, and chastity, the empires of a woman's world, were gone; that the lover, the serpent, for whom she had sacrificed all, spurned her from him, that he would not throw her a crust, as the beggar does to the mongrel by his side.

But again she made one frantic effort, one frenzied appeal to him for mercy. Trembling with passion and excitement, but too weak to let it be her master, she rushed to his side, and taking hold of one of the elegant jewelled hands, pressed it passionately to her lips, exclaiming,—

'Herbert, look at me! look at me as you used to do! Once you loved me! I love you still, Herbert!'

She screamed. He had wrenched his hand away from her feeble grasp with a terrible oath.

A sharp cry of despair rang through the room again and again, and then she flung herself down and invoked his aid and his love.

'Get away, you snivelling idiot,' he shouted, with a coarse imprecation, and he put out his foot to kick her.

She grew deathly pale and gasped out,—

'Brandy, give me brandy. I am dying—quick—quick!'

'You're drunk more likely,' said Herbert Clifford. 'You'll get no brandy here. Get up, I tell you, or I'll make you.'

A shriek—a shuddering moan—another shriek.

'Look, look! What is this? she cried, terrified, holding up her handkerchief, now dyed deeply with crimson blood.

She fell forward, and a stream issued from her lips which made Herbert Clifford, selfish and hardened as he was, utter a stifled groan. He rushed to the bell. The affrighted valet helped his master to place the bleeding woman on the sofa. She tried to speak as he touched her, but the lamp of life had burnt too low.

A doctor was soon on the spot. She was still breathing, and convulsive tremors passed over now and then, but she never spoke. Language was gone for ever, for death was waiting to claim his victim. Just before the end she opened her eyes and fixed them with a horrible stare upon Clifford. So terrible was her look that he turned away, awed and mute, frightened at death in its most awful form.

More glassy they grew, and she followed his every movement until at last a look of unutterable agony came into them. She gasped feebly, and one moan came from the pale lips, and then the pulse of life was dead.

All was over.

When the doctor pronounced her dead, Herbert Clifford turned to him and said,—

'Now, I suppose, there'll be the bother of an inquest?'

The doctor looked up at the speaker, recoiling in disgust at the callous way in which he uttered the words, and replied,—

'Knowing so little of the case, I cannot give any certificate.'

'Cannot it be avoided anyhow? It will be a most infernal nuisance for me. People chatter so,' said Clifford.

'Well, you must find out who has been attending her, and get a certificate in the ordinary manner. Of course, you know all about the lady?'

'Indeed I don't. I haven't seen her for years. Cannot you take this matter in hand for me and communicate with her friends? The whole thing would do me a great deal of harm if it became a public scandal. A man of my means,' he added proudly, 'is always worried by a parcel of begging women, but I never had one serve me this trick before.'

'I have to find her friends first,' replied the doctor gravely, disbelieving the heartless speech.

After her death a letter from Leila to her mother was found in the pocket of her dress, and then the doctor sent a telegram informing Leila of her death.

Leaving a short note behind for her husband, she hurried off to Southport. Herbert Clifford had left the house. There was no one there but the servants, who sent for the doctor at once upon her arrival. From Leila he learnt the true state of affairs—of her mother's long illness and the reason of her visit to Clifford, with a description of his contemptible conduct.

Before she left she was shown to the room where her mother lay calm and silent in death. None of the passions of her lawless life were visible on the marble face. She looked less worn and wan than in her lifetime, and her features had regained some of the traces of her refined beauty. Leila stooped and kissed her, the last token of a daughter's love. Then she withdrew, shuddering at the thoughts which would come—of the blighted life, the unredeemable remorse of years, and then the awful death with heaven so far away, for the voices of the angels had not called her home—and Leila went her way troubled and maddened by the thought of her sinning and dead mother.

That evening when Castelli came home she said to him,—

'My mother is dead. She lies in the house of the villain who betrayed her. With his money he will lay her in the grave, for I have none to give so that I can spare her memory that last degradation. Must the curse rest upon her even in the grave? Will you not help me to give her the last care the dead can receive? He must not, he shall not,' she cried excitedly, 'let his sullied gold buy her grave. Let her sleep without a stone to mark her resting place if you like, but, Emilio, let me take her from his charge, dead though she is—it will make me happy to feel I laid her in the grave,' she cried appealingly.

But he made her no reply.

Later a letter came from Leila's father in response to the urgent plea for forgiveness for the erring, sinful wife. It contained these words:—

'I can offer no pardon for such sin as yours— you will go to your grave unforgiven by me.'

She was going to her grave. And as Leila crushed the heartless letter in her hand she murmured,—

'Death has been kindest after all.'

## CHAPTER XV

### IN THE RING.

SIX months had passed since Leila's mother had been laid in her grave. Six unhappy months for Leila. Her husband had refused to bury her mother. He had not even permitted her to attend at the grave.

'She has only come to what you might expect,' he told her brutally. 'Surely you cannot pretend to mourn for her.'

But Leila did sorrow for her mother for all that. Not that she forgot the disgrace brought on them all by her evil course of life, but it was that very sin which had aroused in Leila all her sympathy, if not affection. She saw what cruel suffering her mother's wickedness had wrought, how terrible was her remorse, how weary the days of desertion had been when spurned by her base tempter—rejected by her husband, deserted by all.

Apart from this, there was the tie of motherhood, that no sin can quite sever. Through all the chances and changes of life that undefined and indescribable clinging to a mother, whether she be a sinner or a saint, will exist for ever.

The arab of the gutter seeks his drunken mother and cries to her for bread. The disgraced son feels pity and sympathy for the mother in the dock, for is she not a parent after all? And some affectionate thoughts arise of her kindness long before the awful change took place which made her a drunkard or a felon.

In this all the world is akin. It matters not whether the child is king, prince, peer, or beggar, the link to motherhood is there. No sin on earth has ever snapped it quite apart.

That would be degrading to the child.

Castelli could not understand his wife bearing her mother the least particle of affection. His mother had died when he was quite a child, and his recollections of her were very vague and indistinct, and he had no sympathy with Leila. It was not that he particularly objected to the immorality committed by her mother, it was what he considered the deceit she had practised upon him. His pride had suffered. His wife's want of confidence in him had annoyed him beyond measure, and to show his disapproval of her conduct he declined

L

to assist her in any way in which her mother was concerned.  Even death found him immovable.

But with his determined decision came a change in his wife which he did not expect, and it annoyed him more than he chose to own.

Although not openly declaring her dislike to him, she simply ignored him whenever she dared.  She rarely addressed him beyond actual matters of business, or pleaded for her children when he dealt them a hasty blow for some trivial childish fault.  Immutably cold in her demeanour towards him, she put up with his increasing severity and harshness without a murmur.  Sometimes, when he had been particularly sarcastic and cruel, she would give him a sad, tender look, as if to mutely plead for his love as of old.  But soon the gentleness would die out and a despairing, hardened glance take its place.  And so the weary weeks lagged on.

The hours of rehearsals at the circus she dreaded the most.  It took what little remaining strength she had to carry her through her work with any show of success, and her husband permitted nothing to pass that was inaccurately or carelessly done.

There was no faithful Whanks there to brighten her with a few kind words.  The groom who had taken his place had been a smart young man her husband had picked up in the country, but he was made of different stuff to the patient Whanks, and at the end of the first month he declined to serve so austere a master, and he went his way.  Another followed in his footsteps, an Italian, who did his work well, but who was as passionate and severe as his master.  To Leila he was coldly civil, attending to her horse and his duties in the ring with unfailing skill, but to her personally he was utterly indifferent, and her children never received the smallest kindness from him.

Once she remarked to her husband upon his churlishness, and he replied,—

'He suits me well enough. I don't want a groom making love to my wife. The less he says the better I like him. He knows his place, and that is more than that confounded Whanks did. It was a good day when he took his carcase out of the "show."'

Leila flushed at his words. She had been so fond of the faithful, kind man who had helped her to bear the burden of her life just when the weight of it became apparent. She felt his loss acutely, and as her relations with her husband became more and more estranged, she longed to see him once again. Her health, too, was failing fast. At times she seemed too weak to hold in her fresh young mare, and this brought down the wrath of her husband. It was in vain that she told him how ill she felt, and that it was beyond her powers to accomplish the task.

He did not believe in women's ailments. It was only hysteria, or some crotchet or other. Had not the doctor in Liverpool told him so when he had asked his opinion months ago?

'A little passing weakness, that is all,' had been the verdict, and Castelli was determined nothing more should be made out of it.

But doctors are mistaken sometimes, even when death is very near at hand.

One morning at a rehearsal she pleaded illness as an excuse for her inability to follow his directions, and Castelli became furious. Her horse became difficult to manage, and her power to restrain him was futile.

'Rein her in, do you hear me?' he called.

'I cannot, I really cannot hold her,' she replied plaintively.

The horse continued to snort impatiently and to rear and plunge vigorously.

'Do come and help me, Emilio,' she cried in terror, for her continual and growing weakness had not improved her nerves, and fear often overtook her when the horse she rode performed some strange freaks.

Once she had laughed and enjoyed the fun, but now apprehension and dread had taken hold upon her.

Her husband stood in the ring watching the prancing animal and the affrighted woman, but he never moved towards her. He was perfectly calm and self-possessed, and her fear did not touch him in the least. But his face grew more white and set; his passion was rising beyond his control. She looked round with an anxious glance to see if succour was near, but the circus was deserted except by her husband's groom. To appeal to him would be practically useless; but her alarm was so great that as a last resource she would try it.

'Ticino,' she called, 'come to "Champion's" head; I cannot hold her.'

The man looked towards his master as if awaiting his instructions. Castelli interpreted the look, and answered curtly,—

'Remain where you are. My wife is quite capable of managing the horse if she chooses.'

The man obeyed; and this treatment gave the finishing stroke to Leila's nervous tension. Her despair at being alone with those two merciless men was too much for her, ill and weak as she was. The reins dropped from her trembling hands, and lay listlessly upon the horse's neck. The animal, finding itself free, was about to rush to the stables, when Castelli, quick as thought, stopped its wild career.

'Let me dismount, please,' pleaded Leila; 'I am so frightened,' and the tears came into her eyes.

'Dismount, indeed! I'll teach you to make a fool of me!' cried Castelli, white with rage.

'Ticino, come here and hold this horse. Be quick, do you hear me?' he roared, stamping his foot impatiently.

The man obeyed, and then Castelli raised his thin whip and struck his wife sharply across her shoulders and arms. Again and again the cruel cuts fell with biting force.

'Now then, my lady, we'll see who is master. Once more, are you going to do as I tell you?'

But she never spoke, she only stifled a moan of pain and drew her breath in gasps, and became white and terrified; but her lips were closed, no sound came from them.

'Answer me, you fool!' roared Castelli, his passion stifling all sense of decency or respect for his wife. 'Answer, do you hear!' he exclaimed, exasperated with her silence.

Still no words issued from the quivering lips, and then in his fury his whip fell again upon her with remorseless energy.

She winced and shuddered under the cruel blows; the beating of her heart could be seen against her habit; its thud almost choked her, and a deadly cold feeling was stealing over her.

But Castelli was too angry to note the change in his wife's face until Ticino called his attention to her.

'Madam is fainting, you'd best take her from the saddle,' said the man coolly, not evincing the slightest sympathy for the suffering woman.

'Curse you, hold your tongue!' said Castelli.

But one glance at Leila's face told him the man was right, and he lifted his wife from the horse, and turning to the groom said,—

'Take the brute to the stables, and bring a glass of water here, and look sharp about it.'

Finding herself on the sawdust, she recovered somewhat, and in a feeble voice she cried,—

'How could you? How could you do that? Take me home. The pain—the pain has made me faint and sick. Do let me go home,' she pleaded.

He held her firmly round the waist so that she should not fall; but there was no pity in his face, no anxiety in his voice as he spoke.

'It serves you right,' he replied, 'fooling about as if you were an idiot. In future you will understand what is in store for you.'

A moan—like the cry of a wounded animal—that was all her reply.

'Hold that infernal noise, and drink this water.'

But her teeth were firmly set, and he could not get her to take a drop.

'You obstinate devil!' he cried, 'you want another good hiding. Come here, Ticino, and give me a hand.'

Together they led her to her dressing-room and placed her in a chair.

'When you feel well enough to walk home you can let me know,' he added with a sneer.

'Don't leave me, Emilio; I can go home now,' she said. 'I'd rather get home.'

'I'd rather you stayed here for a time,' replied Castelli with determination.

And so she sat on alone for one weary hour, suffering acute pain, dazed and faint.

At last, with faltering steps, she reached home. At the door her two children met her with outstretched arms and laughing, happy faces. Their presence caused a terrible and sudden reaction to set in; she burst into uncontrolled fits of tears, then she laughed and showed all the signs of hysteria.

Castelli, his passion gone, brought her wine.

Don't come near me; go away—go away. I hate you, I loathe you—I wish I was dead!' she panted.

The children slunk away terrified.

'Hold your tongue, do, Leila, unless you want all the house up here, and don't go on in this absurd childish manner. Be off and lie down or you will not be able to ride to-night, and that won't suit me by a long chalk.'

'Ride to-night,' she repeated his words mechanically, 'I cannot, I cannot. I could not sit in the saddle.'

'Oh, we'll see about that,' he replied severely. 'I'm not going to let you do the invalid business, I am determined. Go to your bed at once, do you hear me?'

Afraid to disobey, and yet trembling until she could hardly stand, she staggered to her feet, and managed to drag her weary limbs to her room. Degraded, deprived of the dignity of womanhood, struck as men strike dogs, disgraced before a servant—no wonder her heart was broken.

That night she was made to rise from her sick-bed and go to the circus as usual.

The people were waiting. The band struck up a lively air, and Leila, side by side with her husband, entered the ring to display her celebrated trick horse, but so thin and wan was her face, so wild were her eyes, so great her effort to keep her seat and manage her horse, that she drew the attention of the whole house to her suffering condition. Yet no one liked to mark their disapprobation; they were afraid to be the first to do so; it might be all a mistake. After all, they supposed the woman knew best herself, and so silence fell on the sightseers.

It was not until Castelli threw one angry flash at his wife, and a low muttered oath, which did not escape the watchful eyes and ears of a few who sat in the front row of the stalls, that suddenly a hiss rose from a lady's lips, which was taken up by one or two of the most daring in the vast assembly.

But the applause broke forth with renewed force, the hisses were lost.

Humanity was crushed by the cowardice of the people.

It is the same to-day.

Oh for a humanity strong enough, deep enough to tread under its feet the cravens, the poltroons, the timorous pleasure-goers who would rather let suffering live than they should speak. Oh for a humanity which dare plead for the pains of girlhood, for the degradation of womanhood. Away, away with the faddist, away with those who offer a lukewarm sympathy but *dare* not cry, 'I will help the slaves of the sawdust, I will save those who suffer for the pleasure of the people.'

Away with those who have so far fouled the name of philanthropy by standing aloof when their much vaunted services were most needed.

Philanthropy is one thing in name, another in action. The one *so* easy, the other not *very* pleasant. And so the agreeable way has been chosen, and the emotional minds left in peace.

But the dawn is at hand, the faint flickering of the morn is growing nearer, the light will burst, the night be gone for ever, the brilliant day will break, and truth shall bask in her rosy hues and light the path of suffering and misery.

Then it will be well.

At last the 'show' was over and the weary woman had left the ring, and the careless audience were discussing her pale looks and despairing glances. But the next act soon took their attention. After all it was nothing to them.

Castelli was about to turn on his wife with an oath, for the hisses had reached him as he rode, and he was annoyed that Leila should have brought such a slight upon her horsemanship.

But the proprietor of the circus came up to him, with a look of determination upon his face, and said,—

'Castelli, you must not take your wife into the ring again at present. I cannot permit it. The audience have begun to notice how ill she is, and surely you must know she is not fit to ride.'

'She is not so ill as all that,' replied Castelli with anger. 'It's temper, not illness. It's duced cool to tell me my wife is too ill to perform. I'm the best judge of that, I should guess,' he added with scorn.

'I don't mind whether you are capable of judging or not. She cannot appear in the ring here. I forbid it. You had better take her home and fetch the doctor.'

With these words he walked off, and Castelli, using a foul oath, took his wife home. But he did not fetch the doctor, neither did he remain by her side to comfort her in her sickness.

Left alone, she seemed almost stunned by all she had undergone during that terrible day. She seemed hardly capable of thought. But after a great effort she reached her children's room, and kissed them passionately as they slept. Suddenly some awful truth seemed to strike home to her, and she cried: 'I am dying—dying, and who will care for them when I am gone? His lash has fallen on me—their mother—his wife. Some day it will fall on them. What shall I do with my children?' she cried with pathos.

Maddened with this thought, she never slept throughout the long night, and the morning found her wearied to the soul. As the day grew her trouble seemed to rest upon her until she could hardly bear the slightest word spoken in her presence, and in her despair she moaned,—

'My children, my children! How shall I save my children? I must die and leave them all alone. What will become of them? What *shall* I do?'

Her restlessness grew worse as the evening approached, and her husband asked her with a sneer,—

'Are you mad, Leila?'

'I think so—I think I must be,' she said slowly, a wavering and indecision being apparent in her voice.

He smiled calmly.

But she took no heed.

## CHAPTER XVI.

### MAD FOR LOVE.

THAT night he had left her with an oath upon his lips.

She could not work now—she was too weary, too ill.

The tender flower was crushed, shattered, its glory gone for ever.

She had thrown herself upon the bed, and with closed eyes she lay trying to gain some rest. Her fair hair hung wildly about her shoulders, her arms were thrown behind her head, and through the thin dressing-gown could be seen the slim contour of her limbs. All traces of the plump, fine-grown woman had long since disappeared.

She looked very fair and fragile as she lay there almost as still as death.

At last, after a restless struggle, she fell asleep, growing more white as the moments sped on, with a look of unutterable pain stealing over her face, as if animated by an undying consciousness of some horrible thought which had reached the inmost recess of the mind. Some terrible scene come to disturb her brain with acute suffering wrung from the fierce despair of the days that were past.

Sometimes her white and compressed lips moved as if she were speaking, but the murmurings, if any, were too low, too soft to reach the human ear.

That was well, for perhaps her spirit was roaming in memory's land, bringing back to her tortured heart the remembrance of happy days, and far-off friends and charms, which died all too soon.

Suddenly she awoke from her distressful slumber, and with a strange glare, her eyes wandered round the deserted room, resting at length upon a large photograph of her husband. This seemed to infuriate her, and she sprang up, wildy exclaiming,—

'I'll do it—I'll do it to-night—now—I've plenty of courage, plenty—it won't take long—they will just scream a little—but it will soon be over. Let me see,' she said, 'I shall kill Vanda first, she is sure to struggle most—and then the boy. The angel who fetches Vanda must wait for Adrian; he would be afraid to go without her—the way is so very long, the night so dark. To-day, sin, sorrow, care, and curses,' she hissed; 'to-morrow, music, light, golden harps, and flowers,' she cried with exultation. 'I'll do it now, at once—it must be done before their father comes back—now, now is the time.'

With slow and noiseless step she moved to the sideboard and with eager hand drew a knife from the drawer.

She ran her fingers down the blue blade, making a gash, and letting the blood fall upon her gown.

For a moment she stood awed and dejected at the sight.

But her eyes did not lose their glitter—passion still bore the sway. She flung her disordered tresses on one side, marking them as she did so with a crimson stain.

She hurried to the table, and clutching hold of one of the candlesticks with impetuous haste, she moved to the door, the bright steel of the knife flashing as she went. Beautiful, but terrible in her frenzy, she crept along the ill-lighted passage until she reached the room where her hapless children slept. Putting the light down, she fixed her eyes upon the bed where the little ones lay. Gradually she moved towards them, hiding the glistening knife behind her as she went.

She saw them resting side by side, with their golden curls all tossed and tumbled in childhood's dreamless sleep, their white chubby hands showing in relief against the brilliant crimson coverlid, their fingers twitching now and then as if to clasp some much loved treasure. How peaceful they looked; but she only whispered hoarsely,—

'It's best—it's best it shall be done,' her desperate purpose shaking off her fears. 'It's best,' she almost hissed. She took another gliding footstep, repeating, 'Death is freedom—escape from pain and suffering. I must save them—I will,' she panted.

She drew so near that the breath of the sleeping boy was warm upon her hand; the colour deepened in her cheeks, her breath came rapidly as she drew the knife from the folds of her long trailing gown. She hurriedly put back her sleeve from the once rounded arm—now was the time—the gleaming knife was just ready for its ghastly work. Another moment—another terrible moment and it would be besmeared with blood and thick with gore—the dreaded deed, with impetuous haste, complete—the chainless spirits gone—now, now. The knife just touched the little girl. She started, with a cry of terror on her lips.

'Mother, mother! Oh, where is mother?' she cried, half asleep.

'Here, here,' Leila whispered hoarsely. 'Here, here,' she muttered frantically, stepping back appalled, terrified, awe-struck. The voice of the child had stricken her to the heart, and its thrill recalled reason in some mysterious way—feeling, love, memory had returned. Quivering in every limb, she exclaimed piteously: 'Vanda, have I hurt you? I must have done so, there is blood on my hands—on my dress—on my hair. Vanda, have I killed you?' she cried out in terrible despair.

The child did not speak—she had fallen asleep.

Leila stooped down until her ear was close to the child's mouth.

'No, she is not dead. I have not slain her. She breathes—she breathes. The knife is clean—no blood streams from the blade. Thank God! thank God! I have not killed my child; but I'll go—I dare not stay with them. I might try again,' she moaned.

Panting with fear, trembling with emotion, shuddering with frantic remorse, she fled from the room. For a moment she fancied some evil spirit was behind her, and not until she was once more alone did she realise the terrible sin she had contemplated, and then an awful horror seized her. It seemed as if a cloud had come between her and life, a something which baffled description, something undefined, which darkened the past and made the future oblivion. She was different—she felt it—she knew it. She rose as if to shake the phantom from her, and drive away the encircling gloom; but how strange things seemed—what had happened? She put her hands to her head and shrieked,—

'What is it—what is it? Am I mad, or has the hour of my death come at last?' she cried, seized with sudden terror. 'I've tried to do something awful—what can it be?' She closed her eyes and sat motionless, as if trying to reflect what had swept over her life. Suddenly, like a spell, the wondrous change became apparent to her, and with a cry of agony she shrieked: 'Heavens, great heavens, what a crime I designed—invented by the devil, restrained by God it must have been—to plunge my children into heaven—my little innocent, prattling babies! My God! my God!'

Her head sank; she was stupefied with dread. Gradually the shadows left her, the hovering between certainty and uncertainty was at an end; she knew then what she was about to do.

She must go to the children at once—perhaps she had harmed them—she would make sure of their safety.

She went back to their room; a shudder passed over her as she entered. She hurried to the bedside as if fearful of seeing some sign of a terrible deed. But they were sleeping, serene and beautiful. She pressed one long passionate kiss on each soft cheek and murmured,—

God forgive me for my would-be crime. May He show me mercy at the last.'

The anguish expressed in that prayer came from a broken heart.

Would Heaven deny forgiveness?

That night when Castelli returned home he found his wife dejected, depressed, and almost too weak to speak. The excitement she had passed through had made a terrible change in her, and he noticed for the first time, with anxiety, how really ill she looked.

With more kindness in his voice than usual, he persuaded her to go to bed and rest, and then she was tempted to tell him of the awful frenzy which had come over her. But her courage failed, and so the sad tale was never told.

That night she sank into a heavy slumber, and a glorious vision came to her.

Before her stood Tom, with a gladdened and tender look in his eyes. She felt his warm kiss upon her lips.

'Leila, my sister, dearly beloved Leila,' he cried in ecstasy, 'we have met at last, all of us together. See, the dark cloud has gone, and only the silver lining is left behind.'

Then she saw a vapour of filmy silver floating on the air, and gradually it rose into space, leaving in its place a magnificent and dazzling light, in which she saw her father clasping her mother to his heart and wiping away the care and sin from her brow. Each kiss he gave her left behind it a glow of happiness, a rapture, a felicity which comes only from those bright realms where all the streams of joy and gladness have their source. She heard a plaintive voice call,—

'Give back my children, let me hear them say, "Mother, I forgive you—I forgive you." Let me kiss them and touch them before I die. Come, come to me, my girl, my boy.'

Involuntarily Leila felt herself drawn with Tom towards her forgiving father and the repentant mother and wife.

As they approached, the light from the silver mist grew more clear, more pure and transparent. The faces of her father and mother became intensified in their beauty, glorified with a great glory

Her father put out his hands and drew them to him, and spoke these words, 'Wife, here are our children. Children, here is your mother. God bless you all, now and for ever.'

A radiant light fell upon them as their father pointed to the mother's brow, and they saw written there in letters of silvern light the single word— FORGIVEN.

Leila put out her hands towards her mother as if to cling to her, but a cloud began to dim the glory, and as it deepened she heard a low still voice saying, 'Leila, this is heaven—heaven at last.' Then the light grew less, and there was silence— silence everywhere. Tom and she were left alone. A darkness enveloped them, the air became heavy, a lurid glare appeared in the distance, lighting deep arched caves, dark gloomy waters, and hideous chasms, from which pestilential fumes rose in great heavy clouds. It rested upon a mighty rock upon which stood a man. His garments were in shreds, showing his bones protruding through his shrunken skin; his face was drawn with fearful agony and distorted into terrible shapes; from his mouth proceeded yell after yell, curse after curse. Above his head were the branches of a bread-fruit tree, its lobed glossy leaves shining in the hideous glare; its globular shaped fruit hung like melons from every stem, then changed in a moment into loaves of bread, crisp and fresh, and the man's great thin fleshless, bony fingers were outstretched to grasp the food. His eyes, shrunken in their sockets, watched with maddening gaze the loaves coming and going. Sometimes the boughs bent so low that he could just touch them, then suddenly they were raised far beyond his reach. Then he would scream, 'Bread, bread! oh, give me bread! I'm a hungered—a hungered. Will no one help me to lull this fearful craving for bread? Give me but one morsel, one taste. I am famished—famished,' he groaned.

As he cried out the trunk of the tree burst in twain, and before him came a fearful picture, all painted in blood. He saw a dying woman pleading to a handsome man for *bread*—a cast-off love supplicating for the tempter's gold to save her from hunger and death. Then came a terrible voice from the picture, saying,—

'There's the workhouse for such as you. The parish will give you bread.'

The picture faded.

There was nothing to be seen or heard but the wail of the lost soul trying to reach the bread which he in his lifetime had refused to others. He knelt at the foot of the tree, gaunt, famished, despairing, rocking himself to and fro in his agony and wrath.

But it availed him nothing.

Suddenly, hovering over the tree, was an angel form with wings of azure tint, and a low, sweet voice fell upon the crouching, miserable sinner, saying in accents fraught with sorrow,—

'I am from the God of love. You have stolen from Him women's hearts. You have sullied His throne with sins too foul, too cursed to bear. You have darkened homes. You have ruined the beloved ones of the earth, the pride of mothers, the darlings of many a home, and now comes your punishment—the retribution of vice.'

'I see her, I see her,' cried the man. 'Take her away. I see her face in every loaf of bread above me—above me,' he gasped.

'That can never be,' replied the voice. 'The face of that woman shall be before you, to horrify you for ever and for ever, and the bread you refused her in her need shall be within your grasp to torment you in your terrible hunger, but you shall not taste of it. So for all eternity.'

Groans, yells, hideous screams rent the darkness, and then Leila awoke. Too amazed to move or speak, she lay wondering at her dream. She had seen Tom, and the unity of the family completed. She had seen swift justice fall with torturing hand on Herbert Clifford, and that gave her comfort.

Was it, after all, only a fanciful, fantastic vision, devoid of reality and truth, just the freak of a sleeping brain?

Who shall dare to say 'Yes'?

Rather, was it not the mystery of the drawing together of kindred souls, of some great magnetic force which bids space defiance and comes to forge the link that death has snapped?

That night Tom in his Transvaal home dreamt of Leila. He kissed her many times.

That night her father dreamt his dead wife was home again, forgiven.

That night Herbert Clifford had gone to his last home. The day of grace was over.

Dreams, only dreams, laughs the sceptic.

## CHAPTER XVII.

### THE GOLDEN CORD IS BROKEN.

SHE was weaker.

The end was at hand.

What is that mystic knowledge which comes to the human mind at the time when the sands of life are fast running out? that profound secret which is far removed from earthly comprehension, and which makes itself known to the sufferers alone, warning them that the days of their pilgrimage are nearly spent?

Concealed from view, hidden from reason, no man has yet found from whence it has its birth. It comes, bringing certainty in its train, a notice which all must heed.

But why it comes, and from what source it has its being, is a mystery unfathomed to-day and for ever.

Leila had felt this strange forerunner of death hanging over her, and with it came the stronger love for earthly ties, the wish to see once more those near and dear to her. A longing for her father grew into a passion. She must see him again before she died, and she determined to make one last effort to satisfy her craving. She wrote him a few lines—the words in places were indistinct, and the letters quavering—telling a sad tale of a weak hand unfit to guide the pen.

When her father received the little missive he was overcome with grief, and he set off at once to see her.

The years had gone past slowly, making him feel very solitary in his old age. As he sat alone in the long evenings, smoking, he would think he had been too harsh with his sinful wife, too exacting with his girl, too ready to part with his young son, more anxious to pass censure as a judge than to be the fond father, the forgiving husband.

Then he would sigh, and murmur, 'Too late, too late. My day is nearly over.'

Whilst he was hastening to her side, Leila had become so much worse that Castelli had hurriedly sent for the nearest doctor. He came, and looked very grave as he sat by his patient. There was no need to ask her questions. All hope was gone. He could see that by the quick, laboured breathing, the hectic flush, and the awful prostration which overtakes the sufferer before the last.

Castelli throughout had watched his face intently, as if to read his opinion, and directly they were alone he asked anxiously,—

'Is she very ill? I should like to know exactly what is the matter, and what is the remedy.'

He spoke nervously, as if he were ill at ease.

'There is no remedy,' replied the doctor gravely. 'She is dying—consumption of long standing. I fear the disease has been coming on slowly but too surely for a long time. All human aid is useless. I can do nothing for her.'

'Dying,' gasped Castelli, too shocked at last to believe the doctor's words.

'Yes, dying,' replied the doctor. 'I am afraid it is a case of hours now. She is sinking fast. I will call again this evening, but I cannot give you the slightest hope.'

He picked up his hat and took his leave, and Castelli was left alone to bear the shock as best he could. The blow had fallen, he could not restore her if he would.

He was smitten. He cursed himself for his folly, for his neglect and cruelty; but that could not stay the hand of death.

'Good God! what have I done?' he groaned. 'I have killed her, fool that I am.'

He recalled all the miseries she had undergone, and the terrible day when he had struck her. The thought of that deed maddened him almost to frenzy. His mental pain was agonising, and his remorse terrible.

When he became calmer he went to her, and going up to the bedside, he said with great effort,—

'Leila, my darling Leila, will you kiss me once again?'

## THE GOLDEN CORD IS BROKEN. 181

She looked at him. Such a happy smile lit up her face—one of the old winsome smiles which he had loved so well.

She put out her thin hands and drew his face to hers and kissed him many times.

'Emilio,' she cried, 'Emilio, you love me now as you did in the dear old days at Sandcliffe. I was so happy then, and now the joy has come again. I am *so* very, *very* glad. Dying won't be so hard now that you love me again.'

'Don't talk of dying, Leila. You must get better, and keep me company. I cannot spare you yet. I love you with all my heart. Leila, my Leila, I have been a brute to you—a vile brute. Can you forgive me for all my cruelty, all the—' But he could say no more, his emotion almost choked him.

'Yes,' she said sadly, 'I can forgive you all, because you are so kind now—that has made up for the past. Once it was hard to bear—but now, what peace. Love at the beginning—love at the last—what can make me happier?'

'I could have made your life happier,' sobbed Castelli. 'Oh, Leila, Leila, you must not die—only live, and you shall never ride again, never. I will care for you for ever.'

Years ago he had promised to care for her 'for ever.'

He forgot that promise. The day was far spent, the night was at hand, promises could avail her nothing.

'Would you, Emilio?' she asked feebly.

He could not speak, and so she continued,—

'That can never be, Emilio. My hours are numbered—you can do nothing but love me for a little while as you used to do. Will you?' she pleaded, looking up at him gently.

'Leila, Leila, don't talk like that,' cried the strong man in his distress. 'I do love you, Leila; believe I do,' and he kissed her passionately.

She rested a few moments before she spoke again. Her breath was short, and talking was becoming more and more an effort.

'Emilio, I want to tell you something. You won't be angry, will you?' she asked in her old tone of timidity, 'but I have written to ask my father to come and see me. I don't expect he will come,' she added mournfully, 'but I should like to wish him a last good-bye. Will you be kind to him for my sake? It is the last favour I shall ever ask you,' she pleaded.

'I hope he may come, my darling. Don't be afraid; I will meet him civilly. I will do anything you ask me,' he added mournfully.

He sat by her side holding one little parched hand in his, raising it now and again to impress a kiss upon it.

She lay watching him, too weak to say much more, but radiant in mind—the early love had returned, he smiled upon her as in the old days, and in her joy she forgot all she had endured. The present was with her—the past dead.

Kind words were to soothe her path to the grave. His love was to illumine the dark valley and cheer her path to the Strange Land.

How thankful she felt.

That afternoon she slept peacefully, happy once more in her husband's love. Her breathing became placid, and Castelli, as he crept into the apartment from time to time, began to hope she might yet recover.

Alas! how soon Hope rises in the human breast.

Whilst she was resting, an old man with snowy hair and beard was shown into the sitting-room, where Castelli was bemoaning a fate which was about to rob him of his wife.

There was no need to ask the stranger's name or to express surprise at his appearance, for Castelli knew it was Leila's father come at last. He rose and put out his hand to give the old gentleman a welcome, and said quietly,—

'You have come to see your daughter? She will be delighted; at present she is asleep. You had better rest here, and have some refreshment; you shall go to her directly she awakes.'

Mr Gurney looked at the speaker as if astonished at his courtesy. He had expected to meet a vulgar, ill-bred man, dressed in black, with a heavy gold chain, and diamonds in his white shirt front and in his sleeve links, with his hat on one side, and generally low and depraved.

He forgot the members of a large circus are not showmen at a penny gaff. For a moment he did not reply; he felt a little restraint come over him before his outspoken host, the husband of his child.

At last he said with an effort,—

'Well, I suppose you are my son-in-law. I am glad we have met, sir.'

Castelli bowed graciously, and then a very awkward pause came in the conversation. The men looked at each other in silence, and then Castelli said,—

'As you will not take any refreshment I will go and see if Leila is awake. I must break the news of your visit very gently or it might endanger her life.'

Castelli had been inwardly planning how he should tell the aged father of his daughter's serious illness.

'Is she so ill as that?' asked Mr Gurney, raising as he spoke a haggard, anxious face to Castelli.

'I knew she *was* ill by her sad letter, but I did not expect to find matters so grave. Is she dying? Tell me the truth,' and his voice trembled painfully.

'She is very ill,' said Castelli sadly; 'it is best for you to be prepared for that.'

The old man moaned.

'I've only found her to lose her again. It's good-bye, is it—another good-bye?'

'I hope not,' said Castelli. But his voice did not fall very hopefully on the eager ears strained to catch the slightest gleam of promising news from his lips.

'God's will be done,' responded the old man with reverence; 'but it's very hard to see her die. My punishment is greater than I can bear.'

Castelli winced. Was he not punished too, was not his penalty far greater?

The father never dreamt of cruelty and neglect, and the husband was silent.

Had they not both sinned grievously towards her?

They knew it.

'She is awake—will you see her?' asked Castelli, returning.

Trembling with anxiety, and filled with silent dread, Gurney entered the room where his daughter lay breathing out her life.

'Father, dear father,' cried the agitated voice, 'dear, dear father, you have come to see me.'

But he did not reply. He stood speechless. The shock of seeing his daughter brought back the bitter remembrance of other days in the years which had passed. Since they had met, Leila had become a living image of her beautiful mother, and he recalled the day when his bride had come home in all her fresh young beauty. It seemed as if he could hardly bear to take his eyes from her face.

Castelli withdrew, leaving father and daughter together.

'Leila, my daughter,' cried the old man in a shaky voice, 'Leila.'

He locked her to his breast, and for a few minutes the silence was only broken by their sobs, then Leila spoke.

'Father, tell me you have forgiven me. Tell me that before I die.'

In the excitement of the moment he had not noticed how ill she looked, and it suddenly struck him like a blow might have done.

'My girl, my girl, to find you like this. I have come to see you die.'

A heavy sob prevented him from saying more just then, but Leila said hastily,—

'Don't fret, father, for me, but tell me do you forgive me?'

'*I* forgive you, Leila. It is for you to forgive me. I forgot my duty as a father, and left you, too, alone when I should have been your guide, your comforter. I see it all now, Leila, when it is too late.'

'Don't say that, father dear. I treated you very badly. I was not a good daughter to marry without consulting you, but love blinded me to all that.'

'And you have been happy, he has been good to you, tell me that, my girlie,' said her father soothingly.

A flush had overspread her face as he spoke. How should she answer that question? She must save her husband's name, none must know what she had gone through, and she replied evasively,—

'Don't you think he is good and kind? There is nothing he would not buy me, nothing he would not get if it would relieve me from pain and suffering.'

The old man was satisfied. He did not know that

such kindness had only been shown to Leila just when all hope of saving her had to be abandoned, and that dark years had been lived through without a murmur.

'Father, bring a chair and sit by my side, and let me hold your hand in mine. Dear old daddie, I wish I had loved you more,' she said with deep regret in her voice.

He did as she desired, and then they talked over the past, Leila giving him all the pleasant descriptions of her travels and the places she had visited, but most carefully avoiding any reference to her mother, until at length she was startled by her father exclaiming,—

'You saw your mother before she died—your husband thinks you were never well after that. Leila, *where* did she die?'

The hectic spots on her cheeks deepened as she answered in a low voice,—

'In the house of Herbert Clifford.'

He turned white, a look of mute agony stole over his face, and then he said,—

'She died there, did she? I'd rather she had died in the street—if only she had been repentant,' he added sadly. 'It is terrible to think she died in the house of her seducer—terrible to me.'

'You are mistaken, father dear; she went to see him but one hour before she died—she went to ask for a home, for bread, which he refused. She did not sin in that. Your letter came the day she died. Thank God she never lived to see it.'

He moaned two or three times as he listened to all the harrowing details which Leila felt it her duty to tell him. When she had finished speaking the excitement had exhausted her considerably, and when her husband and the doctor entered the room a few moments later she was lying with closed eyes and fighting for breath, her father watching her as one too dazed to move.

'Who has been talking to the patient and doing this mischief? She is much worse,' said the doctor angrily.

'I have,' said Mr Gurney; 'I'm her father, and there has been lots to say to her, and the time will, I fear, be short. Surely my place is here?'

'I must request you to step into the other room at once,' said the doctor severely, 'and you must not see her again to-day. Will *you* see she is kept quiet?' he asked, turning to Castelli.

'Yes, I will watch her,' and then he led the old broken-hearted father from her room.

As the day faded and the night grew Leila became restless, and at times her mind wandered, and Castelli hardly left her for a moment.

It was late the next day before the doctor gave permission for Mr Gurney to see his daughter, and then he strictly forbade him to worry her with questions, and on no account to excite her.

'It is cruel to add to her sufferings,' he said; 'let her have all the peace we can give her.'

And so her father crept into her room softly, but not too softly to escape his daughter's ear. She was weaker, and her eyes were closed, but she opened them directly he entered.

'Father,' cried the feeble voice, 'come here.'

He went up to her, and then she said,—

'Do you think Tom has forgiven me? He has never written since I married. Do you think he loves me still? Has he ever said anything about me in his letters to you?'

She was too weary to say more.

'I must tell you the truth,' replied the aged man, tears running down his furrowed cheeks. 'Tom wrote to you a great many times; I don't think a mail passed without bringing a letter for you. When you never replied, he asked me if I had sent them on. In my anger, in my wish for revenge, I said I had done so. I wanted Tom to think badly of you. After that no more letters came for you. I had my way, but the secret of that sin has lain on my soul until at times I felt I must write and tell him the truth. My child! my child!'

A terrible look of despair and grief had come over Leila's face as her father made his confession, but she only said quietly,—

'Will you write, father, and tell him I never had his letters? And tell him—tell him—I am a wife—that I have not sinned—that I was married in the church. My husband has my lines in a desk. Ask him to let you see them, and then tell Tom, with my last love, that I have never disgraced him. Promise me, father, you will do this for me—promise,' she added faintly.

'It shall be done at once,' replied her father, deeply moved. 'I will tell him the truth—the sin is mine.'

'No; wait just a little while,' she pleaded. 'Wait until the end, and then write and tell him that I died happily, believing in his love.'

He could not reply.

That afternoon a change came over her. She grew much weaker, and she felt her death was fast approaching, so she called her husband and father to her bedside and said gently,—

'Sit down close to me, quite close, or I shall not be able to make you hear, and I have a few last wishes to tell you both. My hours are numbered, and the welfare of my children'—she paused for breath—'is very near my heart. Emilio, dear Emilio, will you promise me one thing—only one?'

She waited for his reply.

'I will promise you anything, Leila, my darling. What is it?' he asked sadly.

'Promise me that neither Vanda nor Adrian shall be apprenticed to your profession—that they shall never become acrobats or riders. I could not rest in my grave if I thought they were likely to fall into cruel hands — like — like — that man Horrox. Promise, do promise, Emilio,' she added plaintively. 'Promise before I die.'

Castelli stood holding her hand. He stooped and kissed her, and said slowly and gravely,—

'My darling, I promise.'

'Thank you, oh, thank you!' she murmured gratefully. 'I have been thinking that perhaps you would let father have them when you are on tour. The journeys are so long and tiring for little children, they would be best at home. May he have them, Emilio?'

'Yes, Leila, yes, your father shall have them the times I am travelling on the Continent, but when I am at home I should like them with me. Will that satisfy you, my darling?'

'Yes, if father is agreeable.'

'That will suit me,' said the old man rapidly. 'Don't fret, my girl; the little ones shall be looked after. I won't forget them, trust me for that.'

'They have plenty of clothes,' continued Leila feebly, 'and everything is in order. When they want more, I think Ringens's wife would get them. She has little ones of her own; but you will see what is best, Emilio. Come to me, both of you together, and take my hands in yours, and kiss me, and say once more that you will care for my children—our children,' and she looked lovingly at her husband. 'Promise—promise.'

'We do,' said both the men together.

'Now I shall die in peace,' she murmured, a lovely light coming over her face—'at peace, for they are safe. I should like to sleep now. I am very tired—so tired,' she said sadly. 'So—tired,' she repeated.

They sat down, one on each side of the bed, and watched her as she slept.

She had been resting for some hours in a trance-like sleep. Suddenly she awoke, and turning to Castelli, she said faintly,—

'Fetch the children. I must wish them good-bye. I am dying,' she gasped.

'Take this first, my pet,' and he held a cup of beef-tea and brandy to her lips. She sipped it, and then said eagerly,—

'Fetch the children before it is too late—and, father, will you leave me with them?'

Both men hurried to do her bidding, and Castelli led the children into the room and placed them on the bed.

Vanda gazed with large wondering eyes at her mother, and a terrible fear came over the childish heart, but Adrian began to cry. The darkened, silent room, the white pinched face before him, the awful stillness frightened the tiny child, and he shrank from the loving arms put out to take him.

His cry awoke the greatest anguish in the mother's heart, for he had been her darling.

'Adrian, don't you know it's mother? Kiss me, my own pet.'

The charmed voice acted like a spell. His fears dispelled. The child fondled up to her, and in another moment his chubby arms were round her neck. She kissed him frantically. It seemed as if she could never stay raining her love upon him. Her husband stood by the door watching the sad scene. Cold and severe as he was it touched him to the heart.

'Good-bye, Adrian—good-bye, my boy. Kiss me again—again—once more.'

'Are you going away without me, mother?' pleaded the little voice. 'Do take me with you.'

'I cannot. I would if I could,' she panted. 'Oh, my child, my child!'

Castelli saw the effort was getting too much for the dying woman, and he took the child gently from her.

Adrian uttered a sharp cry of anguish as his father lifted him from the bed.

'Take him, Emilio. He is yours now, for I must die.'

'Mother, mother, I want mother,' wailed the little one. 'I will have my mother,' he sobbed, and he put out his arms towards her.

She uttered one faint moan, and Castelli, overcome with grief, hurried away, leaving Vanda alone with her mother. He could not bear another parting scene. He would comfort the boy and the aged father.

'Vanda,' said the weak voice, 'mother is going away from you. Will you promise to be a good girl and do all father and grandfather tell you?'

The child's voice was choked with sobs. All through her mother's farewell to her brother she had sat as if stupefied, hardly understanding at first, but she knew now that it was good-bye to her too.

Poor little child!

Leila continued: 'Will you take great care of my Adrian? Will you always love him, darling, because mother wants you to do that? You are nearly seven years old, Vanda—quite a little woman —so you must promise me to help Adrian all you can, and never be unkind to him.' She paused, her words became more weak, her strength was fast failing.

The child cried passionately.

'Don't fret, my girlie, but promise to do what mother asks you,' and Leila tried to draw the trembling, sobbing child closer to her.

'I will, mammy dear. I will always love Adrian best. I will kiss him like you do, and he shall have all my toys,' said the child sadly.

A wan smile passed over Leila's face, and she stroked the child's golden curls lovingly and said,—

'That's a dear good child. Remember, you are to be his little mother. Never forget your last promise to me, Vanda darling—come closer and kiss me.'

The child laid her little soft cheeks against her mother's moistening face and kissed her many times.

'Good-bye, darling, good-bye. Be a mother to my boy, and don't for—' She paused, her head fell on the pillow. She moaned once or twice, and then the child, frightened, scrambled off the bed calling as she went,—

'Mother is dead! Mother is dead! Oh, do come!'

Castelli had heard his child's cry of fear, and he rushed to the room, followed by the trembling father, and then Vanda took Adrian on her lap, and they both crouched down in the corner of the sitting-room and sobbed together.

They had loved her very, very dearly.

She was not dead—she had fainted. The last sad farewells to her beloved children had overcome her. The pain had been so acute that it had almost sapped her life.

Her father and her sorrowing husband stood watching the prostrate form. They both knew the end was at hand—the presence of death was making itself felt.

They bathed her forehead and raised her gently to ease the struggling breath, and Castelli put his strong arms around her. Her head fell heavily upon his shoulder. She opened her eyes and smiled upon them and murmured,—

'Good-bye, father; give—Tom—my—message,' and then she looked up at her husband and spoke. He had to stoop down to hear her last words, for they were too feeble now to be caught readily.

'Emilio, tell me once more you love me—tell me—'

Her voice grew silent. Her breath came faintly. She never heard his passionate reply

It was too late.

There was a rustling as of silvern wings, a rush as of angels' feet.

Neither heard nor seen—yet present.

The breath of Deity was there, showing a golden path from earth to heaven, and an angel stood on either side.

But human eyes were blind; they could not see the radiance—the glory was not for them. Peace shed forth its hallowing light, and rested on her alone.

She was dead.

A groan of despair and remorse from the strong men—husband and father—violent sobs from the old man were the only sounds which broke the silence in the chamber of death.

Then they went to her children.

A few hours later white roses were strewn over the still, cold form.

Had she not loved them in those days at Sandcliffe? Had she not given them to him as a token of her love long ago?

He would give her his last love gift, and that should be roses—white roses.

## CHAPTER XVIII.

### SHADOWS AND DUST.

She had been dead two days.

There was a terrible blank in the home.

Her father had left the house and taken rooms in the town, where he intended to remain until after the funeral. Castelli had begged him to stay at his lodgings, but he could not rest in the same place with his dead daughter. He begged, however, for the children to keep him company.

'I shall be so lonely now she is gone,' he said sadly.

'You can take Vanda, but I must keep my boy with me. He was *her* pet; I cannot part with him even for a few days.'

So Vanda went with her grandfather, and the landlady good-naturedly promised 'to see after the little dear'; and his days were less long and dreary because the child was with him. He heard from her lips how good 'mother had been,' how she had taught them to pray every night and morning, and to bless grandfather and grandmother and Uncle Tom.

The evening before the funeral he sat nursing her. To him it was a great pleasure to watch her, she was so like her dead mother. Even her voice brought back to him his irreparable loss, and he loved to hear her talk of his daughter, and as he fondled her he said,—

'Tell grandfather something more about mother.'

The child looked up at his face and replied,—

'You didn't love mother much, did you? because once she *did* say, "Vanda, I wish grandpapa would come and see us, but he does not love us well enough." Don't you, grandad?'

Oh, what remorse her words brought to his anguished heart!

'Of course I love you, Vanda darling,' he added sorrowfully.

'Then why didn't you come and see mammy when she was in trouble and so sick?' the child persisted.

'She had no trouble, darling. She told me so. Father was good and kind to mother, and I am sure he is to you.'

'Father wasn't,' replied the child. 'He used to make mammy cry often, and he beats me and Adrian, and once, when grandma was dying, mammy asked father for money to buy her bread, then he used wicked words and mother did cry. They forgot I was in the room.'

Charles Gurney was horrified. His eyes were opened to the true character of the man whom his daughter had wedded. She had not been so happy after all, but the truth lay hidden in the shroud, and it could never be unfolded; but to test the child's words he said gravely,—

'Little girls must always tell the truth. I don't think mother cried much, did she?'

'I have told the truth. Mammy did cry very very often, and once, just before she was ill, I was in the room when mammy told daddie she could not ride 'cause she was so tired, and daddie *did*, *did* say he would give her another beating if she did not—and I know he beat her hard once, 'cause I saw the marks when she took her habit off—and mammy did go and ride, and when she came home she went to bed, and the next day the doctor came, and he said, "Now, little girl, will you be nurse?" and I said, "My name isn't little girl, it's Vanda"; and now mammy is dead. How long will she be gone? When shall I see her again?'

'Some day, Vanda, if you grow up good enough,' replied the old man sadly.

'But daddie won't see her again, will he?' she asked with joy, "'cause mother said she should be glad to die if it wasn't for us, then daddie couldn't go on at her. I suppose she is too far off now to hear him even if he shouts, isn't she, grandad?'

'She is in heaven,' he replied gravely, 'where there is no work, no sorrow, no tears—all happiness, Vanda.'

'No circuses?' asked the child.

'No, Vanda. God is there, and all the angels.'

'Is mother an angel?' said the little child with curiosity.

'Yes, darling.'

The child pondered for a moment, and then she asked,—

'And has she wings like a robin, and can she sing and fly about?'

'No one can tell you that, Vanda; but if you are a good girl you will go and see some day.'

'And Adrian too?' said the child, not forgetting her promise. 'I couldn't leave him behind.'

'Then you must teach him to be good.'

'Yes, mammy told me that. How do you make a boy good? By giving him sweets and things?' asked Vanda innocently.

'By being good yourself. Whatever you do he will do, and if you vex your daddie then Adrian will do the same.'

The child grew grave, and then she said,—

'But daddie isn't good. Mammy used to say hush, hush when he would say naughty words, and once when she said that he told her to be damned.'

'Be quiet, Vanda,' said the old man, terribly vexed and horrified. 'What would mother say if she could hear you?'

'But she can't,' replied the child quickly, 'because she has gone away; but I won't say it again—no, I really wont,' she sobbed, as if the sudden recollection of her mother's death was too much for the tender heart to bear.

He kissed the child gently, and something like tears rose in his eyes.

He knew now the sad truth which Leila had hidden so skilfully, and his mind was full of contempt and loathing for the man who called himself husband, the man who had led him to believe that his daughter's life had been one of happiness and mutual affection.

At first he was strongly tempted to go straight to Castelli and charge him with cruelty and neglect, and learn if he could whether there was any truth in the childish statements.

Had they come from older lips he would have doubted the accuracy.

But little children are all truth until the world teaches them the ready lie, and then the petals of the lily are injured—then ruined for ever.

He felt sure Vanda had spoken the truth, yet he decided to be silent. He was convinced that Leila would have confided her sad secret to him had she wished him to be aware of the misery of her married life.

But she had whispered no such words.

Neither would he.

So impressed was he with the child's story that he mentally resolved to keep the little ones with him as much as possible, and to save them from all unneccesary pain and trouble. At the same time he was determined to avoid Castelli, and in future to be polite and nothing more.

He was sick at heart.

The last sad rite was over. The circus rider was

left alone in a silent grave in a great bare cemetery, one amongst thousands. The earth had fallen with a thud upon the coffin, crushing the white roses which lay upon the top, and then the mourners turned away and went back to the desolate home.

In the country the autumn day had been glorious. The voice of the ring-dove had broken the stillness of the woods with its gentle 'coo coo.' The fields were waving heavily with coming corn, amongst which the poppies grew apace. Along the hedges the berries were crimsoning, and the lanes were strewn with fallen leaves, all ruddy and brown they lay, and the robins warbled forth the first carol of the winter.

Nature was so happy.

But in the town there was only the heat and dust, the rattle of traffic, the endless passing to and fro of pedestrians, the ceaseless flow of life.

The pulse of the great town never grew faint. And Leila lay dead amongst the living.

When all was over, Charles Gurney bade farewell to Castelli, asking if he might return for the children in a month.

To this their father consented. He had no wish to take them with him to Vienna; besides, his promises to his dead wife were as fresh as the sods upon her grave. They should go to their grandfather, and this being amicably settled, Mr Gurney prepared to return to his home. There was much to do before the arrival of the little folks in his country cottage, and he must see his solicitor and alter his will in favour of the motherless children.

But first of all there was a letter to be written to Tom, that must be done.

He was full of new desires, and the sooner he began to put them into practice the happier he would feel.

Alas for earthly hopes!

Destiny, which overtakes all, stepped in, and brought with it inevitable doom, which must come sooner or later to end the lives of all mankind.

Does not Clotho for ever wield the distaff, and Atropos spin the threads of man's life, and Lachesis divide it just when least expected and apparently most needed?

These three deities hold the world, and man *must* die when they will—mercy there is none. So say some.

They had destined that Charles Gurney should die.

Travelling from Liverpool to London, an accident occurred to the train; it ran into another which was at a standstill. Luckily for the other passengers the train was proceeding at slow speed or the results would have been disastrous. As it was, Charles Gurney was travelling in a third-class carriage, close to the engine, thus he received the full force of the shock, which pitched him against the opposite seat. He was the only occupant of the carriage, and when the train came to a standstill he was found to be dead. His neck had been broken.

They took him on to the next station, and thence conveyed him to a room at the inn to await the inquest.

But who was he? That puzzled the people, for no papers or memoranda were found on his person, and his identification seemed hopeless.

But Castelli had read of the accident in the daily papers, and he went and identified the body, making at the same time all the arrangements for the funeral.

He had refused to bury her mother, but for the sake of the wife whose memory was so fresh in his mind he would pay this last tribute of respect to her father.

She had not been dead long enough to be forgotten.

That was to come.

Charles Gurney was the only one who met his death in the railway disaster, the only one of those travelling to meet such an awful end—the one man, who had the future welfare of two innocent children in his hands.

Why should he have been chosen and others left?

Surely there is a fate, after all, which guides the footsteps of life.

Who can doubt it?

We may disbelieve, we may scoff, mock, and jeer at those who put their faith in destiny. But contempt must fall when truth stands out so clearly.

That must always be.

Leila's dream had come to pass. Father, mother, and child were home at last.

They were waiting for Tom to share their bliss.

But the hour of reunion was not yet.

## CHAPTER XIX.

### TOM TRIES HIS LUCK.

'YES, sir, I shall try my luck with the rest,' said Tom to Mr Bates one morning, intimating his intention of quitting the store for the diamond fields.

'Well, you were getting on all right here. It seems to me as if this boom at the De Beers mine has turned everyone's head. You are smitten, too, and throw up an appointment for an uncertainty. I don't think it will be a good thing for all. Some will lose; everybody cannot make a fortune out of the diamonds,' said Mr Bates with caution.

'I mean to try,' persisted Tom. 'I mean to do some business for myself if I can. I shall go up to Colesberg Kopje and see what is going.'

'You'll find things in a terribly rough condition. I know food will be a pretty stiff item. You'll soon spend all you've saved. You'd better stay where you are.'

But Tom shook his head and replied,—

'No, I've made up my mind to purchase a tent waggon and an outfit and go to the place. I might be successful. Somebody must. Why not I?'

Mr Bates made no reply. He saw that Tom would never settle down again to life at the store and that all he might say would be in vain. At the same time he was honestly vexed that Tom should wish to leave him for what he considered was a rash undertaking. He had grown much attached to him, and a strong friendship seemed to be established between the two men. Tom had done his work well. There had been no scamping of duties, however hard, and Mr Bates had no fault to find with his assistant, and his going away was a source of great distress to him. However, he was of far too generous a nature to use any undue influence over his comrade; and so Tom went his way, and left the roadside store which, if lonely, had at any-rate sheltered him during the years he had most needed a home. The business had enabled him to forget, in a measure, his mother's disgrace, and a feeling of intense regret came over him when the last good-byes had to be said, and his voice faltered a little when Mr Bates came to the waggon and wished him God-speed and shook him once more by the hand.

Tom was by no means ungrateful for all the

kindness which had been shown him, but he was seized with a great desire to possess a 'claim' at New Rush. He had visions in his mind of untold wealth, of a certain sweet girl whom he longed to call wife, so with these ambitious projects in view he commenced his journey.

He was prepared to find things very rough and extremely uncomfortable, but the true state of affairs was far beyond what he had pictured. When he reached New Rush the desolation of the place was depressing beyond description. There were only some thousands of tents, waggons, a few wooden framed canvas erections, and plenty of wretched canteens, the resort of the lowest grades of society, and Tom feared that he would be practically alone even among many. He managed to buy a claim for one hundred and twenty pounds, a lucky chance, as already the original owners, who had pegged out claims when the rush took place, were selling portions of them—an eighth, a quarter, or a half, as the case might be. He drew up his tent waggon close to the spot and prepared to make that his home.

All around him were those who came in search of diamonds—thousands and thousands eager to try their luck—farmers, shopkeepers, clerks, masters and men of all sorts and conditions; but the respectable members of the crowd were largely in the majority, and the rest were, as a rule, fairly law abiding; their one object was to obtain the precious white stones hidden away in Mother Earth. Day after day they toiled in the heat of the blazing sun, many to return to their canvas homes cruelly disappointed; but when another day broke they began again to scrape over very carefully the earth, hoping to find a reward for their labour. Hour after hour the patient scratching went on, hope keeping up the heart of the weary labourer. But Tom was so bent upon success that his surroundings were of little discomfort to him. Indeed, his zeal was so great that nothing was likely to upset him so long as his health stood him in good stead, so he determined to make the best of matters and set to work with a will and begin operations without further delay. His claim was thirty feet square, and with the help of two Kaffir boys, whom he hired to do the digging, he soon got to his new venture. Very hard and monotonous it was at first to Tom, who had been accustomed to a much easier life at the store, but he had taken out his digger's licence and made all arrangements to work the claim, and he determined to continue through all difficulties and to wait for the luck he felt sure must some time come.

Every day, for two long months, he had sat at a rude wooden table, with the bright burning sun above his head, scraping with a piece of old hoop iron the earth carried to him from his claim by his two Kaffir boys, who continually kept bringing basket after basket and depositing it on one end of his table. Very patiently he had toiled, but so far he had seen no trace of a diamond, and a decided depression was fast creeping over his ambitious hopes, so there were hours when he wished himself back at the roadside store.

One morning, when Tom was more than usually depressed and down-hearted, a stranger came up to his table, and stood watching him silently for a few moments, then he spoke.

'Well, governor, trying to make a fortune? Pretty hard work, isn't it? I heard of the "boom" so thought I might just as well "rush it" with the rest. Had any luck?'

'No,' said Tom rather grumpily, and he went on scratching at a mass of earth with hasty vigour.

'Takes time and patience,' replied the stranger, 'and if there's no luck the expenses run pretty high. I never heard of such confounded cheek, charging a fellow a bob for a loaf of bread, and five bob for a little bit of a cabbage which would be called a stalk with a couple of outside leaves in England. A cove at the canteen asked me three shillings for a dozen eggs, and seven bob for a bushel of potatoes. "Thanks," I says, "I'll give you three bob for the hen, but I'm blest if I will for the eggs, and as for the potatoes, well, I can go without." Strikes me a goodish few diamonds are needed to keep the pot boiling in these parts,' said the stranger heartily.

'Yes, you'll find everything pretty dear,' replied Tom, without evincing much interest in the man, who continued to watch his movements.

Nothing daunted by his cool reception, the stranger continued,—

'I don't know much about this blessed diamond digging, but I'm going in for a "claim." My aunt left me some money, so I shall try the speculation. "Nothing venture, nothing win"—good old adage that. But, I say, what's the licence cost for a digger?'

'Seven and sixpence a month,' replied Tom, shortly.

'Oh, seven and six! Anyone would think we were dogs. But there, I'll pay that on the chance of scoring a few thirty-carat diamonds. Now what's the worth of a good diamond?' the stranger asked.

The question was so direct that Tom was obliged to give a distinct reply, though he did so most unwillingly, for he was tired, heated, and very sorely disappointed, and the intrusion of a stranger just at that time annoyed him considerably.

'A good-sized diamond of—let me see, well, of thirty to fifty carats, is worth, if "off colour," about four pounds a carat; if good colour, twelve pounds a carat; but you have to find them first,' said Tom wearily.

'Just what you are trying to do, by the look of you,' said the stranger with good humour.

Tom was in no mood to be joked, and to show his displeasure he swept a mass of the earth from the table on to the ground.

'Here, I say, governor, you'll never find diamonds at that rate. Can't you do it more gentle like?' and as he spoke the stranger looked down at the heap of upturned earth.

'By Jove! what's this?' he cried excitedly, as he stooped to pick up a bit of soil which Tom had so ruthlessly swept from the table.

'A diamond! a diamond!' shouted Tom in his joy. 'Hurrah! a diamond at last!'

'Hurrah!' said the stranger, 'I'm in luck. Just fancy me finding that after you shoved it down. 'By Jove!' he cried excitedly.

'The first found on my claim, too—what a jolly lucky fellow you are! Shake hands over it, old man,' said Tom warmly, and come to the canteen and have a drink on the strength of our luck—come along.'

'No, thank you, governor; I'm deuced pleased I was the one to find the first diamond on your claim, but I'm "sworn off." The drink it's been my curse, and I mustn't touch a drop,' said the stranger with determination.

'Oh, just this once you can,' said Tom persuasively. 'One drink cannot make much difference. You needn't take another. Just think of our luck.'

'Just think of me drunk as an owl, that's more to the point. I guess there would not be much luck in that—eh, governor?'

Tom was decidedly pleased at the man's refusal, but anxious to show him some hospitality, he replied,—

'Well, come to my waggon and have some tea and a chat,' said Tom.

'I most certainly will with pleasure. Tea is tea, and drink is drink. The one keeps me a man, the other a fool,' replied the stranger.

Together they went to the tent waggon, and after many gloating looks at their precious find they settled down to enjoy tea and a chat.

As Tom talked the stranger kept his eyes fixed on his face. Surely there was something familiar in the large fearless eyes, and something in the clear ringing voice which he had heard before?

But how could that be in the great strange land? And yet he could not rid himself of the fancy, and as his companion continued to chat the feeling grew almost into a certainty.

'I say, governor, what is your name?' the stranger asked at last.

'Tom Hesketh,' uttering the surname as if he would rather have left it unsaid. 'And what is yours?' he continued.

'Whanks, I'm called just Whanks, and nothing else. So you are Mr Tom Hesketh, are you?' he said quietly. 'Oh, I fancied I knew you, but I find I don't. Got any relations?'

'Yes, a father,' replied Tom evasively, 'and one sister somewhere in England, but she turned out a great disappointment to us. I have no other relations,' he continued, ignoring his mother entirely

Whanks was puzzled. He had never known anyone of that name, and yet he could not dispel the feeling that they had met before.

Tom and Whanks spent the rest of the hot, languid day in talking over the future. Something in the frank, outspoken stranger made Tom reluctant to part with him, and finally he decided to let Whanks buy a portion of his claim, and they arranged mutually to share the tent waggon and throw their lives into one partnership.

After the first chat Tom and Whanks never referred to their past lives. Both of them gave all their time and attention to their work, and both men were the happier for each other's company in a strange land. They were drawn together because they both came from the dear old country so far away. Surely that was a link which nothing could bend or break?

Tom's luck seemed to have taken a turn after Whanks had joined the undertaking, for several fine diamonds were found on their joint claim, and Tom began to picture himself a rich man. Buoyed by this hope, he worked with greater vigour than ever.

Whanks laboured too. But he did more, he infused a healthy, merry tone amongst the rough and often abandoned men around them, and without in any way joining in dissolute fun. He managed to become a general favourite—playing tricks upon his companions, and generally making fun amongst those who had left home and friends to search for riches.

So much was he liked that one day when it became known that he had gone alone, gun in hand, towards the kopjes, and a storm seemed inevitable, the greatest consternation reigned in and around the canteens, and Tom was questioned many times as the heat grew more heavy and the air more still and oppressive; and although Tom laughed at their fears, he felt seriously uncomfortable to think of his friend, alone and without shelter, if the terrible storm should break before his return.

Suddenly it burst upon them, and the whole stretch of land, as far as the eye could reach, seemed a livid mass of fire, whilst the thunder crashed and roared as if it would destroy all the earth with its might and its anger.

The men in the canteens stood huddled together, silent with fear. But Tom repaired to his waggon, growing desperately uneasy about his companion.

At last there came one blinding, curling flash of lightning, which seemed to envelop everything in its vivid tongue of flame, this was followed by a heavy crash, which died away in angry mutterings, and then there was silence and a calm. Tom ventured to look out of his shelter; everything was like a deluge, the water, from the excessive rain, coming to the height of his waggon wheels, and at the canteen he saw a man on a horse which swam down the path with the current. But above him the sky grew rapidly blue, the sun shone out resplendent in his glory, the storm had passed on its way. But where was Whanks? As soon as the water would permit him, Tom descended from his waggon and went to the canteen to see if Whanks had gone in there at the last moment.

But no, there was no sign of him, and the men shook their heads and expressed their opinion that no man could live out in that storm.

'He'd be scorched to a cinder,' said one burly man.

'He be drowned like a rat,' said another.

'Dead as a flounder by this time if he ain't in quad somewhere,' called a third man in a conclusive tone.

'We can only hope for the best,' said Tom at last; 'he is no fool,' he added.

'Fool or no fool,' said the first speaker, 'the lightning don't care—it would as lief kill one as t'other.'

As they talked Whanks was seen approaching the canteen, gun in hand.

'Here he is, here he is!' cried a chorus of voices, and they went towards him.

'Well, old fellow, got home again?' cried one.

'Where did you "turn in?"' asked another.

'Where did you shelter?' chimed in Tom.

Whanks stood before them smiling, dry, and with a cheery look upon his face, now crimson with the heat of the day.

In his hand he held his gun and one solitary hare.

'Here, ask one question at a time,' laughed Whanks; 'a fellow cannot answer half of them. Now, I'll tell you just where I've been, and how I escaped, if you care to hear.'

'Go on,' they shouted.

'Well, I had made up my mind to have a bit of an excursion up one of the kopjes and bring down what I could, and this is the result,' he added, holding up the hare for his companions' inspection, and then he continued: 'I got to the top of the kopje, the sky above me was lovely, no sign of storm, but when I looked down across the basin beyond I saw the clouds in great masses, and the lightning playing in the distance, and the thunder was coming nearer. I cut down that blessed ridge as hard as I could pelt, sticking to the gun and the hare like death. By Jove! how hot it was! In a few moments the storm clouds covered the sky, it was coming nearer every second. I tore on for very life, half blinded by the flashes of lightning. Suddenly I felt a great dab of rain, and holding on to the gun and this blessed hare, I spurted all I knew, for sixty yards away I could see the Kaffir kraals. I reached a hut just as the storm broke, and shot in at the entrance, hare and all. You should have seen the look of astonishment on the faces of the women and children as I floundered in; but they turned a tub over to make me a seat, and there we sat, two

Kaffir women, five kids, and myself, gun, and hare. They all talked, so did I, but we didn't understand a word each other said. By Jove! how hot it was in that hut! I was nearly sick, and the lightning was a treat I can tell you. For two blessed hours I stuck on that tub, gasping and perspiring until I was all of a sweat. When I looked out after the storm the hailstones were as large as pigeon eggs. I'm blowed if I'll go hunting again in a hurry. I've waded home like a duck in a thunderstorm; but no more of it—thanks, gentlemen,' said Whanks with a bow.

A round of applause and two or three hearty cheers rose as Whanks finished his narrative, and then, much amused, they turned to go to their claims, when Whanks called out,—

'Hi! here! we'll have a raffle for the hare by-and-by. what do you say, gentlemen?'

'Put the gun in with it,' responded one of them. 'And then it'll be worth havin',' called another.

'Here, look out!' cried Whanks, and as he spoke he flung the hare at the group of men. A scuffle took place for its possession, which ended in several of the men securing portions of the unfortunate animal, and amidst peals of laughter the party scattered to their labours, and the incident of the storm was forgotten in the anxiety for gain.

Days, months, and years sped on, and time brought ruin to some and wealth to others of the toilers. Many had left their claims, weary, saddened men, broken in health and spirits, with all their hopes dashed into nothing, even as the foam which crests the waves, and though beautiful to the eyes, sinks away from sight on the seashore.

Others had worked perseveringly to the last with but little regard to their disappointment, but there were some who made great riches, and amongst that lucky number Tom and Whanks stood almost first on the list. On the average, three hundred diamonds in ten months had come to their share, a fair number only a little off colour, and a small per cent., say three or four per cent., quite perfect. This continued for some years, and one night Tom said to Whanks,—

'I don't feel inclined to go on diamond hunting much longer. When shall we go back to the old country? I haven't heard from my father for a long time; I think I shall go and see the old man.'

'And your sister, too, I suppose?'

'I don't know about that,' replied Tom quickly.

'Well, I shall go home soon, because a friend has written to me that a someone I knew is dead, and the children are left quite at their father's mercy, and I should like to see to them. But I sha'n't go until I hear again. Maybe there is some mistake as to her death,' said Whanks quietly.

'Her!' replied Tom, dwelling upon the *her*, and smiling sadly. 'There is a lady in the case, eh?'

'In her coffin, you mean,' said Whanks bitterly. 'Ah! Mr Hesketh, you don't know the circumstances—poor Miss Leila, Miss Leila!'

He dropped his voice almost to a whisper.

'Leila, Leila! What was her other name?' asked Tom, turning white.

'Leila Gurney once, afterwards Leila Castelli. Poor thing, poor thing! I ought never to have left her.'

'What had you to do with her? Tell me, tell me quickly, was she married?'

'Married!' said Whanks. 'Of course she was. Are you an old sweetheart, then?'

'No,' replied Tom. 'No; I am Tom Gurney. My sister's name was Leila. Tell me all—all there is to know. Tell me, is she dead?'

Whanks and Tom sat that night through, and when the pale stars waned, and when the glories of another waking day were at hand and ready to burst with hues of splendour, they still sat talking.

There was so much to tell.

But it was all sadness, for Leila Gurney had known little joy. And as Leila Castelli still less.

Was the light of her life dead?

## CHAPTER XX.

### IN SACRED AISLE.

THE months had measured out their span—the years had run their course. Springtimes had changed to winter, summers succeeded each other since Leila had been laid to rest. Many glorious dawns had lit up the lonely grave marked by the plain marble slab, and the last lingering beams of day had, unnoticed, shed their softest light where the circus rider lay.

Dead and gone, almost forgotten amongst those with whom she had lived and toiled; forgotten by the applauding audiences, for there were others to take her place, others to do all that she had done, and the people were satisfied.

Are the dear dead to be cast out of mind like a vision which passes by and is lost to remembrance as time goes on?

The widower cries 'Yes,' the widow is ready to smile at the new fresh love, and to forget the old days when the now dead man had wooed her and made her his bride. Alas! alas! Such is death—such is life.

Leila's children had passed through the years

happily enough. Their father, if not actually indulgent, did not ill-use them; he had never used personal violence to them since his wife's death. He had so far fulfilled his promises to her. They had been his constant companions in all his Continental engagements, and he left them to follow their own pursuits without much restriction, so long as they caused him no personal annoyance. He had devoted neither time nor money to their education, nevertheless the children had managed to pick up a fund of knowledge, acquired by visiting foreign cities and through the girl's natural taste for reading. Vanda had inherited all her mother's refined nature, and she had an intense love for nature and all that was beautiful, and eagerly she sought to understand everything that came before her. Child as she was, she did her best to teach Adrian all she knew and read. But his tastes were somewhat different to those of his sister. She could spend hours reading, but Adrian loved nothing but pictures and poetry, and in books he evinced very little interest—unless they contained the life of an artist he could not be persuaded to read them. He showed no taste for his father's profession, and seldom asked to go with him to the circus. He had made up his mind to be a painter some day, and to paint great pictures like those he had seen in the cathedrals.

Castelli, to humour him, had bought him a paint-box, and for hours the lad would sit making little sketches with his brush, rude in construction, but showing genius and originality of design. Vanda treasured these boyish paintings, and very carefully she stowed them away at the bottom of her box; they were the dearest and most precious of her scanty possessions.

Poor little child, all the love of her heart was

centred upon her brother; there was nothing she would not sacrifice to ensure his comfort. He was her one thought day and night, and in return for this strong affection Adrian gave her a most devoted love. Thus the days passed, and the children happy in their tender feeling towards each other, never deamt of sadness coming to cast its shadows over their brightness.

But the gloaming was at hand. The days of joy, peace, and rest were fast drawing to a close.

The hereafter was to be for a time hell upon earth.

It was in the festive city of Brussels that the cloud first appeared upon the horizon of their young lives.

The circus had been there some time, and the children had enjoyed the sights of the great gay town. Adrian had spent much of his time at the cathedral, and once he found his way to the Wiertz Musée, and for hours had stood rooted to the spot with wonder. One picture, representing Napoleon Buonaparte in hell, fascinated him beyond description, and when he reached home he attempted to portray the well-known figure, in its white coat, with the cocked hat drawn down over the brows. Vanda was delighted with his efforts, and Wiertz himself never received half the praise for his great masterpiece that Adrian did from his proud and loving sister.

At the cathedral Adrian found more difficulty in watching his beloved pictures and statues, for the verger had found out they came from the circus, and several times he had sternly ordered the children from the building when he found they did not come to pray to the Blessed Virgin or to bring offerings to some saint.

Vanda was afraid to go again; but one afternoon Adrian had been gone some hours, and she began to grow anxious, and at her father's suggestion she went to look for him.

Very softly fell her footsteps as she entered the dim, still Cathedral of St Gudule et St Michael. She trembled and started nervously when the heavy oaken door gave a creak as she closed it. Very cautiously she entered, looking around after every hasty footfall. Once she paused to listen to a sound, but perchance it was only the pit-a-pat of her own anxious heart. She gained a little courage as she went, and at last she stood opposite one of the great stained windows. She listened again; all was silent. The last notes of the organ had died away after the solemn vesper hour, the worshippers had gone homewards, only a faint blue mist remained over the Altar of Mysteries, for it was not long since the incense had arisen to purify the earthiness around the tabernacle, and now its fragrance had floated down the choir and reached the nave beyond.

The perpetual lamp before the sacred Host flickered now and again, making the brilliants on the cross reflect gleams of purple, blue, and crimson, yet they, too, were somewhat veiled in the shadows of the incense cloud. Suddenly the setting sun broke through the painted, figured windows, which tell the story of the stolen wafer, spreading a ruddy glow over transept and aisles, and resting on the deep bays, lighting niches and statues with glittering hues, seeming to rest longer upon the representation of the Saviour of the People. But the shadows came betwixt the ruby tints and the cross of gold, and then the rays lit up the last resting places of many a noble house, brightening the dim vaults of the Princes of the House of Austria, which grew brilliant with blue and crimson. Intense and changing grew the colours as they glided over the polished marble floor, and then lingered almost lovingly over the girlish figure standing alone beside a mighty column. A halo of brilliance rested upon and around her head. She was crowned with glory as no earthly crown can ever shine, clothed with divers colours with which no artist can ever clothe his model, for were they not the offsprings of a light which never fades or grows dim.

Despite her fear, despite her somewhat untidy apparel, Vanda was absolute in her beauty. Even when the sun sank behind the summer clouds, and left the cathedral dim and lonely, even then Vanda was beautiful. She knew that, for did not the groups outside the cafés whisper as she passed.

Suddenly she paused, and her small voice broke the actual stillness of the spot where she stood. Her voice was so soft that it could not have reached the altar, where the body of Christ, in the form of the wafer, rested in the Tabernacle waiting for the 'Adoration of the Faithful.'

'Adrian!' she called, 'Adrian!'

But no reply came from behind the massive pillars, no voice answered that plaintive cry. The silence seemed the greater after her voice was hushed, as in the valley when the echo has died away.

She listened. The light in the cathedral was growing dim, the cloud of incense was gone, the figures of the disciples looked white and cold against the deepening twilight.

She would call once again, for Adrian often came to watch the changing lights, the pictures, and the altars, with their flowers and gems. She moved towards the Lady Chapel. There, high above the altar, stood a life-sized figure of the Virgin Mother, robed in spotless white. Behind the canvas a light burnt dimly, and in the gloaming the beauty of the figure stood out in bold relief. For a moment it startled her to see that living picture. She had seen it often before, but somehow it looked more pure, more still than she had ever remembered.

She wondered if *their* mother looked like that now she was an angel.

She gazed awe-struck for a moment or so, and then she called in a louder voice.

'Adrian! Adrian! are you here?'

But there was no response, only a rattle of keys, a heavy footstep, a cough, loud and prolonged, Vanda knew it was Tosè come to light up for the Benediction service. If he caught *her*, a child of the circus, unbaptised, a child who had never confessed to the priests or knelt at the communion! How often before he had found her lingering there with Adrian! How often had he told them to be gone, and not to turn the cathedral into a promenade! So she knew it would be useless to ask him to let her find Adrian, and she turned and fled. And whilst she wandered down the steep hill to the bright boulevard the candles blazed upon the altars, and the organ poured forth glorious strains, and the kneeling people raised their voices in the *Ave Maria Stella*, and priests bowed before the consecrated wafer and worshipped, but Vanda never prayed now.

When she reached home she found Adrian there; he had come in whilst she had been seeking him in the cathedral.

'Father has been gone ever so long,' said the child, 'and I couldn't think where you were. Will you read something to me, Vanda?'

'We will have some supper first, Adrian, and then I will read to you about Zeuxis,' replied Vanda.

'Who is Zeuxis?' asked the child. 'If he is a horrid king out of the history of some place I don't want to hear anything about him.'

'Zeuxis was a Grecian painter, Adrian.'

The child's eyes brightened at once, his interest was aroused, and he said,—

'A painter! Tell me some more about him, and where did you see about him?'

'In a book which Ringens gave mother long, ever so long ago. Zeuxis painted a bunch of grapes so like real grapes that the little birds came and pecked them, and then he did another picture, a boy, I daresay like you, holding a bunch of grapes, which the birds also flew to and pecked; but this made the painter very angry, because he said his picture was not natural, and that if he had drawn the boy as well as he had planted the grapes, the birds would have been afraid of him. Was not that funny, Adrian?' she asked, glad to have something to tell him which gave him pleasure.

'Is he dead?' asked the child.

'Years and years ago; he died from laughing at the picture of an old woman he had painted,' replied Vanda smilingly. 'But I sha'n't tell you any more until we have had supper.'

They sat down together to eat the portions which Castelli had prepared for them before he went to the circus, and then Vanda set herself the task of reading and amusing Adrian until their bedtime.

Whilst they chatted happily at home a man and woman were walking slowly under the trees in the Boulevard de Waterloo. The gas lamps flickered on the splendid beauty of the woman and on the fierce, cruel face of the man, who was talking with great earnestness.

'If you can get round him the thing can be arranged easily enough—get them into my hands

I am determined I will at any cost,' said the man, with a fiendish gleam in his bright, cold eyes.

'You still bear the mother a grudge, do you?' asked the woman, smiling sweetly.

'You know I do, Cleo. I swore I would have my revenge for taking that summons out against me. I lost a good engagement over that cursed business—had to "cut" for fear of what might come out if she went into the court. I hate her memory,' said Horrox with a hiss.

'And so do I,' replied Cleo. 'If it had not been for her infernal scheming I should have been Castelli's wife. She took the only man I loved from me, and if I can plan revenge on her children, trust me for doing so. You shall get them into your power before long, I bet. The girl must be about twelve or thirteen, and the boy a year or so younger. They told me down at the circus that Castelli lets them do just as they please, and they spend all the blessed day at picture galleries and idling away their time. Neither of them have been brought up to earn a penny, but they are stunners—just lovely children. When did you see them last?'

'Yesterday,' replied Horrox. 'You see I don't open here until Saturday night—neither do you—but I thought it best to scheme out the future and get matters settled, and then we shall see what they will *have* to earn for me. I'm damned if they will go to any more picture galleries. They will have to keep *me*, and take your oath my training won't err on the side of kindness—revenge is sweet—and I long to get the handling of them. It must be done somehow,' replied Horrox determinedly.

'But Castelli will never give them up to you,' said Cleo with certainty in her voice.

'Who the devil supposed he would,' replied the man with anger. 'You must get him to apprentice them to someone, and I will arrange for them to be handed over to me, and then we'll see what hard work and the whip will do. I sha'n't spare them; the mother had her turn against me, and now it's my turn against her brats. If I don't have my revenge my name isn't Horrox.'

'Right you are,' replied Cleo with a satisfied air. 'Castelli has been sweet enough to me since his wife died, but that goes for nothing—it's his way with women; but I'll bring about the matter somehow. Leave it to me.'

'I'll stand you something handsome when you have done the job; but whatever we do we must keep quiet, and don't hang on to me down at the circus. And when you suggest to Castelli that his children should be apprenticed, lay it on strong that they should go to a man who will take care of them; at the same time *we* must choose him, and make arrangements with him to pass them over to me.'

'That's a matter for detail later on,' replied Cleo; 'we have to get them first.'

They walked on some distance, then turned into a café and refreshed themselves with coffee and cognac, and before they parted that night the ruin of two children had been planned, two happy lives were to be marred by cruelty and brutality, two more white slaves to be added to the ranks of those who suffer for the pleasure of the people.

Slavery, of course, it is not called—it owns the respectable name of apprenticeship, but what else can it be? There is, after the training is over, a weekly wealth for the master—for the little children, hard work, drudgery, blows, torture, and no pay.

But perhaps that is not slavery after all.

Christian England cannot yet decide.

It may some day.

## CHAPTER XXI.

### A BROKEN PLEDGE.

STEALTHILY and ingeniously Cleo set about her task of taking Castelli's children from their home. She put forth all her talons, and like a bird of prey she was determined to seize her spoil at the first opportunity.

Cruel and heartless, and burning with an unquenchable revenge, no tender feelings arose in her heart for the young children whose happiness she was planning to destroy.

Many women are born without that most priceless gift, a tender heart. In them stillness reigns where yearning sympathy should live; a hollow void chills passions which nature would gladly obey; they know not the feelings which soften life and give joy to the eyes and balm to the sorrow-stricken.

There are too many such.

After Leila's death Cleo had thrown herself continually in Castelli's way. At first he treated her with silent contempt—the remembrance of his dead young wife was too keen to permit him to take much notice of any woman, for he honestly mourned her. But Cleo was patient, and contented herself by waiting until his affection for his wife had passed off. She contrived to procure engagements wherever Castelli happened to perform, and thus they were constantly thrown together. As time went on he grew more civil towards her, and would even enter into short conversations with her at the rehearsals. At such times she used all her powers to fascinate him. Once or twice she had offered to go and see his children, but this Castelli had sternly refused, for he was sufficiently honest to own to himself that she was not the sort of companion Leila would have chosen for her little ones.

But, like the water-washed stone, time wears away the rough surface of sorrow, and life comes to look very much as it did before the great grief came to shadow it with care.

And as the years sped on Castelli unconsciously began to find delight in her society, and a strong and exclusive friendship sprang up between the two, she gaining influence over him gradually but surely. But still he showed no indication of wishing to make her his wife, and Cleo, try as she might, could not bring him up to the desired point.

One morning after a rehearsal Castelli stood in the ring talking to Cleo.

'You're going to Bombay—you're joking surely?' said Cleo.

'I have had the offer to go out to a circus there, and I am sick of England, so I think I shall go.' He paused as if anxious to see how the proposition affected his hearer.

'When do you propose to start?' she asked curtly.

'After the Christmas holidays are over,' he replied. 'It will be a change altogether; yes, I am sure I shall take the engagement. There is only one obstacle in the way or I shouldn't hesitate a moment.'

'The children, I suppose you mean? You can't drag them to Bombay, the expense would be just awful, and it wouldn't be good for them,' answered Cleo cautiously.

'You've hit it,' replied Castelli; 'it's the children I am thinking about.'

'Oh, you don't mind leaving me, that's plain,' said Cleo as a try on.

He hesitated before he replied, and then he said smilingly,—

'I shall miss you, Cleo, but I cannot expect you to go out there.'

'Why the deuce not?' she asked, looking him straight in the face.

He hardly knew what to reply, and then he said,—

'You might find it rather difficult to get an engagement at your business; it's a toss up whether they need anyone in your line. I'll try and find out through the agent if you like.'

She paused before she spoke again; the chance was too good to be lost by want of tact or by being in too great haste.

'I don't know that I should care to go so far alone. You see if I was married and had someone to look after me I shouldn't mind how far I went. Don't trouble to inquire at present, I must consider,' she replied quietly.

'I'll look after you,' said Castelli quickly, really anxious to have the clever southern woman as his companion.

'Oh, yes, and then go and get married like you did before, and leave me to get on as best I can. Oh, no, thanks; much obliged for the offer.'

The sarcasm in her voice struck Castelli painfully, but he replied sternly,—

'I shall never *marry* again; I could not find another Leila if I sought the world over,' and a shadow of sadness came over his face.

Cleo noticed it, and a very bitter feeling of resentment against the dead woman rose in her heart; but she stifled it, so that he should not see how annoyed she was at the praise he had bestowed upon his wife.

'That's true enough, I daresay, but there are

other women who would be just as fond of *you* if you gave them half a chance,' she added as a hint.

'Yes, but that isn't much good if I don't love them. Love doesn't grow on every tree, by a long chalk; you can't find mistletoe on every branch. No, no; I'll look after you, Cleo, with pleasure, but the wife business is out of the question.'

Cleo grew crimson as he spoke, and replied angrily,—

'*I* don't want to be your wife if that's what you think I'm driving at. I only said I did not want to be chucked up if you married again, and then the children they must be th—'

A crack of a whip, a thud of horses' hoofs. A young girl and a powerfully built, severe looking man left the ring. He turned to Cleo, saying brusquely,—

'Here, clear out of this quick; it's my turn here now.'

'You be hanged with your sauce!' she retorted, angry at being disturbed, but she moved away as she spoke, whilst Castelli remained to talk with the manager.

As she passed out of the circus Horrox was standing on the pavement, and he came up to where she stood.

'It's no go yet,' she said, shaking her head; 'he's off to Bombay. He doesn't intend to marry again. He can't forget the blessed Leila. It's my belief he'll take the brats with him, and if so you may whistle for your revenge,' she answered with a sneer.

'The devil! Did you ask him to marry you, then? You seem darned put out,' he replied calmly.

'No; I hinted it to him just to see which way the land lay. You may trust me, I'll get him somehow. I don't care which way it is,' she said with anger. 'But leave it all to me, and to-night

I'll think what will be the best means to work the dodge. He says he does not know where to leave them, and to-morrow I mean to make him an offer.'

'You! He won't leave them with you,' said Horrox quickly; 'surely you're not such a fool as to suggest that?'

'Leave it to me. Either let me manage the thing or do it yourself, and go to the devil for what I care,' she added with passion.

'Not to-day, thank you; perhaps I may some other day,' he replied flippantly.

She ignored his remark and said coolly,—

'Well, *au revoir*. I shall win the game yet.'

An oath fell from his lips, but Cleo had passed out of hearing.

'She's a perfect devil, there's no mistaking that. Castelli is too wideawake to marry her I bet. He'd be a blarned fool if he did.'

He uttered another vile oath and sauntered towards his apartments.

Castelli, walking hurriedly, passed him. He gave Horrox a curt nod as he passed. There was no fellowship between the men.

A mutual but silent hatred existed, and they seldom exchanged common civilities.

When Cleo went home she thought out many a crafty plan, and after sitting quietly for some time she said aloud,—

'Le Sale, he's the man to send them to at first, and then Horrox must bargain with him; that's his part of the show. But I shall have to go pretty gingerly to work with Castelli.'

It was some days before another opportunity occurred for her to speak to Castelli, and in the meantime he had been thinking how much he should miss Cleo when he had left England.

Somehow the handsome Spanish woman always fascinated him, and his thoughts were constantly wandering to her. She had won his heart, but he was loth to own it.

She looked unusually handsome when she walked into his room at the circus one evening when her performance was over. His 'show' was over and he was preparing to leave.

'Don't go, Castelli. I want a word with you,' she said eagerly.

He looked up at her bright, cheery face, and at once remained to hear what she had to say.

'When you spoke of going to Bombay the other morning you led me to think that your children were the bugbear. I have thought since why not let Le Sale have them? He wants apprentices, so I hear.'

She paused and waited anxiously for his reply

'Put Vanda and Adrian to the show business? That is impossible. I promised my wife that neither of them should be apprenticed to our work, and I mean to keep to it,' he said firmly.

'But I think Leila must—'

Her sentence was interrupted by Castelli exclaiming impatiently,—

'Don't speak of my wife by her Christian name. You were not her friend, and I object to it, once and for all.'

She saw all would be lost if she did not humour him in his present frame of mind, so she replied sweetly,—

'I beg pardon, I meant no offence. You see her name figured on the bills, and we all seemed to best know her by her Christian name, but I didn't mean to upset you. I must be careful in future; but I am sure Madame Castelli only meant you to promise they should not fall into bad hands.

She was not the sort of '— person she was going to say, but she substituted—' lady to wish them to do nothing. Suppose you died, what would become of them? They would be much better earning for themselves than left to starve in the streets.'

'That may be so,' replied Castelli, ' but she made me promise all the same. You see the Horrox affair upset her, and after that she made up her mind to keep the children clear of it.'

'Oh, Horrox is a *brute!*' Cleo replied cunningly, 'but Le Sale is very kind to his children; he encourages them by kindness. I have heard that he has never "flicked" his whip at any of his apprentices. Perhaps your wife was not aware such masters existed among us? I bet Le Sale would suit any mother. Have you seen him?' she asked quickly.

Castelli smiled and then replied,—

'Yes, I have met him at lots of Continental circuses; he is a fool. I should like to know what he has scored with his pupils. Why, none of them have been big successes; he reminds me of a tame cat in the ring. Once when Belainè was ill he asked Le Sale to put his celebrated trick horse through his performance. Well, I never saw such a beastly muddle as he made of the show. He stood in the middle of the ring more afraid of the horse than the horse was of him, but " Wainfleet" knew his work, and when the music changed he understood what came next, and just went on without any master. Le Sale cracked his whip feebly now and then, and bowed nervously when the people applauded. The horse just went on as if the man wasn't there, and that old fool got as red in the face as if he was going to have a fit; and when he came out of the ring I asked him for fun how he had got on, and I'm darned if he didn't answer as meekly as a modest curate : " Oh, the horse got on all right—if he had forgotten, I don't quite know what I should have done, but luckily he didn't." A man like that can't train. I've heard him trying to check some of his girls when they have been impertinent to him, but they don't care a hang for him. Vanda would do more harm than good with such a noodle.'

'Oh, she'd like the fun, without the worry and brutality of training,' replied Cleo. 'It must be dull work for the children, alone nearly all day. Le Sale may be a fool, but he is kind, and you seem to be able to provide for them now, so it does not much matter whether they "score big" or not, and they must be a dreadful nuisance to drag all over the country.'

As she spoke Castelli called to mind what a daily anxiety his children were. There was their food to order, their lodgings to pay, their clothes always seemed to want repairing or renewing, and his landlady ran him up high bills for 'attendance,' and when he complained she told him 'children were a worrit, and kept her on the run all the blessed day,' and so he settled the accounts with an oath.

He began to think that Cleo's suggestion was a good one, and that the children would be better off employed, and of course Le Sale was not a man like Horrox. He might do well to consider the matter.

'Yes, they are a bother when I am travelling,' said Castelli. 'I'll think over what is best to be done with them before I go to Bombay.'

'You *are* going then?' asked Cleo, 'and all alone too?' she asked inquiringly.

He looked at her, their eyes met, and then he spoke.

'Would you care to come with me, Cleo?' he asked her gently. 'I am very lonely, and if the children go I shall be quite desolate.'

He smiled almost sadly as he spoke, and the

pathos in his voice would have touched any heart with sympathy, but Cleo was not moved to compassion.

'Yes, I will go with you, Castelli, but as your wife, or not at all.'

'Then it must be not at all,' replied Castelli firmly. 'I shall never marry again, never.'

'Well, I suppose we must wait until I can persuade you to marry me, but I think you're awfully shabby,' said Cleo with a sigh.

'Not at all,' answered Castelli. 'I am just telling you truth, and giving you the choice. You must accept me on my conditions or give me up.'

She could never do that; her passion for him was too strong, and her desire for revenge on the dead wife was still more strong—and perhaps he might marry her some day, and she would not let him go.

'I cannot give you up,' she cried passionately. 'I will go with you to Bombay, or anywhere else in the world. Do take me with you, Castelli,' she pleaded.

He hesitated for a moment and then said,—

'Very well, it is settled; I will treat you well, and in future we will share and share alike, and I must do my best, Cleo, to make you happy.' He stooped and kissed her.

'I'll help you all I can, and you settle the children up with Le Sale, and then we shall be free.'

Castelli answered,—

'If you like, Cleo. I suppose it's best; but mind Horrox must on no account get hold of them. If Le Sale likes to have them he may, but no one else shall.'

'I'll see to it, Castelli, trust me,' and she kissed him again and again.

The bargain was struck, and Cleo began life

again with the man for whom she had waited many a long year.

'Better go anyhow if I can't be his wife. But I'll marry him yet, be hanged if I don't.'

She forgot the resolute nature of the man with whom she had to deal, and that if she was determined he could be equally so.

A week later Vanda and Adrian were apprenticed to Le Sale. Their few things had been packed, and under Cleo's charge they had been taken to England and given over to the keeping of their new master. They had shown little regret at leaving their father. He had been away too much to have had a chance of gaining their affections, and Vanda did not mind where she went so long as Adrian was with her. Added to this, their inexperience of the life before them made them quite innocent of any trouble or suffering which might be their lot in the future.

At first they missed their freedom, and in consequence they pined a little. The air of London seemed to oppress them, and there were days when Adrian cried to go home; but on the whole they were not unhappy. Le Sale had a wife and three little children, who were all nice and gentle to the strangers, and their master himself was very patient and quiet over their first lessons on horseback. Vanda rather enjoyed them, but to Adrian they were a perfect torture. He wanted to paint and be an artist, and it was with great difficulty that Vanda persuaded him that 'all grand painters knew how to ride.'

'Yes,' replied the child; 'but father said we should have to stay here until we were twenty-one years of age. I should be too old to be a painter then, and I hate the circus—I hate it all,' and the tears welled to his eyes as he spoke.

Vanda did not reply, but that evening she told her master how much her brother loved drawing and painting, and Le Sale patted the boy kindly on the back and told him he might be a painter some day, but that he must do his best to learn to ride and then he could paint in his leisure time.

For Le Sale's apprentices were not slaves. There were many hours in the day when their time was their own, and Mrs Le Sale was particularly motherly, and grew very fond and proud of Vanda, and the child clung to her with all the warmth of a young heart. Once, when Le Sale looked grave because Vanda had given him infinite trouble in the ring, his wife openly took the child's part, saying, 'You cannot expect her to be perfection, Charles. She's only a child, and has no mother nor home to go to. I won't have her upset, so there!' and Le Sale smiled kindly again at Vanda, who was sobbing aloud.

'There, don't cry any more, child,' he said sadly. 'I am afraid I did get cross, but you were very naughty indeed.'

'Yes, yes, I know I was,' and fresh sobs almost choked her.

'Be quiet, do, Charles,' repeated his wife. 'Don't keep on jawing at the child. Can't you let bygones be bygones. I daresay she will be good to-morrow, won't you, Vanda?'

But the child could not speak. Her sobs came faster and faster, and then Mrs Le Sale said,—

'Run off to bed, there's a dear, and Adrian shall bring up your supper, and don't cry any more.' When she had left the room Mrs Le Sale turned to her husband and said fretfully: 'I do wish we could do without apprentices. I hope none of my children will ever be trained for the ring. I'd rather they stood at the wash tub in a laundry all day.

It worries me to death to see Vanda cry like that. I hope you didn't beat her down at the circus.'

His face flushed painfully and he replied,—

'Annie, how can you ask me such a thing? You know I shouldn't do *that*, but she must do as I tell her or she may meet with a terrible accident. She must not play tricks with a horse. I cannot allow it,' he said more firmly.

'Well, I suppose you know best,' replied Mrs Le Sale with a sigh, for she almost worshipped her gentle, delicate husband. 'But when I see a child cry I feel as if my chest was being turned inside out. I can't help it, Charles,' added the good woman.

'You're a dear kind soul, but I assure you Vanda had no need to be so upset. I am beginning to fear she is not very strong. She tires so soon that sometimes I feel she ought to be resting with you, but I must train her, or Castelli will be down on me like death.'

'You're looking pretty bad yourself, Charles. I wish you could get strong,' and she looked up anxiously at his pale, thin cheeks, and for the first time it struck her how much more delicate he looked lately, and a sudden horror came over her. 'Do you feel worse, dear?' she asked kindly.

'More tired every day,' he replied with a sigh. 'I could hardly bear the fatigue of giving Vanda her lesson to-day.'

'Well, you shall rest to-morrow. Surely someone at the circus could attend to her for once? Anyway, you sha'n't,' she added decisively.

He smiled at her loving words and promised to rest for just one day.

Alas! it was a long day of rest, and only ended when death called the toiler home.

## CHAPTER XXII.

### ANOTHER CHANGE.

HORROX, at Cleo's suggestion, had procured an engagement in England so that he could keep his eyes on the children and make his own plans to get hold of them. It was some months before he saw his way at all clear, and Castelli and Cleo had sailed for Bombay, and he was left to manage the scheme as well as he could without Cleo's aid.

Wandering down to the circus one morning, he learnt that Le Sale had broken a blood-vessel and had been conveyed to the hospital, where he lay in a precarious condition. He hurried thither and found that the authorities of the consumptive hospital allowed their patients to see visitors each day at three o'clock in the afternoon. Duly at this hour he presented himself to the sick man, and with many protestations of sorrow at his misfortune, he offered to undertake his apprentices during the enforced absence from his duties. Le Sale, feeling weak and ill, readily accepted what he thought was a kindly offer. He forgot, in his extreme suffering, the character he had heard of Horrox and the severities practised upon those who came under his *régime*, and the smiling, bland man standing by the bedside did not remind the dying artiste of any such danger to his young apprentices.

'If you will take their practice I shall be very grateful,' said Le Sale feebly. 'They can live with my wife and go to you at stated times. Annie wouldn't like to part with them,' he added with great effort.

But this did not suit the plans of the cruel and

revengeful Horrox, and he replied with well-feigned kindness.

'Of course I'll take their practice, that is what I came to offer to do, but I think it would be a great relief to your wife for me to take them to my house. You see it will save her much expense now you cannot work. It costs a sight to feed two hearty children. If they come to me there is an end to that, until you are strong again.'

Horrox knew too well that Le Sale would never be well; but to gain his dastardly ends he held out the hope.

'Yes, I forgot Annie has not much money It will be best for you to take them for a bit, until I am about again; but I am afraid Annie won't like them going,' he answered in a tired voice.

'I think she will see it is best,' replied Horrox curtly.

The sick man lay back on his pillows, gasping for breath, and did not reply for a moment, and then he said,—

'I daresay she will. Two mouths are a great deal to fill, and I can earn nothing now'

'Very well, then, I will take them over, but you had better just write a few lines telling your wife they are to be given up to me until such times as you can undertake them again.'

Horrox, as he spoke, drew a sheet of paper and a pencil from his pocket, and placing the materials as handy as he could for Le Sale to write, he waited anxiously for the letter which would empower him to take possession of the two hapless children.

Tremblingly Le Sale held the pencil and tried to write the words which Horrox dictated, but he was powerless to do so, and said feebly,—

'I am afraid I cannot write—all my strength has gone,' he said sadly.

## ANOTHER CHANGE.

'Well, suppose I write it and you sign it,' said Horrox cheerfully.

Le Sale nodded gratefully, and then Horrox wrote:—

'It is my wish that Vanda and Adrian Castelli, apprenticed to me until they come of age, shall be handed over to James Charles Horrox, to be trained by him as acrobats and riders, until such time as I can undertake them, when they shall be given up at my demand, and all claims of James Charles Horrox to the children's services shall be at once forfeited.'

He laid down the pencil and read the document over to Le Sale, who said, quietly,—

'Yes, that seems fair enough. I am satisfied.'

'Now, you'll try and sign it, and then I will,' replied Horrox kindly.

After many attempts Le Sale managed to put his name in faint letters to the agreement, and then below it Horrox wrote his, in a fine bold hand, agreeing to take over the apprentices—a sad contrast to the quivering, shaky signature above.

'Now, you need not worry about them whilst you are ill,' said Horrox gently; 'they will be all right with me.'

'You must take care of Vanda,' whispered Le Sale, for the business anxiety had made him feel exhausted. 'Vanda isn't very strong, don't forget that,' he said pleadingly, and then after a pause he continued: 'The last evening I was at home she cried dreadfully, I remember that, and when she came here with Annie to see me she—looked white and ill.'

He could say no more, and Horrox replied,—

'I will take care of her, Le Sale. It wouldn't pay to do otherwise.'

At that moment a nurse came up to Horrox and

explained that his presence was disturbing her patient and that he must be good enough to leave him to rest.

Horrox was only too glad to follow her wishes. He had got all he could from the sick man, and now he did not care how soon the interview was ended. The nurse followed him towards the door of the long ward, and then Horrox asked her what chance there was of the recovery of Le Sale.

'None at all,' she answered promptly; 'it's only a matter of days. He is much weaker than he was.'

'I am sorry,' said Horrox cutely. 'The poor fellow and I belong to the same profession, and we have met off and on for many a year.'

The nurse expressed no sympathy. Death to her was nothing more than an event which occurred daily—merely 'part of the business' for which she had been trained.

Love and commiseration are not to be found in hospital wards.

True all that human skill can devise is done for those who lie at death's door—true that nurses and doctors 'do their duty.'

Can one imagine it quite possible that tender-hearted women could remain day after day within sound of the moans wrung from the agonised sufferings of their fellows, and witness sights which make the blood run cold in the veins and the heart sick with pain?

After leaving the hospital Horrox wended his way to Lambeth to claim his victims, but he met with the greatest opposition from Le Sale's irate wife.

'My husband sent you here for Vanda and Adrian? I don't believe a word of it, so there!' she replied in answer to Horrox's demand for the children. 'You think, because my husband's ill, you can come here and worry a forlorn woman, but you've reckoned on the wrong card, my man. You've no call to come here at all, so there!' she panted.

'I've come for the brats, and I mean to have them. I hold your husband's authority to take them with me at once,' replied Horrox severely.

'He hasn't got any authority now he's laid low, and you'll have to leave as you came, without 'em. So just take yourself off my doorstep; I've got quite enough worry without cleaning it twice a day. That's the worst of being ground floor lodger, you've got to do the cleaning down stairs.'

Horrox took no notice of these remarks, but he said more sternly,—

'My good woman, I've come for Vanda and Adrian Castelli, and I shall not leave without them.'

'Then you'll stand there till you die. They are not yours to have, and as to coming from my husband, that's all gibberish.'

Mrs Le Sale had grown excited, and her voice in consequence had risen to a high pitch, and much to Horrox's annoyance a small and curious group had collected to 'hear the fun.' The dairyman had ceased his cry of 'Milk ho!' so that he could stand to listen; an errand boy whistling 'She lives in Camden Town' paused in his melody, and putting his basket on the pavement, leant against the iron railings to see what was 'up.' Suddenly he caught sight of a 'pal,' and he yelled out, 'Come and see the old woman a-going it,' and in answer to the invitation a telegraph boy sauntered up, and forgetful of the importance of the missives stowed in his little black pouch, he took his stand by the side of his companion.

'What's the row?' he asked.

'It's a lodger that hasn't paid his rent, I guess,' said the errand boy with glee.

'I bet it's a broker as can't get in,' answered the other.'

These and other remarks at last reached the ears of Mrs Le Sale, and she exclaimed to her visitor,—

'Come in, do; can't you see how we are being stared at? We shall have the police here directly, or the fire engines, to see what's the matter. Wipe your shoes,' she continued, 'and look where you are going, the passage isn't over light.'

Horrox followed her into a small but well furnished sitting-room, and when he was seated she said,—

'You can't see the children. Vanda is lying down, she isn't strong, and Adrian is painting—and I sha'n't disturb them,' she added defiantly, looking at his cold, cruel face with distrust.

'Very well, madam, then I shall call in the police to assist me. I hold a paper here which gives me absolute control over your husband's apprentices until he is sufficiently recovered to continue their training.'

'Let me see it,' she asked with determination.

He pulled it from his pocket and showed her the signature of her husband, and then he added,—

'Can you deny my claim now? The best thing you can do is to get the children ready, and their clothes and in half-an-hour I shall take them, ready or not ready, or call the police.'

Horrox had no intention of calling in any aid, or to call attention in any way, his scheme and his document was far too shaky to do that. But Mrs Le Sale did not know that, and after seeing her husband's signature she collapsed entirely.

'He always knows best,' she cried, the tears in her eyes, 'but it's like parting with my own. I don't know what I shall do without Vanda, she is so useful just now. Couldn't they sleep at home, sir? You could have them all day,' she pleaded.

'They are going to Selchester with me this evening, so once more let me remind you there is no time to lose,' said Horrox firmly.

Stifling her sobs, yet anxious to carry out her husband's wishes, she left the room and told the children of the sudden change in the arrangements. Both of them cried most bitterly, but Mrs Le Sale told them how much her husband wanted them to go, and that they should come back directly he was well. 'You may only be away about a month after all.' Thus reassured the children prepared for their journey, and soon they were borne away from the happiest home they had ever known, and their lot in future was to be left to the tender mercies of a brutal master.

'Revenge at last,' he muttered with an oath. 'They are mine.'

Later a telegram was sent to Bombay. It bore one word: 'Settled.'

Cleo was standing talking to Castelli when it reached her.

She knew the meaning too well, but she told Castelli it came from her English agent, and he believed her then.

A week later Charles Le Sale died, after making his wife promise that his children should not follow his profession. This she gladly acceded to, and then she was left to struggle on as she could.

Once, now and then, she grew anxious about Vanda and Adrian, and thought she would write to Castelli and tell him who had taken them from her husband; but one thing after another delayed her kindly intention, and it was a very long time before Castelli knew his children's fate.

Alas! for them earthly happiness was over, and joy was turned to mourning.

Is it not always so?

Why should hell, the oft favourite theme of poets and painters, be portrayed beyond the limits of this visible universe? Why should its terrors, its thunders, its curling flames, its forked lightning find footing on speculation, and Fancy be used to depict pain of soul and body, when hell is on the earth? Can it be necessary to go to unknown realms to find a hell, where the future of the sinner is to be portioned out according to the manifold sins committed? For does it not exist around us in various sections and forms, and are not Alecto, Megæra, and Tysiphine, the supposed fiends of hell, around us in other and natural forms, making our streets the veritable paths of hell for the rake and the giglot, the murderer and the thief? Is it not the hell of earth which drives women to the dark, cold river, and men to the cursed drink, and daughters to the lair of the destroyer? Is there not hell for men, women, and children in our slums, in the bitter poverty, the cold and terrible sufferings of sickness and death? Are not the mysteries of hell at work when little children are murdered, beaten, and tortured by frenzied and drunken men of the earth, or torn from loving hands and hurled into the great chaos which makes up life, so that their youth and beauty may pander to the amusement of the morbid and the selfish? For them, as for others, hell is everywhere on earth. Its existence lies in the mental and physical agony which must be the lot of all.

Surely there is no need to paint another hell, full of mythical sorrows, with awful and everlasting punishments and pain?

There can be but one hell, and that has its abode

on earth, casting amongst the people terrible vices, the scourge of sickness, the agonies of death, the cruelties of separation, the hardships of poverty, broken hearts, discarded love, disappointed hopes, and ruined lives.

If these comprise not hell, what does?

Vanda and Adrian soon realised the horrors of what was before them, and Horrox made no secret of his brutality.

The first night he made Vanda turn out her box, and then was discovered Adrian's drawings, in a small packet.

'What's that?' demanded Horrox fiercely.

'Adrian's sketches,' replied the child timidly.

'Give them to me.'

Vanda hesitated for a moment.

'Do you hear me?' he thundered.

She handed him the treasures, so dear to her heart, without speaking.

He unwrapped them, and the paper fell to the ground, and then he quietly proceeded to tear them across.

'Don't—please don't do that, they belong to Adrian—don't tear them,' she pleaded, quivering with excitement.

'They belong to me now,' he replied with an awful oath, 'and you'll both have something else to think of now than a lot of damned daubs, and so here goes,' and he ruthlessly tore the rest asunder.

Vanda burst into tears; she was speechless with fear and astonishment.

'Now, if I ever catch your brother daubing here I'll thrash him until he can't stand, or you—it doesn't matter a curse to me which it is—and give me that paint-box and those books,' said Horrox, looking down into the box.

Vanda did as she was told, and then she ventured to plead for her brother.

'Adrian is so fond of painting. Le Sale said he would make an artist some day. Surely he may paint when his work is over?'

Horrox did not reply, excepting by an oath, and giving Vanda a heavy blow.

She reeled for a moment and then fell to the ground. She had fainted.

Nothing daunted, Horrox stood by until she had recovered consciousness, and then he said,—

'I shall paint you black and blue if you give me any of your cheek—get off to bed.'

Vanda and Adrian shared one room, and very miserable it was after the clean apartment allotted to them at the Le Sale's; but they were too miserable to care much, and it was the small hours of the morning before they cried themselves to sleep.

Horrox had a permanent home near Selchester, and in an outhouse at the back, he conducted all his training. It was there that his hapless apprentices had to go through their bending, splits, flip-flaps and other feats enough to cause injury and strains to the strongest children, for terrible is the nervous tension necessary to perform them accurately and gracefully. Locked in this building, the absolute property of the master, what outside help could reach his unfortunate victims? Safe from public inspection, safe from the intrusion of any, the training goes on to this day without let or hindrance.

The secrets of the Inquisition were never more carefully guarded than are the practice hours of children preparing for the 'show' business, where they work continually until they are sufficiently advanced for public exhibition.

To this room Vanda and Adrian were taken the

day after their arrival, and Horrox began his brutal 'instructions' for the contortion business, the most painful and degrading avocation of all, the training for which makes modesty die for ever.

Oh! the labour and pain of these feats, which the public applaud, cost the weary little children and the languid, growing girl, whose tender frame has to assume positions which are absolutely contrary to those for which nature has fitted her.

It is time that those who enjoy such performances should realise this, and understand what has been endured for their selfish edification.

But the multitude have taken no counsel as yet, and the wisdom which would prevent young children from performing such hazardous feats is still wanting; it will be found some day, and then the dark shadows will pass from girlish hearts, and child labour for the amusement of the people will cease for ever.

But the time is not yet.

## CHAPTER XXIII.

### BEHIND THE SCENES.

So strong was the spirit of revenge implanted in Horrox that he was ready to inflict any punishment on the children to exact satisfaction, under a sense of injury which he felt sure their mother had been the means of doing him. His anxiety to return evil for evil had grown with years, and now his opportunity had come to wreak vengeance upon Vanda and Adrian. In his malignant spirit he forgot that kindness might make them 'score big,' and that they might prove a gold mine to him, for both were gifted with refined beauty, but for the first time in his life he did not care whether his apprentices survived their severe training or not.

Revenge, for once, was sweeter than great gain.

Is it not true, as has often been remarked, that Providence seems to darken the understanding and to depress the spirits of criminals, and hence the origin of misery and depravity? And was not Horrox's a hideous crime, which deserved the greatest punishment that earthly judges can inflict? Should they not say with Cicero, 'perish that power which has been obtained by evil means, retained by similar practices, and which is administered as badly it was acquired?'

But the law does not help weak children when training for the people's amusement, because it cannot penetrate into the haunts where the children undergo their suffering. The masters take care of that, and smile in secret at the protection which their hapless apprentices could rightfully claim.

Who is there to hear the stifled sobs of suffering? Who can catch the plaintive voices crying for mercy, and pleading vainly to the taskmaster? Who can save the children from the cuts of the thin white thong?

As yet, no one. For alone and in secret the deeds are done, so that the people may rejoice and pass pleasant hours in watching dangerous and degrading feats; from which they would guard their own precious, petted offspring, who cry because they have every selfish whim gratified, and fret because they cannot think of some further luxury.

True there is a law for the protection of children in the slums and alleys, in the baby farm, in orphanages and public schools — true a licence must be forthcoming before a child can perform in a play.

But *where* is the law which protects the children during the months of training which is conducted in private? Surely a public performance is nothing compared to the hardships of training? Yet there is protection for one, but not for the other. The law offers its aid when the evil has been accomplished.

But there is One above, says the Christian, who guards little children from harm?

In luxurious homes, yes.

But why is mercy meted out to some and not to all? Why should shame and labour fall with merciless hands upon two sinless children? And why does it not come to the lot of those who to this day *make* pleasure for the people?

Is it fair that some children should labour and suffer that others may sit and enjoy?

The weary ones could cry with Codrus, who had served God all his life, when he found his beautiful library at the Palace in Forli razed to the ground, with all his valuable treasures, his speeches, letters, and poems gone to ashes: 'Christ Jesus, what mighty crime have I committed? Whom of your followers have I ever injured that you thus rage with inexpiable hatred against me?'

From the sawdust that expression of pain and distress should rise, for have not the children the right to ask where is the God which Codrus served? And are the joys of heaven, His mercy, and infinite power reserved only for those who are rich in this world?

What reply can these placid Christians give to the overworked, wan, sickly girls who pander to their amusements? The Church of God is largely represented at all circus performances.

But those who have a knowledge of spiritual things are discreet, and silence reigns where the voices should rise with one accord, crying: 'God is everywhere. His love shall shield you, His strong arm shall protect you, His peace must rest upon you now and for ever.'

But instead there is an awkward pause—a cessation of voices, for they dare not give that answer to the 'slaves of the sawdust.' Alas, alas! though such is truth as taught to the rich, does not the existence of the evil prove the fallacy of the teaching?

There is very little mercy shown to-day in the methods pursued by some of the masters behind the scenes, and Vanda and Adrian received none.

Friendless and alone, in the hands of a brute who would disgrace any respectable circus, the children underwent the greatest pain and degradation. Attired in tight-fitting 'fleshings' only, Vanda and Adrian were made to practise all the indignities necessary for those who become contortionists. Their limbs had to be made supple by the most cruel and artificial means, and to these measures Horrox for spite was delighted to resort.

One morning, when he had forced Vanda into a most unnatural position, she fainted away from the effect of the intense torture it caused her.

She lay on the hard floor deathly white, and only the slight heaving of her chest showed she still breathed.

Horrox took no notice of her. He knew perfectly well that her age made it more painful for her to undergo the straining of limbs and back than if she had been younger and therefore more pliable. At the same time he was aware that suppleness and grace for the trapeze could be acquired no other way, and therefore it must be done, even if the agony of distorting her limbs made her suffer the greatest possible pain that could be borne. He knew she would faint every time he put her through the 'splits,' but it did not disconcert him in the least, and he turned his attention to the boy.

'Now then, you young rascal, it's your turn,' he cried fiercely.

'Look at Vanda, she must be dead,' said a weak voice, whilst the tears coursed down his wan cheeks. 'Vanda, Vanda!' he repeated; 'dear Vanda, do speak to me!' he sobbed.

A stinging cut came from the white thong, causing him intolerable pain.

'There! take that for your answer,' he said with an awful oath; 'and now to your work—quick, or you'll get another stroke.'

Adrian recommenced his performance of walking on his hands and feet with his body bent backwards, the pain of the horrible distortion making great beads of perspiration break out on his forehead, saturating the curly locks which had been so dear to his mother's heart.

'Oh! you've come to your senses again, have you, you confounded fool! Now, we'll go at it again,' he said cruelly, utterly regardless of the girl's white face. He took hold of her roughly; she was cold, and trembled very much. But Horrox took no notice beyond remarking that 'he would give her something to make her hot if she didn't leave off.'

'I cannot do the "splits" again to-day,' she said with anguish in her voice; 'the pain is terrible.'*

* However kind the master, the pain suffered by those girls undergoing training for the contortionist's business is simply torture, and a disgrace to Christian England. The 'boneless' man or woman has had to suffer hell upon earth before the wrenching of the muscles is complete and they are fitted to accomplish their degrading feats. 'Splits' for women should be prohibited by law from exhibition in public amusements.

'Oh, won't you come? Well, here goes,' and he placed her in position, extending her legs sideways until she was sitting on the floor. He then put a powerful hand on each shoulder, and kept her firmly to the ground, regardless of her cries to him to let her move, if but 'for one moment.'

But he was relentless, until her head fell forwards on her chest; she had fainted again.

'You cursed fool!' he hissed, 'I will break every bone in your body if you don't leave off this game.'

But Vanda never heard his threat, or the volley of oaths which fell from his lips. She only moaned feebly once or twice, when Horrox roughly put her into her natural shape again. Adrian meanwhile stood petrified at his sister's condition, but not daring to speak one word on her behalf.

Vanda continued so long in her faint that Horrox at last became alarmed, and he hurried from the room to fetch a glass of water. The very moment he was gone Adrian rushed to where his sister lay motionless, and throwing himself down in a paroxysm of grief, he cried,—

'Vanda, Vanda, dear, dear Vanda, do look at me! Open your eyes, Vanda! Don't you know I am Adrian? Do, do speak to me!' he pleaded, and the child's hot tears fell on the pink cotton fleshings, leaving great spots here and there.

But Vanda neither moved nor spoke, her lips uttered no words of love to her distressed brother.

With a grasp of despair he flung his arms around her, and shook her gently, but still she showed no signs of returning consciousness, and when Horrox returned he found Adrian sobbing loudly and bending over his sister, distraught with grief.

'Get up, you howling fool!' said Horrox grasping the child and flinging him away from the prostrate form, uttering a fearful oath as he did so.

With no gentle hand he poured the cool water down Vanda's throat, and at last she opened her eyes and a faint colour returned to the haggard cheeks.

For a moment she forgot where she was, and she just murmured,—

'I thought it was Adrian standing by me.'

'Then, you see, it's me, so just get up,' he said roughly. She rose with an effort, and he placed her in a chair. 'Sit there till I am ready for you.

The child obeyed, too ill and weary to be afraid of what was to come, and then Horrox went up to Adrian and demanded fiercely,—

'What were you blubbering about just now, making a fool of yourself—eh, answer me? Do you hear me?' he roared as the child ventured no reply.

'I was so sorry for Vanda, sir; she will die here, I am sure,' and he sobbed again.

'Sorry, were you, now I'll make you sorry for yourself.'

And he took the boy by the arm and dragged him to the table where the white-thonged whip lay, and then he applied it mercilessly about the child's body, until the youthful crimson blood came through the 'fleshings,' leaving hideous marks on the pale pink covering. Vanda closed her eyes. She could not bear the sickening sight. His suppressed moans of pain struck a chill to her heart. She did not want to see the blows descend.\*

'There, now,' said Horrox in a satisfied tone, laying down the whip, 'that's what you get for interfering and whining like a puppy, as you are,' he said with contempt.

The child sobbed, he was too weak to speak.

'Now, then, both of you, come along,' called

---

\* The incident of the beating until the blood came is no highly coloured imagination, but a positive fact.

Horrox, walking towards the bars, and then Vanda dared to protest.

'My hands are too sore for that to-day,' she replied gently, looking down at the large wounds across the palms, caused by the broken blisters which had weeks before been raised by the friction of the powdered resin on her hands and on the bars. These sores take weeks and weeks to heal; but Vanda suffered no worse than the rest in her initiate.

'You must jolly well get used to that,' replied Horrox. 'No nonsense, begin at once.'

Delay and protestations were alike unavailing, and the children began their practice. Very soon the bar bore traces of blood. Vanda's sores had been broken again; but Horrox took no heed of the incident, and he relieved her no sooner from her arduous task.*

And so the long days dragged on, the night came, but the children dreading the dawn, because another awful day must be lived through. One morning, during the hurried breakfast hour, Vanda ventured to ask Horrox when they were likely to return to their old master Le Sale. The hope of that had kept up their spirits during many a saddened day.

'He's dead weeks ago,' replied Horrox with a smile. 'You belong to me now, my lady.' he said with a sneer.

Vanda turned very white; she gave Adrian one hopeless look of despair, which Horrox noticed at once.

'Ah, I don't spoil you like Le Sale did, do I?' he asked meaningly.

'He was very kind to us,' replied Vanda quietly

---

\* A celebrated lady gymnast has told the author that the bars of the trapeze have blood stains upon them, until the hands of the young performers are hardened.

'Made regular noodles of you both,' said Horrox; but we don't go in for that sort of cant here, do we?'

Vanda gulped down a lump which had risen in her throat and said,—

'I should like to write to Mrs Le Sale, if I may?' she pleaded.

'No, you may not, so there is an end to that,' he replied curtly.

Vanda said nothing, but she determined to write a few lines, and trust to some chance of posting them. She would not give the address for fear Mrs Le Sale had left the old home and the letter should be returned, and then the fury of Horrox would fall upon her, and some dreadful punishment would sure to be her lot for disobedience to his orders.

Adrian and Vanda talked over plan after plan in whispers when they went to bed. At last Vanda determined to try if the dirty little 'slavey' of their lodgings would post her letter and hold her tongue, but the difficulty was to find out whether she was loyal or not.

Sally had been taken from a London workhouse, and had unfortunately fallen into the hands of a hard, selfish old woman who let her rooms to professionals. Two years before she had come across Horrox, and he had decided to make her house his headquarters, so that she withdrew her advertisement in the papers under the heading of 'professional apartments,' and settled down, prepared to take her rent and mind her own business, and she took good care that Sally should do the same.

'You talk to my lodgers, and I'll take the skin off your back.'

This suited Horrox, for there was no chance of his apprentices finding sympathy from landlady or drudge.

But Sally Pike had a heart; the workhouse schools had not quite robbed her of that, and although she was only known as one hundred and two, and sent out into the streets with the uniform which stamps children as homeless and poverty stricken, she retained an affectionate disposition if anyone cared to win her love.

In the workhouse schools love lies dead. It in no way enters the curriculum of the educational advantages. It is not considered necessary for 'pauper children,' yet Sally had loved in her heart one or two of her companions, and when she went to service she was anxious to love her mistress; but, to her bitter vexation, Mrs Jane Carter resented what she called familiarities, and Sally soon became the slave of a harsh woman. From early morning until late at night she toiled, receiving no thanks, and bearing constant complaints with stoical indifference. Once or twice she had smiled at Vanda and said a kind word to her, but the chance came very seldom. One day, however, Vanda caught sight of Sally coming upstairs, and putting up her finger, she beckoned to her, whilst she placed a finger of the other hand on her lips to let Sally understand she must be silent.

Sally put down her brush quietly, and stole noiselessly to where Vanda stood, her poor thin shoes being excellent for that purpose. A slatternly figure she looked standing by the unique beauty of Vanda, with her erect figure and refined bearing. Sally's hair was red, and hung about her face in rough clusters, whilst the rest was gathered together and tied with a piece of black tape at the back of her head; her apron was ragged and dirty, and her old black dress was pinned over to make it fit, for it had been made for her stout mistress, and had undergone no alteration. To shorten the length, it was tucked under the band, making the child look like a dancing dervish. Her sleeves were tucked up to her elbows, leaving her red and begrimed arms quite bare; her hands were raw looking, with cuts and unhealed chilblains, and were greasy and black from washing the household saucepans. When Vanda beckoned her, the girl had put up her hand to tidy her hair, leaving as she did so a smudge on her freckled, uncleansed face.

'Where is Horrox?' asked Vanda cautiously.

'A-quarrelling along of the mistress,' said the girl in a whisper, a smile coming over her woebegone face.

'Where is he?' said Vanda hurriedly,

'In missis' best parlour. He says as how we's took the tea for our own use, and he ain't going to buy two pounds a week for we to use it. Missis often do borrower his tea; she calls it borrower, but she don't ever put it back. It's like the brandy—she nips up a drop of his now and agin, when you's all out; and we often has a shovel or two of the coals sint up to you, but she charges for a scuttle all the same; and she puts one egg into the pudding and charges Mister Horrox for two. "Perks" she calls them, but I guess it's stealing, ain't it?' and she grinned all over her face, as if it was some satisfaction to tell of her mistress's misdeeds.

'Never mind all that,' whispered Vanda; 'come into my room, I want you. Horrox may be here directly.'

'No, he won't. When he hollers at mistress he's a good time coming round, and she'll 'ave to take somethink off the bill. A real rumpus takes a good time to settle. Missis won't, Mister Horrox won't, and that's how they gits to a rigular row.'

She followed Vanda, and when the door was closed she waited for her to speak.

'Sally, I want you to do me a *very great* favour, and not to tell anyone. Mind, not a soul is to know; it's quite a secret between you and me.'

Sally nodded her shaggy, unkept head and whispered mysteriously,—

'Is it anything to do with a young man, miss?'

Vanda gave a sad smile and replied,—

'No, Sally, I had a very dear friend once, and since I came here I must not write to her. Her husband is dead now, and she has no one to love her. It would make her happy to have this letter. Will you post it for me?' said Vanda, holding the precious missive in her hands.

'Yes, sure I will; but s'pose the hanswer comes back, they'll want to know who posted it, and then I shall git it pretty 'ot,' said the girl in a frightened voice.

'I have given no address; it's only to let her know I am alive.'

'Was you *ever* so fond of 'er, miss?' asked Sally sadly.

'Yes, yes; she was a mother to me,' responded Vanda wearily.

'Give it us,' said Sally. 'I'll post 'im, and hold my tongue. I'm blowed if I'll split.'

She took the letter and put it down the neck of her dress, and shook herself once or twice until it slipped between her underlinen and her unwashed skin.

'There, 'e'll rest there, safe as a gun, until I gits out, and then I'll post it in the first piller I gets to,' said Sally, satisfied.

'But when will that be?' asked Vanda, anxious that her letter should not be delayed or be left to fall into other hands.

'Well, missis 'ad some 'errins in this morning, and she said as 'ow I had to go and change 'em—they smells orful, and we give three harf-pence for two of 'em—they's for dinner, so missis must send me soon, and then I'll go in the scullery and wrop them up, and betwixt the two your letter 'ull set nicely. None of them 'ull guess that a letter is in with the 'errins, and I'll take it out afore I gets to the fish shop,' said Sally with a chuckle.

'And you will tell no one, Sally?'

'No fears of that. I writ to the baker's boy once, and missis don't know to this day, that she don't—Sally Pike ain't a fool.'

'I have nothing to give you, Sally, for your trouble—I wish I had—I haven't another penny left. The stamped envelope I had by me; Mrs Le Sale put it in for me to write to say we got to Manchester safely, but I could not manage to post it before.'

'You can give one thing, miss, if you will,' said Sally shyly, 'it don't cost anything, not even a penny.'

'What is it, Sally?'

'A kiss, miss, just one kiss. I'm awfully lonely at times, and I often wishes there was some one to give me a good hearty smack. I ain't 'ad a kiss since I came here, and that's nigh on two years. I'd like to 'ave one just to see 'ow it feels,' she added with pathos.

Vanda looked at the dirty face before her, and for a moment she shrank from the task.

The girl saw the look, and read the truth in a moment. Taking up her apron, she passed it across her mouth once or twice, saying,—

'There, it's quite clean now, Miss Vander.'

Vanda was ashamed of having hesitated, and she kissed the girl two or three times passionately, as if glad herself to have found a friend in the squalid little slavey.

'That's real like 'eaven,' said the girl. 'Now,

I don't care if I don't git another kiss till I'm married, that I don't.'

Vanda smiled and replied,—

'I will always kiss you when I can, but you won t mind if I ask you to go now, will you? I am afraid we may be caught.'

''Pon my soul, I'll go, and now—' But before she had finished speaking heavy footsteps were heard coming up the stair case.

'That's 'im,' said Sally, and Vanda turned deadly white with anxiety.

'Do go, Sally, go; do go at once,' she urged. But Sally whisked off her apron and made for the window, which she began to clean with vigour. At this moment Horrox opened the door in search of Vanda.

He looked at her, and then at the servant, but he could read nothing in their faces to lead him to suppose that they had spoken to each other. Vanda looked as depressed as ever, and Sally seemed absorbed in her work; apparently they apppeared innocent of each other's presence.

'Come into the sitting-room. What right have you to be in the bedroom? Get out at once,' said Horrox, angrily pushing her as he spoke, 'and come to your work, both of you, quick.'

Even Horrox's love of revenge was satisfied as he watched them droop day by day, pitiable wrecks of their former beauty.

But help was at hand, the days of their suffering were drawing to a close. Many other children's days of labour would be ended if selfish sightseers would only say they should be.

But they will not.

Yet these people writhe in holy horror and indignation at the mention of a Spanish bull-fight, and protest loudly against the iniquitous cruelty.

Nothing would persuade these fastidious, highly cultured ladies to witness a scene likely to upset their delicate nerves. 'They really couldn't.'

But they enjoy seeing young girls perform at perilous heights, there can be no *harm* in that; but bull-fights are so *cruel*.

Why? Where is the difference? Where does the definition of cruelty commence? where is the limit? These people reply with one accord, the bull may kill horse and rider, its own gore will run in a crimson stream in the ring where it stands to be goaded to despair and frenzy, this they must see; but the gymnast has bled in secret, and been goaded to pass through perils often beyond her physical endurance, but as this does not occur in public, so the previous torture is nothing to these sentimental beings, who detest cruelty when it interferes with their personal comfort. They do not even insist upon what that enlightened emperor Marcus Aurelius commanded, that persons performing on tight-ropes, and otherwise, at daring heights should be protected by a net underneath.

But he was humane.

They are not.

---

## CHAPTER XXIV.

### ON THE TRAIL.

' I AM tired of wandering, Whanks. I think I shall go back to the old country and see who are living and who are gone for ever. There may be some mistake about Leila being dead; reports are never very trustworthy, and if she is dead, poor thing, there are the children to see to; it is the least I can do for her.'

'I'm afraid it's too true, sir. Ringens is the only one I have written to from here, and he sent out every particular of her death. It was a comfort to think your father was with her. I'm sure, sir, it was best that we heard of both their deaths through his letters, or maybe going to the old country would have been a chapter of disappointments. We know the worst, and that's something to be grateful for,' said Whanks with gratitude.

'But there's always hope, Whanks, that some mistake has arisen, and then, as I said before, there are the children.'

'Yes, and there's the cuss of their father to deal with. I reckon they are with him, and being made useful by this time. Circus folk don't keep the children at home with nothing to do—you see, sir, it's business to make every honest penny they can.'

During Tom and Whanks' acquaintance very little had been said of Leila or her married life. Before Whanks had come across Tom he had received full tidings of Leila's death and that of her father from Ringens, who had from time to time written out to the faithful servant such news as would be likely to interest him.

'I believe she died from a broken heart,' he wrote, and Whanks repeated that over and over again, the tears often coursing down his cheeks, and he would cry with sorrow,—

'I wish to God I had never left her to face it out, poor thing; but my aunt's money tempted me out, and the drink would have ruined me at home. Oh, Miss Leila! Miss Leila!'

He tore up the letters which bore the sad news.

'Bad enough to have to think of it without having it in writing, as if I was likely to forget her,' he said with bitterness; and so when Tom asked to see the letters Whanks had none to show him, and from that time Tom refused to believe his sister and father were dead.

'But surely the father won't mind their uncle seeing them. There's no mystery, I suppose, is there?' he asked impatiently.

'A goodish deal, I expect, sir, a goodish deal,' he repeated mechanically.

'Don't you believe my sister was married to this infernal rider, or ring-master, or whatever he is? If she was, where can the mystery be?' said Tom with rising anger.

'I told you, Mr Tom, that I saw Leila Gurney made Castelli's lawful wife. If going to church and swearing to do this, that, and t'other makes man and wife, then your sister was married tight enough. I've said many times, sir, that I was one of the witnesses at the ceremony, and if you think I wasn't, well, you must,' said Whanks in an injured voice.

'I don't doubt you, Whanks, but when you talk of mysteries, and the children as if there was a doubt of my getting at them, I don't know what to think,' he replied doubtfully.

'Not evil of my Miss Leila, anyway,' said Whanks, waxing hot, 'and the mystery is soon put right. When Miss Leila died, God bless her! the little ones would be left on Castelli's hands, and I bet he wouldn't be bothered with them, and very likely he has parted with them to some man for good and all.'

'Done what?' said Tom in astonishment.

'Given them over to someone to train for the ring or the trapeze; that's quite common amongst our set,' replied Whanks coolly.

'Well, if he has parted with them, I suppose they are to be found,' said Tom with determination.

Whanks shrugged his shoulders.

'Ah, sir, you don't know as much as I do about the "profession." No convent ever kept young women as close as the artiste does his apprentices. There isn't much chance of the outside world seeing what goes on, I can tell you, and ten to one Vanda and Adrian are kept hard at work, and never allowed out of their trainer's sight, that's the rule.'

'All the more reason why we should go to England at once. Should you have any idea where to begin to search for them, Whanks?' asked Tom with anxiety.

'To a T. I bet I could lay my hands upon them in a week, provided they were in England. I know one or two who could put me up to the dodge at once. If they are to be found, I'm the man,' replied Whanks with confidence.

'Then I hope you will agree to come along back to the old country, and I propose we start as soon as possible with the mail bags, for although not too comfortable, I am fidgeting to get on, for in my present state of mind "trecking" would simply drive me mad.'

'All right! I shall be just as glad to see her children as you can be, God bless them!'

A few days later found them well on their way—perhaps as comfortless a journey as could be taken in any part of the world, for when Tom and Whanks tried it; there was no accommodation for passengers with the mails. They had to do the best they could, and sit or lie about upon the bags, irrespective of hard, angular parcels which were being borne to friends far away. At various posts the horses and drivers were changed, but the miserable passengers were never changed—no such luck befel them, rest there was none, and the only sleep they could obtain was short, and taken alternately, when one would watch that the sleeping comrade did not fall into the road, as the callous drivers on passing a piece of rough road would suddenly whip up the team of horses with their long rhympie whips. To suit themselves, the drivers could often be most tantalisingly slow, which maddened Tom almost to frenzy, but like their *confrères* at home they had the happy habit of coming up to the post-station as though the whole journey had been conducted at the rate of twenty miles an hour.

Everything pleasant, everything miserable has an end, either on the earth or in the grave—even such a journey as Tom and Whanks had experienced—and both were glad to find themselves on board one of the Donald Currie steamers, where Whanks in particular appreciated the luxury of the saloon after the years of roughing it in different circuses and in a strange land.

He was a rich man now, and riches not birth bring comfort.

During the voyage home Tom had made up his mind to know more of Leila's domestic life, and of the life she had lived amongst the circus folk. Like most people he had no idea of the 'behind the scenes,' and there was much he wished to be made acquainted with. Sitting on the deck one day with Whanks, he broached the subject.

'Whanks!'

'Yes, sir.' Whanks had always adopted a tone of respect towards Tom, and once when Tom had told him that they were friends, and not master and servant, Whanks had replied,—

'But you are Miss Leila's brother, and that's enough for me,' and he never omitted the 'sir' when addressing him.

'Tell me candidly *was* Leila happy with her

husband? Don't hide the truth.  I wish to know exactly how she lived.  She was my only sister.'

Whanks hesitated.  He did not like to tell Tom how the beautiful girl had grown daily more white and thin ; he was almost afraid to repeat the words of anguish which burst from her lips one morning at the circus, when she thought no one was near:  ' My God, spare me more misery; I cannot bear it.'

Tom noticed his reluctance, and continued,—

'Are you afraid to tell me of all my sister suffered?  Have I not the right to know?' he added sadly.

'You have the right, sir, I can't deny that, but she's gone now, poor thing, and what's the use of making your life miserable as well as hers?'

'Then she *was* miserable?' said Tom ; 'you have acknowledged as much.'

Whanks nodded, and then added,—

'She was, so there's no use to make out otherwise.  She was gentle, good, and kind ; he was brutal, perfectly brutal, and didn't understand her.  I've heard him use the most filthy language to her.  At last she grew quite afraid of him, and a coldness seemed to spring up between them  The fact was, he soon tired of his lady wife—the pig and the dove can't mate together: you may try it, but I reckon the pig is a pig to the last, and never learns the coo of the dove.  And so it was with Castelli.  He couldn't learn Miss Leila's sweet ways.  When she cooed, he grunted, and so matters grew worse.  She never *said* much to me, but I twigged a good deal, and I watched her pretty closely ; but I think the worst trouble of all was that her husband took a good deal of notice of a woman, Cleo by name, whom he saw a good deal of—a regular bad one, I can tell you, who did her best to get my master to take on with her.  Ah, she was a bad one,' he repeated.

'And did Castelli do anything so vile as to pay attentions to this Cleo woman and to forget my sister? Poor Leila! what degradation she must have endured,' said Tom with sorrow in his voice.

Whanks smiled sadly.

'Ah, Mr Tom, he didn't forget Miss Leila, and neither did he forget Cleo. He was proud of his wife, but he played fast and loose with the other, and then they quarrelled, and when Miss Vanda was born he steadied up a bit, and then all of a sudden he put her in the "ring," and became master instead of husband, and after that he treated her like an apprentice, instead of a wife. In my humble opinion, sir, she is best dead, and it would please her much better, if she could but know it, if we looked after the children. Bless her, she loved them madly. It's best to seek the living, and leave the dead to rest, sir. I am afraid Vanda and her brother may have fallen into cruel hands. It's odds he's married Cleo, and the children may be suffering terribly now with some harsh master. The right thing is to find the little ones,' said Whanks.

'But surely they may have fallen into kind hands? Are all the masters cruel?' asked Tom almost too pained to speak.

'Some are pretty hard when the training is on,' said Whanks. 'I never knew but one kind trainer, and he was kind if you like. His name was Le Sale. I don't know what became of him, but he had a heart like a child, tender as a new potato. I remember Castelli used to laugh at him and call him a fool, but he was the best of the bunch for all that. I never saw a better, kinder man to beast or apprentice; but it is not likely the children are with him. I don't feel very comfortable about them. But for Miss Leila's sake I shall ferret out what their father has done with them.'

'You seem pretty sure their father has parted with them,' said Tom with some indignation.

'Sure as the sun shines. I know my customer, and time will prove which way the land lies,' replied Whanks quietly.

After that day the conversation was never renewed until they landed on English shores, and then Whanks suggested they should go to London direct.

'It's no use dangling about in the provinces. If we stop in London we shall get on the right scent at once, and save ourselves no end of bother.'

And so Tom acquiesced in the arrangements.

Both men felt strange and lonely when they arrived in London. There were no happy faces to greet them, no one to bid them welcome, no hospitable board waiting for them to partake of the feast, with friends and neighbours smiling upon them and bidding them to eat, drink, and be merry. There were no such things for the weary travellers, so they drove to a hotel and put in their lot with strangers.

How many like Tom and Whanks return after long years to the old country to find no smiles of love to greet them, no outstretched hand ready to press theirs? Yet how eagerly that long-desired home coming had been longed for, how impatiently waited. The vision of the joy of seeing the old home again is perfect. They forget time will have wrought changes in people, places, and things; that the sunlights and the shades can never be quite the same; that the past has been lost in the current of years.

Like the anxious man who left his home to gain riches, and returned suddenly after ten years' absence, kissed his wife fondly, and then said: 'Now, where is baby?' 'Here,' cried a bright, girlish voice, and the father beheld a tall, handsome child. He had forgotten the lapse of years, and replied: 'When far away from you all I have always thought of home as I saw it last, my bonnie wife holding up "baby" to say good-bye, and now she has grey hair, and baby is changed into a young lady.'

How true it is that the mind carries with it to distant climes the last picture of home life upon which the eyes have rested—all else seems lost but the long farewell.

But alas! how many others have found the cottage home shut up, the honeysuckle dead, the green, sunny garden, where the roses bloomed and the pinks and lupines grew in profusion, left to neglect and decay. The path up to the little porch grass grown, the gate padlocked, for two more stones are in the churchyard hard by.

The old folks rest there.

The day after Tom and Whanks' arrival in London they commenced their search for Leila's children. Whanks bought an *Era* newspaper. He ran his eyes down the first page, but there was nothing to his satisfaction. He turned to the back sheet but one, and eagerly scanned the column headed 'Circus Artistes' Wants.' At last he chuckled to himself, 'Ah, that's the game, is it?' and he read two or three times over:—

'Wanted known Emilio Castelli's performing horses great success at Wyatt's Grand Circus, Bombay.'

'Wanted known Mdlle Cleo. greatest success on record—Wyatt's Grand Circus, Bombay.'

'Now, where are the children, that's the rub?' he said aloud. 'I guess they're not out in that locality. Let me see. Ringens might know, or Le

Sale—or—' But Whanks could think of no one else. He had grown rusty about circus matters. 'I'll be off at once and see some of the agents, and find out what I can,' he said in a loud whisper.

The first agent he called upon told him that Le Sale was dead, and that Ringens was at El Circo, Valencia, Spain, and that his engagement was a long one. That was all he could glean, and he began to fear that he must return to the hotel without much news for poor, anxious Tom. He sauntered about considering what would be the best means of finding out Leila's children. Suddenly a woman dressed in shabby black passed him. She was carrying a bundle in her arms, and she seemed tired and weary. She looked very hard at Whanks, as if trying to recall to mind who he was.

Whanks noticed the look of inquiry and thought to himself,—

'That's some of the blessed crew. I know the face I believe.'

He turned to look back at her. She was standing watching him, and their eyes met. Then she advanced towards him and said,—

'Excuse me, but I think you are Mr Whanks, as used to be ring groom with Castelli down at the circus where my poor dear husband was—was engaged?'

'Yes, I am Whanks right enough,' he answered, 'but 'pon my soul I don't know you.'

'I'm Mrs Le Sale. Poor Le Sale is dead, and I have to get on as I can. Ah, there's been a lot of changes since you left,' she added with a sigh.

Whanks put out his hand and took hers, saying heartily,—

'I'm very glad to see you, Mrs Le Sale, very, and now suppose you come in somewhere and have a bit of dinner.'

Together they went, and Whanks was a very patient listener to all she had to tell; but his interest rose considerably when she told him that Castelli's two children had been apprenticed to her late husband.

'Where are they? Where are they now?' asked Whanks excitedly, jumping up in his eagerness.

'I don't know. I wish to God I did.'

Whanks' hopes fell like lead falls to the bottom of the deepest well.

'You don't know? You must know, my good woman, if they were in your house?'

Mrs Le Sale told Whanks how things stood, and that she had given them up in deference to her husband's wishes, then she continued,—

'A month ago I received a few lines from Vanda. She gave no address, so I guess it was posted on the q. t., but the postmark was Selchester. The letter broke my heart nearly, and yesterday I wrote out to their father, for *I* don't believe things are straight.'

'So that villain Horrox has them, has he? Well, it won't be long before they part, or my name isn't Whanks. Selchester—that's good enough for me. Now, where do you live, in case I want you?'

'Over the tobacconist's in the Waterloo Road, Clye is the name. You can't mistake it; and very nice people they are.'

'Well, here's something for the children, for the sake of the old days,' and Whanks slipped a five-pound note into her hand. 'Now, look here, Mrs Le Sale, you hold your blessed tongue over this business and I'll make it worth your while. I may have to bring the children up to you. If I do, don't breathe one word who they are, or we sha'n't be able to get them over the water. Do you see what I mean?'

'He won't give them up, I'm sadly afraid,' replied Mrs Le Sale.

'Then I shall break his head open, and there'll be bloodshed. One of us must get the worst of it, and I lay a quid he'll be the one. Now, good-bye for the present, and wait further orders.'

Mrs Le Sale thanked Whanks heartily for his generous gift, and then they parted.

Whanks scrambled into a cab, and called out to the driver,—

'Tavistock Hotel, and hurry up that skinny old horse. I'm in a deuced uncertainty about the trains, so look sharp, cabby.'

'Oh, yes, I daresay you'd like me to drive 'im like a racehorse, and get locked hup by the society for the prevention of cruelty to 'osses—no fear.'

'Here, just you start, and there will be an extra bob for you at the end of the journey,' said Whanks cheerily.

With a grunt of satisfaction the cabman whipped up his horse, and in due time he arrived at the Tavistock Hotel.

Tom was sitting reading in his bedroom when Whanks blustered in in a state of great excitement, calling out hurriedly,—

'The children are in Selchester. Here, make haste, and let us chuck the things in the portmanteau. I'll do that if you'll go down and find out what time the train goes.'

'Thank God, we have found them,' said Tom gravely.

'Well, we just haven't yet,' replied Whanks, 'but I am going to, so just be quick, sir, or we shall lose the next train. I'm all of a tremble to be off.'

He opened the portmanteau with a wrench, and pushed in sufficient things to last them both for some days. Then he closed it with a bang, and waited impatiently for Tom's reappearance. At last he came.

'There's a train at five-thirty,' said Tom, 'will that suit you? We've just an hour before we need start, so let's get some food and pay the bill.'

Whanks took no notice of this remark for a moment, and then he said,—

'I wonder if Miss Vanda is like her poor mother?'

'I hope so,' said Tom; 'it is nice to see the picture of the dead in the living.'

They were soon on their way, each hour bringing them nearer to the children of the dead woman so dear to them both.

Little did Vanda and Adrian dream that night that friends were so close to them.

They slept after the work and torture of the day, while Tom and Whanks spent hours in arranging what were the best means to ensure success in their undertaking.

When the sun came out over the great city, Vanda and Adrian went to their work as the galley slaves go, without hope.

But peace, joy, rest, and happiness were at hand.

The days of toil were nearly ended.

But they did not know it.

## CHAPTER XXV

### PAID IN FULL.

WHANKS soon found his way to the circus, which was then in Selchester, and going down early, when he knew the rehearsals were on, he asked to see the ring-master.

'Who wants to see me? I'm busy; tell the man to come again.

'He told me to say, sir, that he was engaged with

Signor Castelli for years, and must see you,' said the groom.

'Does he want a situation? If he does, say we are full up, there is no vacancy,' replied Daspar impatiently.

'He looks like a gent, sir; he's come in a cab, and is dressed wonderful well. In fact I'm sure he is a gentleman.' The man was thinking of the tip he had received as an inducement to venture to disturb Signor Daspar at his duties as ring-master.

'Go and fetch him, and be quick about it,' he said to the man.

Whanks entered the ring, and a strange feeling came over him. It seemed as if the old life had come back again, and he half expected to see Castelli and Miss Leila there waiting for him. Daspar smiled when he saw his visitor and said,—

'I'm hanged if it isn't Whanks. Well, who would have guessed you would turn up? It seems like old times again. Come out and have a drink with me?'

'No, thanks, sir. When I came into my aunt's money I vowed I'd never drink another of "mild or strong," and I never will, thanking you all the same. I came down here to ask you if you could tell me where Horrox hangs out—you know Horrox the gymnast—I want to see him particularly,' said Whanks nervously.

'He was here a few minutes ago. He is going to bring two children out in January, and they will appear here. I don't know much about him. He is no favourite here, and his apprentices look pretty bad. He brought them down once or twice. But I'm half afraid he's gone. John, John!' he called, and a groom came hurriedly forward.

'Yes, sir.'

'Has Horrox left the building?'

'Yes, sir, some minutes ago.'

'Where does he live, John?'

'Don't know, sir, but Sam knows.'

'Go and ask him, and be quick.'

The man went off with alacrity, and returned almost immediately and said,—

'Sam says as how he lives in South-Side. He's getting the name of the street and the number, sir.'

At this moment Sam appeared, bearing a piece of crumpled paper in his hand.

'There's the name of the street, sir, but no one here is sure of the number. Tim thinks it's forty. I think it's one hundred and forty. We're sure it's something with a four in it.'

'Thank you,' said Whanks, slipping a shilling into the man's hand, 'I shall soon find the house. The street isn't too long, and the time is my own,' he said proudly.

The men walked away, leaving Daspar and Whanks alone in the ring.

'How has time served you, Whanks?' asked Daspar.

'Splendidly,' replied Whanks. 'I left England with four hundred pounds, I have come back to the old country with thousands, rich enough to buy this blessed circus and all in it, and a good many other "shows" into the bargain.'

'You're a lucky fellow,' said Daspar. 'How did the riches come to you?'

'From my claim in the diamond fields. It's been no joke sitting there scraping and scratching like a hen all the day long, but it's better than working in a circus after all.'

'Well, I am glad to hear of your luck. I should not object if I could boast of a trifle more than I earn here; and deuced hard work it is, never done morning, noon, and night—one long toil, always the same, not Sunday free even. But here I am, so it's no use to grumble; but I get pretty dead beat at times.'

Whanks, after a few words of simple sympathy, left the circus, and returned to Tom.

'I've found out the villain lives in South-Side, but no one seems sure of the house, so I think we'll start for that locality. Bring your thin walking-stick, sir, we may want it; he'll be a pretty rough party to deal with, I dare bet a quid.'

'I'll give him the most thundering thrashing he ever had if I can only catch him,' said Tom quite fiercely.

'What a villain he must be to get the children from Le Sale; but we'll make him confess to his dirty tricks, the unscrupulous scoundrel,' continued Tom, his anger rising as he thought of the sufferings to which his sister's children must have been subjected. Mrs Le Sale had told Whanks sufficient to make them both very uneasy about the welfare of Vanda and Adrian.

'They couldn't have fallen into worse hands,' said Whanks to Tom. 'Horrox is about the cruellest man *I* ever knew, and added to that is his hate for your sister. He never forgave her getting him summoned, and all this blessed trouble starts from that I bet.'

Whanks' knowledge of the hardships of the training, even under the most favourable circumstances, had aroused Tom's worst fears; but when the character of the man, and the ill-feeling he bore Leila became facts, his anxiety knew no bounds, and he in his turn was determined to have revenge for the sake of the dead mother—the only sister, and the sole companion of his earlier days, who had clung so lovingly to him when the great disgrace of their lives had fallen upon them both.

Together the men started, resolved to rescue

the children before many more hours of suffering had passed over their heads.  They could not fix upon any certain plan of action until they found out more about Horrox and his surroundings.

At the corner of Humphrey Street was a public-house, and into this Whanks turned, followed by Tom.

'You must have a glass of bitter,' said Whanks to Tom, ' or I sha'n't get out of them what I want. I mustn't take a drop; if I begin the old game I'm done for, and when my aunt's money came I vowed I wouldn't touch another glass, and I won't.'

'Glass of bitter,' said Tom to the stout, red-faced woman at the bar.

'Small lemon,' said Whanks.

The woman pushed the glasses towards them and banged down the change with an injured air. 'She didn't believe in a customer as went in for lemonade,' and she made it a rule to be particularly short and disagreeable to those who occupied the 'private' bar and who ordered nothing but small lemons.

She was turning away when Whanks, nothing daunted by her manner, said,—

'I say, mum, I want you a minute.'

She looked at the speaker, she looked at Tom and wondered whether he was an excise officer, and that thought brought her back to the counter where they stood.

'My name's Smith, Mrs Sarah Smith, if you want to speak to me,' she said loftily.  'I ain't used to be called after in that fashion, and pray what do you want with *me?*'

'I'm sure I beg your pardon,' said Whanks hastily, and Tom lifted his hat.  That won the heart of Mrs Sarah Smith, and a smile broke over her face, making her look more low-typed and coarse than ever. 'I want to know at which number in Humphrey

Street Mr Horrox lives. I have particular business with him. Does he ever come in here?' asked Whanks.

'Let me see, I think it's fourteen. George,' she called to a burly man, who was filling glasses rapidly one after the other, 'George, which is the house that man—what's his name?—you know, the chap with a roaring name like a wild beast.'

'Horrox,' put in Whanks.

'Ah, yes, that's the name. Horrox,' she called to her husband.

'Forty-four, I think; but the gal will be in here soon for the beer. It's nigh on one. Ah, here she is.'

Mrs Smith went over to the other counter and said a few words to the child, who left the bar and came round to the door of the private bar, upon which was written 'No jugs, glasses only.'

When Sally saw Whanks and Tom standing at the counter a frightened look stole over her face. In her childish mind visions of policemen and prison came before her, for had not she, at the landlady's orders, taken what belonged to the lodgers? And she fancied now that she was found out.

'These gentlemen want to ask you a question, child.'

'You live in the same house as Mr Horrox, my dear, don't you?' said Whanks very kindly.

'Yes, sir, please, sir.'

'Who else lives in the house?' put in Tom, as if afraid to hear her reply.

'Mistress, and Miss Vander, and Master Adrian, and me,' answered Sally.

'Are you fond of Miss Vanda and her little brother?' asked Whanks.

'Oh, ain't I just, that's all,' answered Sally, her grimy face breaking into a look of real pleasure and love. 'Miss Vander kisses me now and then when the old brute is out of the way.'

'Who is the old brute?' asked Tom.

'Mr Horrox, to be sure. He do whack her about! She looks pretty bad, nigh on dying I think.'

'Would you help Miss Vanda if you could?' asked Tom. 'Would you help her friends to find her and make her happy?'

'Wouldn't I just! But she ain't got no friends, I think. I posted a letter for her once, took it out 'tween the 'errins, but she said as 'ow it were to someone she'd once lived with. It wasn't a mother or anyone of that sort, 'cause she'd have told me. She ain't happy enough to 'ave any friends, please, sir, leastways I don't think so, please, sir.'

A look of deep pain passed over Tom's face as the child finished speaking, and Whanks looked much distressed.

'We are her friends,' said Tom, 'and we are anxious to know at which number in the street you live.'

'You belong to Miss Vander? I'm blowed if that don't beat all! The number is four, the 'ouse with the yeller blinds. My hi! what a lark!' and Sally, in her ecstasy, gave a hop and a jump round, which spilt the beer down her apron, and it trickled to the floor. Then the happiness died from her face, and she exclaimed piteously, 'What will the missus say? I daren't go home without the beer. Oh, dear! oh, dear!'

'See here,' said Whanks, 'I will give you half-a-crown, and pay for the beer, if you will help us. Now, what time of the night should we find Miss Vanda, her brother, and Mr Horrox at home, and where would they be sitting?'

'They mostly practises until eight o'clock, and then sometimes Mister Horrox goes out to a music 'all. Sometimes they goes too; sometimes he locks them in the drawering-room till he gits back, ever so late. They never gits to bed until after twelve. I 'eard Mister Horrox tell Miss Vander " she wasn't a-going to spend her time in bed," and she gits up at harlf-past five—'taint much rest after a-clambering over them bars all day, and she looks ever so white, but Mister Horrox don't mind. One blessed night he come 'ome from the music 'all and found Miss Vander asleep, she were that dead tired, and he just did whack her!'

'Well, look here, can you be outside the house about eight this evening and let us know whether they are at home or not?' asked Tom with great anxiety.

'No, I'm sure I can't,' said Sally convincingly. 'I'd be nearly murdered if they caught me out of a hevening.'

'Can you give us any sign from the house?' asked Whanks.

Sally thought for a moment and then she said,—

'If they's at home, and all tergether in the drawering-room, I'll put the broom out of the top winder and twirdle it round and round, and if you stands under the lamp-post oppersite to number four you'll see it hard enough.'

'Very well, and if we see the broom we will come to the front door, and will you let us in without ringing or knocking?' said Whanks eagerly.

'Can't do that, sir, mightn't be able to git to the door; but when I twirdles the broom I'll drop the latchkey in a piece of paper, and one of you gents must look in the gutter for it. But you will have to look sharp, 'cause I mustn't contract the neighbours.'

Attract she meant, but Tom and Whanks were too full of business to notice the ludicrous speech of the child before them.

The matter seemed arranged, when Sally suddenly broke in,—

'What are you going to do when you gits in to missis' house? 'Cause if I'm found out they'll nearly kill me, I know they will,' said the child in distress.

'We are going to fetch Miss Vanda and her brother,' said Tom, 'and if you will really help us you can come along too, so just have your bonnet and cloak handy, for everything must be done quickly.'

'You'll take me along of Miss Vander?' said the child aghast. 'Do you really mean that, sir?'

'Yes, child, you shall go too, that is, if you carry out your promises for to-night.'

'If they's at home I shall, and when you gits in you'll find the drawering-room the furst door you comes to up the stairs. Mister Horrox allus makes a goodish rattle with the latchkey, and if you does that missus will thinks it's he.' Suddenly she looked at the clock. 'Lor' 'av' mercy! it's nearly a quarter to two. What shall I do? What will the missus say, and Mister Horrox wanted his dinner at half-past one sharp?' and such a terrified expression came over the girl's face that both men felt ashamed of the time they had kept her, and Tom said kindly,—

'Never mind; if you stand by us you will be off to-night with Miss Vanda. Be brave till then, and don't forget to-night at nine.'

The child nodded her head and hurried off, and the two men went out of the bar.

'I say, George, them's a queer party. They're planning something to-night at eight; I hope it ain't a murder, or an elopement, because Sarah Smith ain't going into a witness box at the court; it's no fit place for a lady.'

'No one wants you, my dear,' answered a gruff

voice. If they were planning a murder they wouldn't come to a public-house, and if it's an elopement I hope they will enjoy it.'

At five minutes to eight Tom and Whanks loitered near to the lamp-post opposite to number four. The night was damp after a recent shower, but the air was close for the season. The moon peeped out now and again from among the grey scudding clouds, and shone with a sickly wan light upon the long row of dusky houses.

There were but few people about in the side street. A boy passed them, yelling 'Evening paper, special edition,' but Tom and Whanks watched number four with all the sharpness of experienced detectives. They saw lights were burning in the drawing-room and basement, but all the other windows were in darkness. Suddenly the top window was cautiously opened, and a broom came out and was turned round twice quickly and then disappeared, but no key fell with a ringing sound to the pavement beneath.

Whanks looked in dismay at Tom and said,—

'She has forgotten the key.'

'I'd much rather she let us in,' said Tom. 'Breaking into another person's house is punishable by law.'

'We are going to get Miss Leila's children, law or no law,' said Whanks savagely.

They kept their watch on the house as if reluctant to move, when Whanks exclaimed excitedly,—

'The front door is open. She has managed that. Come at once.'

They both walked boldly in. Sally stood in the hall. She did not speak, but pointed to the stairs. In another moment Tom and Whanks stood facing Horrox and his apprentices.

'Who's gone upstairs, Sally?' asked her mistress, half muddled with gin.

'Some gents—friends of Miss Vander's. I'm going up to set the supper now.'

But the besotted woman did not reply, and Sally got her opportunity to get upstairs. Her heart beat, her face grew crimson as she made her way to the drawing-room door to be ready to go if they really meant to take her. But she doubted that, poor child, yet she would hope for the best. The gentlemen might think of her.

The room which Whanks and Tom entered was large, but there was an air of desolation, which struck them in a moment. They saw the faded carpet, the dirty curtains, the untidy appearance of the apartment, and the cheerless air which pervaded the whole room. In an easy-chair sat Horrox, fiercely watching the movements of his two apprentices, who were practising some stage steps. On a chair by his side lay the white-thonged whip. Just as Whanks and Tom entered a fearful oath fell from his lips, and the whip had curled swiftly round Vanda's feet, and they heard her smothered cry of anguish.

'Who are you?' roared Horrox, as the two men stood looking at him. 'Get out of the room this minute; how dare you come in here? Oh, it's you, is it?' he continued, glancing at Whanks, who had stood behind Tom, but both men were quick enough to perceive that he grew a shade paler when he recognised his visitor.

'It's Whanks! it's Whanks!' cried Vanda. 'Adrian, have you forgotten Whanks?' the child cried with joy

'Hold your tongue!' cried Horrox, white with passion and fear.

'I've come for you, Miss Vanda and Master Adrian,' said Whanks with emotion in his voice. He could hardly speak, so terribly unnerved was he to see the thin, haggard, and sad faces of the children he loved so dearly.

'Who are you?' asked Horrox, coming up to Tom, 'and what the devil brought you here, Whanks?'

'I am the uncle of those two wretched children. Their mother, Leila Castelli, was my sister, and I have come to claim my niece and nephew, and they leave this house with me to-night.'

'Ah, ah! I daresay you think you're master here, but you see they belong to me, and they will stay in my charge,' said Horrox.

'We shall see about that. Show me your authority? Where are the indentures signed by their father? I demand to see your right to detain these children. If you have none, the police shall be called upon at once to act in this matter, for you are not only detaining them unlawfully but I am given to understand that you brutally ill-use them.'

'You want my authority do you? Well, you shall have that right enough. It's in this room,' and he moved to his desk.

'Vanda and Adrian, come here. I am Uncle Tom. You must remember your mother speaking of me,' and then he folded her in his arms and kissed her fervently, and for the first time he was struck with the acute misery written upon her face; then he tenderly embraced the boy.

When Horrox came back to where Tom stood, Whanks called the children to his side and kissed them, saying, 'Stand by me, my dears, and listen to what Uncle Tom is saying.'

'There, that is my authority,' said Horrox, showing the piece of paper Le Sale had signed.

'That! Why it's not worth the ink it's written with. Le Sale had the indentures, not you; this paper is a fraud, a lie. The children are *not* yours. Look at them!' cried Tom, his voice quivering with passion, 'look at them, I say! Are you not ashamed to stand there and face *me*, their uncle? Can't I see the pain you have inflicted in their white, sad faces? Dare you tell me they have been kindly treated? You are a villain, a consummate scoundrel; and what does this mean, sir? Is this the instrument of torture you have used on these hapless children? Answer me, or by —— I'll throttle you as you stand!'

Horrox grew livid. He looked at the tall, fine man before him; he saw the broad, thick-set shoulders and the powerful build of the sturdy frame. He was a gymnast, yet he did not feel inclined to show fight with the angry man.

'Children,' said Tom excitedly, 'has this man often struck you with this? Tell the truth, there is nothing to fear. You belong to me, and to your father. Now, speak out.'

There was silence for a moment. Horrox glared at the two frightened children, and then Vanda replied in a low voice,—

'Many times a day.'

'Deny that if you can, you villain!' said Tom with passion. 'You've meted out torture to two helpless children, now, sir, it's your turn,' and before Horrox could defend himself Tom had seized him by the collar. For a moment there was a struggle between the two men, but Tom, strong as a lion, after years of healthy outdoor life in the Transvaal, was more than a match for the trained but more delicate man before him. In the scuffle Tom dropped his thin cane, but Whanks picked it up and handed it to him, and then the blows came down mercilessly on Horrox.

'There, you coward, how do you like that?' cried Tom, dealing him cut after cut. The children turned deathly white, and then Whanks opened the door, and hurrying them downstairs, called to

Sally to come along also, and hold her tongue. A moment afterwards they were in a cab, which Tom and Whanks had left in a side street. All was so quickly done that the children hardly realised that they were free. They were soon in the Stretford Road, and then Whanks called to the cabman to stop. He got out, and walking up the street, entered a small draper's shop, and stepping up to the counter, he said,—

'I want a hat for a girl. I'm going to London to-night, and I want to take a present to my niece. Look sharp, please.'

'What size, sir?' asked the matter-of-fact shop assistant.

Whanks hesitated, he had never thought of the difficulty of size, and for a moment he did not know how to reply satisfactorily.

'She's thirteen,' replied Whanks at last, evading the direct question.

A hat, gloves, and ulster were also selected by the aid of the proprietor of the shop, and Whanks returned to the cab. He then told the cabman to drive on and stop at the first shop where they sold boys' clothes. These clothes, an overcoat and hat, were purchased for Adrian.

'Now, children, pop on these things quickly. We shall be at the station directly.'

The boy did as he was told, but Vanda neither spoke nor moved. She had fainted. Whanks was in the greatest distress, and he called to the driver,—

'Stop at the next public-house,' and then he went in and brought her a glass of brandy and water.

She sipped a few drops and opened her eyes slowly.

'You are with Whanks, darling. Cheer up, and put on these pretty things. We are going to Mrs Le Sale.'

'Going away!' cried Vanda, almost dazed with joy. 'Are we really going?'

'Yes, you and Adrian, and Sally, all going with me and Uncle Tom.'

'Oh, how happy I am! Adrian, kiss me.' And the children, free from bondage, hugged one another and cried for joy, and Sally said, 'Miss Vander, Miss Vander, won't you kiss me?' And then Vanda said, 'Sally, you have been my friend, we must never part again,' and she kissed her lovingly.

Whilst the happy, grateful children were driving to the station Tom was administering what he described as 'a thundering thrashing' to Horrox. At last he let go his hold, and striking him one blow on the temple, felled him to the ground insensible. After waiting for one moment to see that he had done no serious injury, he marched downstairs. The landlady had heard the confusion, and she discreetly locked herself in her sitting-room, murmuring, 'It's naught to do with me. I sha'n't hinterfere.'

After a time Horrox recovered, and then sat down to consider what was the best thing to do.

At length he decided to leave the country.

That night Vanda and Adrian quitted the scenes of their unhappy and cruel training, the faithful Sally and Uncle Tom and dear old Whanks giving them the most unceasing care. Adrian, tired out, slept, but he started up several times, as if afraid of a blow or a harsh word, but he sighed with contentment and fell asleep again when he found the kindly faces around him smiled very lovingly at him. But Vanda lay back white and weak, fainting twice during the journey. Tenderly they chafed the small thin hands, and Tom supported her in his strong arms and kissed her many times, and once he said to Whanks,—

'I feel as if Leila had come back to me. See, she has the same fair hair, the same great eyes. Oh, Whanks, what do I owe you?' and he gulped down the lump that would rise.

At last Vanda slept, and then Tom told Whanks of the hiding he had given to Horrox, and both men were satisfied that he had met his deserts.

When they reached London they stayed there a night to give the children time to recover, and after a peaceful rest they awoke to find luxury and love instead of cruelty and hard work.

The next day Mrs Le Sale came, in response to a telegram, and the children were placed in her charge to be nursed and tended until Tom could take them to Paris.

Vanda was too ill to say much. She put her arms round Mrs Le Sale and whispered,—

'Home, it is home at last. I am very tired. Can I go to sleep now?'

They left her. The blinds were drawn, the room was quiet, and Vanda slept.

Poor, weary girlhood, there was peace at last.

The toil was ended.

There was perfect rest for Vanda.

No more grief, no more sorrow.

Home at last!

## CHAPTER XXVI.

### THE BEGINNING OF THE END.

CASTELLI'S engagement at Bombay was drawing to a close, and he and Cleo were preparing to sail homewards in the *Contadina* when Mrs Le Sale's letter came to hand. He read it carefully many times over, and then he questioned Cleo.

'Do you know what this letter means? Did you understand that Vanda and Adrian had left Le Sale and gone to that villain Horrox?'

He kept his eyes fixed upon her as he spoke.

'Don't ask me such ridiculous questions,' she replied in an offhand manner. 'Why should I know more than you do about your own children? You surely don't expect me to be responsible?'

'Did you hear of Le Sale's death?' he asked, quite ignoring her reply.

'Did you?' she asked evasively.

'No,' he replied brusquely.

'Then why should I have done so?'

Cleo was far too cute to deny her share in the transaction entirely, because she was not sure how far Castelli might go to find out the true state of the case, and to be on the safe side as long as possible was a necessity; but neither would she own that she knew anything of Le Sale or his death, and the subsequent arrangements with regard to the children, for might not the whole thing blow over, and then she would not stand in a false light either way.

Like all who commit dark deeds, she fancied her secret safe in the keeping of an unscrupulous man. She forgot, as others forget, that the day of retribution must come, that the glare of the light must sooner or later lay bare her sin in all its heinousness. But she never thought of that.

Castelli said very little, but he was quite determined to sift the matter to the bottom, and so sure he was that Cleo was in some way mixed up in the affair that he could no longer treat her in the old familiar style, and a coldness sprang up between them which all Cleo's smiles and attentions failed to disperse.

A week before they sailed Castelli received a telegram from Whanks. It ran :—

' When do you return? Children with uncle. Whanks, Falcon Hotel, Selchester.'

To this Castelli replied :—

' Sail *Contadina*. Meet me Selchester.'

After the receipt of the telegram Castelli remarked :—

' Well, Whanks will soon find out the whole thing, if he hasn't by this. I suppose that confounded aunt of his has left him a pot of money.'

' Well, don't you remember Ringens told us that he had made thousands with your wife's brother on the diamond fields. But why he interferes with your children *I* can't understand,' Cleo added in a disagreeable tone.

Castelli knew only too well. He could call to mind how devoted a servant Whanks had been to his dead wife, and how he bestowed much love on her children, but to Cleo he only remarked rudely,—

' It is nothing to do with you; I am much obliged to him.'

' Ah! that's because he is a rich man; if he had been still your groom your thanks would have been pretty scarce I'm thinking,' she added saucily.

During the voyage he took but little notice of her beyond the merest civilities. Both of them were going direct to Selchester to fulfil a long engagement. This Whanks had found out through Castelli's agents, and there he determined to return at such time as Castelli arrived. Vanda and Adrian were in Paris in the kind care of their uncle and Mrs Le Sale, and later he received very cheerful letters from them. One in particular, which came from Tom, announced his engagement to Fanny Herepath.

'I met her in Paris,' he wrote, 'and now all is settled and I am a happy man.'

'So Mr Tom is going to be "spliced," is he? Well, God bless him! I hope he will be happier than poor Miss Leila was. But I'm wondering if he will have the children when he's married. Well, if he don't, I will,' he murmured.

When Castelli and Cleo arrived in England they started at once for Selchester, and then Castelli made rather a startling proposition to Cleo.

'I'm going to put up at the Falcon Hotel, Cleo, for a day or so, and you had better go into private apartments; Miss Taylor may have the same rooms again. I can't have you at the hotel with me,' he added positively.

'And, pray, why not? I suppose I am good enough company for your late groom—the hotel is as much for me as for you. It's public to all who can pay, and you can't keep me out,' she cried excitedly.

'I can't, but your character can,' he remarked with a sneer. 'You've been in Selchester too many times to pose as a saint; take my advice and don't go to the Falcon or they may refuse to take you in, and that wouldn't be pleasant for you.'

'You're a beauty!' she stormed. 'It's pretty cool to tell me that *you* can go where *I* can't. If I am a sinner, I bet you are a greater, and surely where the devil can go his angels can,' she cried angrily.

'Well, you won't go with me. I believe you have deceived me all through, and until I hear what Whanks can tell me we are best apart. Someone has lied, and I shouldn't wonder if it is you. At anyrate, Cleo, you must look out for yourself,' he added without relenting.

'Thanks,' she replied with sarcasm, 'I will.'

Castelli had not expected Cleo to take his decision so quietly, but she had a good reason for doing so. For some days she had been wondering how she could get out of the meeting between Castelli and Whanks. She knew he would probably accuse her of a great deal which she knew to be true, but which would bring down Castelli's wrath. She would rather put off the evil day, for she dreaded what she knew must be the result if Horrox had 'split' upon her, a parting from her handsome lover; therefore it suited her best to be out of the way until the affair had tided over. But she played her part so well that even Castelli was unaware of her wishes, and he hoped that he was meting out a just punishment to her by declining to have her with him as his companion. Unwittingly he assisted her to carry out just the plan she desired.

And so each of them went their several ways.

When Castelli and Whanks met, the greeting to each other was somewhat cool. Both of them felt how much had happened since last they saw each other. Whanks recalled to Castelli his dead wife, whilst the presence of his old master brought back to Whanks the vision of a beautiful, happy girl on the seashore at Sandcliffe, afterwards of a pale-faced, weary woman, dying of a broken heart, and he could not put out his hand and welcome him, as the old servant felt he should like to have done.

When Castelli thanked him for being the means of helping the children, Whanks replied,—

'What has been done by me and Mr Tom has been done for Miss Leila's sake.'

Castelli winced. He felt the implied rebuke, but he made no reply, and a silence fell on the two men. At last Whanks spoke.

'It's better, sir, that you should know just how things were after poor Le Sale's death, and then you can judge what is best to be done.'

The two men sat down, and Whanks told Castelli the history of Tom and his going to Selchester, how Tom had thrashed Horrox unmercifully, and how the coward in his fright had begged for mercy, putting the chief blame upon Cleo.

'It appears,' said Whanks, 'that Cleo and Horrox were hand and glove in the affair from the beginning. The villain paid her for her share of the transaction, and getting your consent to sending them to Le Sale was the beginning of the cruel scheme.'

'The devil!' muttered Castelli.

'Yes, she is devil enough and to spare. It broke my heart to see those children, Miss Leila's, worn as thin as laths, and looking like death itself. They've been treated most shamefully. I'm not sure as Miss Vanda will live long. It's pretty nigh killed her, sir.'

Castelli turned white as Whanks spoke, but it was with anger more than regret for his children's sufferings.

'I have done with her for ever—for ever,' he hissed.

'She's a bad lot, sir, take my word on it, sir She will bring you more trouble than joy. You'd best rid yourself of her once and for all,' said Whanks boldly.

Castelli did not, as of old, tell Whanks to mind his own business. He was a rich man now, and no longer the drunken servant of the old days.

'I intend to,' said Castelli angrily. 'Cleo and I have done with one another from to-day.'

'I hope you'll keep to that, sir, for Miss Leila's sake. She'd have fretted had she known how

T

things had turned. God bless her! But the children are safe enough now, and Mr Tom and I will be glad when you can go over and settle things. Somehow Mr Tom and I don't like the idea of parting with them,' said Whanks anxiously.

'I daresay they can stay with you,' said Castelli rather vaguely. 'But where is that villain Horrox? He and Cleo must be polished off before I think of the children.'

'I've been inquiring. He's gone abroad—bolted. I guess he is in America. He used to hang out there a good deal at one time. He actually owned that he sent a telegram to Cleo the very day he got the children into his power.'

In a moment flashed across Castelli's mind the receipt of a telegram by Cleo which she had declined to show him. He had no doubt now as to whom it came from, and his face grew whiter still with passion as Whanks ceased speaking.

'Well, I'll go down to the circus,' he said, his voice trembling with rage. 'I'll go and see what she has to say for herself, the devil! and if ever I catch Horrox there will be murder, as sure as I stand here. Here, give me my hat. Give it me at once,' he added with his old peremptory manner, forgetting in his anger that Whanks was not his servant to do his behests.

But Whanks did as he was asked, and did not attempt to interfere with the irate man.

Castelli went to the circus, more of a fiend than a man in his terrible passion.

Whilst this was going on in Selchester Tom and the children were in Paris, awaiting the coming of Castelli and Whanks, when Tom was going to make the former a definite offer for the charge of Vanda and Adrian. After much persuasion on the part of Tom, Mrs Le Sale had consented to leave her children with her married sister and come with them all to France.

'The children must have someone with them,' said Tom. 'Look how ill Vanda is.'

'Ill, I should think she is! It will take months and months before the marks of that fiend's terrible lash disappear. She is terribly scarred and marked, and so is Adrian. I think Horrox ought to have been put in prison, that I do; but as to going to Paris, I don't know, it seems to me an awful journey. What with crossing the sea, and the language being all of a muddle, and my children left behind, is more than I can lean to,' said Mrs Le Sale.

But eventually Tom persuaded her to make arrangements and come for a few days, until he could find someone else to be with them.

'Would you leave them motherless and ill, with only me to look after them?' asked Tom gently.

This speech touched Mrs Le Sale's motherly heart, and she exclaimed,—

'I'm sure poor Le Sale would have told me to look after Vanda; he thought a world of Vanda. Yes, I'll go if the sea is the death of me, so that's agreed,' and she went to try and nurse back life and spirits to the two almost heartbroken children.

One evening Vanda was resting on the sofa in a pleasant room at the Grand Hotel in Paris. Mrs Le Sale was sitting by her, when she said suddenly,—

'Do you think many children are treated like we were, Mrs Le Sale? Sometimes I cannot sleep for thinking of it.'

Adrian was sitting at the table, once more at his beloved drawing. He had almost forgotten the hardships of the past, although his face looked very thin and white. He looked up as Vanda spoke, as if her words recalled the days of horror and misery.

'Don't worry about that, Vanda,' said Mrs Le Sale kindly. 'There's very few in the world as cruel as Mr Horrox. You see, my dear, he hated your poor dear mother, and so he had his spite on you.'

'But the masters are not kind, are they, even if they are not as bad as Horrox?' inquired Vanda, not to be put off.

'Well, my dear, Le Sale was, but I am afraid there's few like him. They have to be strict, and keep their apprentices hard at work. You see the people go to circuses to be amused, and so the children *must* be made to do their work properly. Horrox would have been kinder if it hadn't been for his grudge against your mother; but it's a dreadful life for a girl—hard, cruel, terrible. My children won't go in for it, I'll take good care,' said Mrs Le Sale with deep feeling.

'Can't anything be done to help the children, Mrs Le Sale? Will no one save them?' said Vanda in real distress.

'I've heard some people are trying, but it will be uphill work. The public won't believe—don't want to. They're afraid it may cost them something. They like to offer opinions, but when it comes to helping those who have done the work they don't see it,' replied Mrs Le Sale. 'If the hardships could be stopped without touching their pockets, they would gladly cry out against it. But no, no, my dear, the children may work and toil to the end if it is likely to cost them a fiver.'

'I wish I had some money,' replied Vanda wearily, a flush of pain spreading over her thin, wan face.

Mrs Le Sale noticed the change, and she said hastily,—

'Try and rest now, Vanda. You know the doctor told you this morning not to worry or the nervous attack would return, and then your uncle would be so vexed. Don't think any more about it just now, my dear,' said Mrs Le Sale.

Just as she finished speaking the door opened, and Tom came into the room, behind him came a bashful, blushing girl.

'Vanda,' said Tom, 'this is Miss Fanny Herepath, my future wife. She has promised to be your friend; haven't you, Fanny?' asked Tom, turning to her.

'I shall do my best. May I kiss you, Vanda?' and she stooped down and caressed her affectionately. 'And will Adrian kiss me too?' she asked, going up to where the boy sat.

He put his arm about her neck, and pursed up his mouth for a kiss.

'Are you going to live with us?' he asked.

'Some day, I hope,' she answered quietly.

Mrs Le Sale motioned to Sally to leave the room with her; she felt sure Mr Tom had something to say, and when they were gone he told Vanda and Adrian the story of his love; how he had seen Fanny Herepath many years before, and how they had hoped to meet again some day; how Fanny's father had returned to England a rich man once more and her brother was studying art in Paris; and how they had all met in the great city, and that he and Fanny would be married soon, and there would be a home for them both, if Castelli would accept a proposed offer.'

'But what will become of Whanks and Sally? I shouldn't like to leave them,' pleaded Vanda.

'Whanks will settle that himself. He is as rich as I am, Vanda. I cannot make him go with us unless he wishes it; but, of course, Sally must go, and learn to wait upon you and Adrian. You see we must get a governess for you both at home, unless your father wishes to take you with him, and, of course, he has the first claim—nothing can be decided until he comes,' said Tom.

'I am glad you are going to be married, uncle. I hope you will both be very, very happy,' she said wearily.

The tone struck Fanny and Tom painfully, and both of them drew near to the sofa and looked at the lovely face, so white and sad.

'Do you feel more than usually tired, Vanda dear?' asked Tom with anxiety.

'No, uncle dear, only the life seems gone out of me. I wonder if I shall ever feel happy again. It all seems different, even Adrian is not the same,' she said, smiling languidly at her brother.

'Do you hear that, Adrian?' said Fanny Herepath; 'come and kiss her, and tell her you love her just as much as ever.'

The boy came, and flushed painfully when he stooped to kiss her, saying,—

'Of course I love you, Vanda dear.'

'Yes, you love me,' replied Vanda, 'but somehow it doesn't seem the same,' she added, with deep regret in her voice.

'Oh, you'll soon be better, and then it will appear just the same,' said Fanny cheerfully. 'And now I shall wish you good-bye until to-morrow, when I will call again, if I may.'

Vanda smiled, and Fanny kissed her again, and from that night a very deep friendship arose between the two—a friendship which was to make life very pleasant for Vanda after the shadows which had marred it for so long.

Later that night Tom, full of anxious love for his dead sister's child, tried his best to find out from Vanda what trouble lay upon her mind, and her reason for supposing her brother's love to be altered; but to all his inquiries she only replied,—

'It is different; there is something come between us. It can never be the same.'

Vanda did not tell her uncle what that sad 'something' was, but she knew, poor child, that the degradation of their training together—the hardships and punishments which they had undergone in each other's presence—had caused a natural shyness to arise between them, and the memory of those days would do away for ever with the old familiar and innocent love.

True brotherly and sisterly affection, deep and lasting, would always exist between them, but alas! the early love was gone, degradation had ruined that; it could not return if it would.

To how many other girls now training in mixed troupes of men and boys, does this terrible feeling of 'something' gone arise to them. As to Vanda, that something means loss of the purity and sweetness of girlhood, and of that priceless gift of modesty which dies for ever in those poor hapless girls whose limbs are daily distorted and bent into unnatural shapes by brutal and coarse masters.

Oh, the misery and sin of a system which permits young girls to suffer such terrible pain so that the people may take their pleasure.

It exists to-day, to-morrow—it is going on now.

And will the people dare still to plead ignorance? Very likely.

## CHAPTER XXVII.

### DEATH UNSEEN.

CASTELLI left Whanks and strode down to the circus, prepared to deal with Cleo as she fully deserved.

He knew he should find her there.

His passion was fearful, it raged within him like an angry sea, and maddened him with its giant power. He was ready to spring upon his prey with all the fury of his fierce nature, for Cleo had deceived him, lied to him for the gratification of her passion, and he had been her lover. These truths filled him with rage. Terrible he looked, with flashing eyes, his strong feelings magnified to desperation as he confronted her practising in the ring.

She saw him coming, and she advanced to meet him with a bright smile. She knew Castelli had a faint suspicion that she had helped Horrox to procure the children, but there had been no facts to establish any actual evidence against her, and only once during the voyage home had he alluded to Mrs Le Sale's letter, and then he had said,—

'I believe you know more of this than you choose to admit; but I shall find it out, cost what it may.'

Now he had seen Whanks, she thought, more than likely Horrox had 'split,' 'for he was always a coward,' said Cleo to herself, remembering his fright when Leila had taken out a summons against him. 'He hadn't the pluck to go to the court and deny the whole thing.'

He stood facing her; she was alone, for the circus was deserted, but she did not flinch from his glittering eyes, which flashed upon her full of hate and scorn.

She knew her game was up, she read her fate in his wrath, which was reflected in his trembling voice, in the clenching of the hands, in the livid workings of his white, set face.

She drew herself quite erect and looked at him calmly. Grand in her splendid beauty, she never quailed; but there was a light in her lustrous eyes which spoke of revenge hiding beneath their depths, of some baffled strife which might wake suddenly and crush with its force the might and mystery of life.

She was prepared for the battle. She had no terror of the furious man before her, even when his anger came towering upon her with relentless fury, like the autumn boreas which carries all before it, blustering, hurrying, rushing, booming on its way. She smiled like the bright ray which shines when the storm has gone. It suited her to suppress her wrath until his had burst and passed away.

She might appease him once more. She could not lose him for ever.

'You impostor! you liar! you cheat!' at last came from his opening lips. 'I've found you out, you false hypocrite! It was you, was it, who planned the dastardly act of taking my children from the home I chose for them? I understand now why you persuaded me to part with them to Le Sale. It was the first step in your fiendish design, the first step, I say, towards having revenge on my dead wife. You and your brutal lover thought to baffle me with your devilish lies, but the hour of reckoning is at hand. I'll set sleuth hounds on his track. He shall be done to death!' he cried in his violent excitement.

She made no reply, and this provoked him to frenzy, and he continued furiously,—

'You who have pretended to love me, you who came grovelling to my feet, you fiend! you she-devil! what have you to say?' he cried, distraught with passion.

The vigour of his vehement speech did not take her by surprise. She knew of the temper which so often distorted his fine face and made him a terror to those in his power. At such times she expected no softening in his humour. He was too desperate, too insulting to listen to reason. But she was not prepared to give him up. She must win him back to her side. His displeasure must be removed from her, so she said sweetly,—

'You are too hard upon me, Castelli. Listen to me,' and she moved a few steps nearer to him, but he waved her back rapidly, as if her presence stung him into unbounded hate.

'Stay where you are. Don't come a step nearer,' he cried. 'I loathe the sight of you.'

'No, no, Castelli, you don't. Love can't change like that. You're making a deal more of it than you need. The precious children are alive and well,' she said, trying to modify his anger.

'*Love*, don't talk to me of *love*! Curse you and your love! They might have died for all you cared, you she-devil! I know how you intercepted letters and papers, and kept Le Sale's death a secret, so that your cowardly plans could be carried out to revenge yourself on my wife. You and Horrox are devils —devils!' he thundered.

'I deny it all,' replied Cleo quietly.

'Don't lie to me, or by heaven I'll do for you! Why, you received money from that villain for helping him. Can you deny that?' asked Castelli with an oath.

'Who told you I received money?' asked Cleo uneasily, wondering how that part of the bargain had transpired.

Castelli's brow darkened, his eyes flashed angrily.

'Who told me? Why, your dastardly lover. He put the blame on you when his own neck was in danger, the cur. But if I can find him I'll kill him with one stroke, and you after him,' he said with violence.

'That would be murder, Castelli; you can't mean that?' said Cleo.

'Murder is too good for either of you,' he added. 'I shall go and search for him, and his fate will be death. I shall stab him through and through for —for—Leila's sake.' His voice grew more quiet as he uttered the dead wife's name.

'Castelli, do be quiet; you are going a sight to far. It is simply absurd to talk like that. What I did was to save you worry. I did for them as if I were their mother, you—.'

In a moment he strode up to her and caught her arm roughly, shaking her with brutal force.

'You like their mother!' he hissed. 'You, a scheming woman,' and he flung her from him, 'a woman with as many lovers as days of the year. She was good and pure, whilst you are as bad as the devil can make you,' he said frantically.

'You didn't treat her as if she was such a treasure,' replied Cleo with sarcasm, for she was angry now, but she kept her temper under control.

He put out his hand to deal her a terrible blow. She saw the action, and evaded it quickly, saying,—

'I am going, until you are less mad and can behave not quite like a fool or a lunatic.'

'Oh, no, you are not; I haven't done with you yet. Look here,' and he lowered his voice and spoke slowly and remorselessly, 'you have longed after my love for years, you took it freely when I had a wife, you would take it to the end, but—but from this day forth you dare to darken my steps and I'll shoot you as I would a dog. I've done with you. You've been confoundedly jealous of "Darkie," well, I am going to make her my wife, and if I catch you dogging me about I'll put a bullet through your heart. Now, get off, and never you come near me again. Be off, I say!' he cried wrathfully.

He had touched her at last, he knew how jealous she was, and it pleased him to probe the wound he had made.

'You are going to marry "Darkie" the rider?' she asked, her face flushing. 'Well, I hope you will be happy,' as a strange look overspread her features.

A change had come over her face; it was not yearning love, it was not despair.

What was it?

'You are a brute, and a savage,' she replied, and then she turned and left him.

The next day she went again to the circus to seek Castelli. He might be there, for both of them had been engaged for the season.

'I'll give him another chance one more—only one,' she murmured.

Her plans were ready, and she intended to put them into effect without delay. She watched him from a safe distance, and she saw him enter a dressing-room, where he had left his overcoat and stick.

In a moment she followed him.

'Castelli!'

His face darkened, his passion rose again when he saw her there. Beautiful but evil she looked standing before him, with her long artistic cloak clinging round her shapely form.

'*You* here again! Do you want me to shoot you?' he asked, speaking rapidly

'Answer me one question, Castelli, and we shall never trouble each other again.' Her eyes grew fixed on his face as she continued: 'Are you going to marry "Darkie"? Is it all over between you and me?' she said slowly, never moving her eyes from his face.

'Yes, we are strangers for ever. Go, woman, begone!' and he glared at her fiercely.

'Are you going to marry "Darkie"?' she persisted.
'Yes,' he replied.
'Do you mean that?'
'Yes. Get out of my way, you brazen devil!'
'You mean that too?' Her voice quivered with suppressed passion and excitement. She went close up to him, so near that he could see her agitation.

'Will you be gone, or by heaven I'll do for you in another minute,' he stormed.

Still she kept her eyes fixed on him, but her hand moved stealthily from behind her cloak. There was a glitter of steel—a white arm raised—a groan—a stream of blood—a voice full of mad impulse, crying,—

'*You* shall never marry "Darkie," my man; you're done for now.'

She had plunged the knife deep into his chest. She knew he must die.

Castelli staggered, then fell to the ground heavily.

He put his hand to the wound to try and staunch the crimson blood which flowed more rapidly.

With one wild effort he tried to wrench the knife from his chest, gasping,—

'Help! help! I am stabbed.'

But he could not move it, Cleo had done her work too well; and so the blood flowed out of the hideous wound. He grew faint, and at last he lay unconscious and ghastly on the floor.

Half-an-hour later he was found by a horror-stricken groom, just breathing and that was all.

'Cleo — has — stabbed — me,' he managed to whisper at last.

The police were sent for, and then Castelli repeated the charge against her, a look of hate stealing over his white face at her name. After the police and doctors had seen him he was removed very tenderly to the manager's office and placed on a sofa. They all felt the hand of death was upon him.

There he lay the victim of a foul deed. All the fury had died from his face. The dews of death were fast gathering on his brow. More handsome he looked ebbing out his strength than he ever did in life.

His eyes were closed. There was silence in the room. No one dared to speak when the hour of death was at hand.

Whanks, who had been hastily summoned, sat by his side. The doctors, the manager, and one or two performers stood about the room, all of them dazed and grieved that such things should happen in their midst.

Castelli opened his eyes and murmured,—

'Whanks—I want—to—speak—to—you—alone,' he gasped feebly.

Castelli's wish was made known, and the men went out softly and closed the door, and then Whanks bent over Castelli to catch his last words.

'Ask her brother—to—take care of—my children —you will see—to that—promise.'

'I will,' said Whanks solemnly, overcome, and much distressed to see his old master dying by a woman's hand.

Castelli lay silent for a few minutes, breathing hurriedly, and then he murmured,—

'The horses—must—be—sold for—the children —and the money in—' But the next words were lost, and Whanks replied,—

'Don't worry, sir, I will see to everything; the children will never want.'

He looked up, and something like a smile passed over his face; but he could not speak his gratitude.

Suddenly he seemed to revive somewhat, and then he murmured,—

'I can see Leila—down—by the sea—the wind blows—the rock is nearly covered—I must—save her.' Then his thoughts wandered to their wedding day. 'You are—mine, Leila—I—will love you for —ever—how dark it grows—Whanks—are you there?—Leila—'

He gasped heavily twice, and then Whanks knew that the great shadow of death had fallen on Castelli.

But there were no angels waiting to take him to the realms where Leila had gone long before.

In sin he had lived, in loneliness he died.

When the officers of the law went to arrest Cleo —they found her cold and dead.

An empty glass, a phial by its side, marked 'poison,' told the oft-repeated but silent tale. A scrap of paper, crumpled in her death agonies, was found in her hand. On it was written:—

'I was with you in life—I am with you in death. Only "Darkie" is left behind, and that is well.
'CLEO.'

A motley crowd gathered at the cemetery. The curious and the vulgar saw the body of the murderess lowered in silence; only the thud of the earth falling on the coffin as it was lowered gratified the lookers-on. But the words of the burial service were hastily read over her victim's last resting place, and then the people went their way. There was nothing more to see.

But there were no tears shed, no flowers left on the newly turned mould.

Unhallowed, unblessed, unloved they lay.

Such is the curse of sin.

## CHAPTER XXVIII.

### FINALE.

It was a lovely spring morning in the early May time. There was happiness everywhere, the joyous birds carolled forth their bright spring notes, the robin trilling with all his might from the branches of the great walnut tree, and in the copse hard by the linnets twittered and flew about merrily in the warm sunshine, and the quivering larks rose from the grass in the fresh meadows, each and all offering a tribute of thankfulness to the profuse springtime. The bees hummed with a pleasant murmur among the newborn flowers and on the blossom laden trees, and the air was full of the fragrance of the growing vegetation and the bursting buds.

Nature was sublime, truly heaven and earth rejoiced, for is not the verdant spring the brightest time of all the year, more beautiful, more enchanting because the cold and mournful winter has past and gone. Surely the most placid must have some love for nature in her supreme moment? But to those who are rapt in wonder by her changing seasons May must be the greatest pleasure that life can give throughout the living year.

May tells of coming hopes and joys; it brings the happy summer tide, and adorns the landscape with brilliant lustre and light. The voice of the cuckoo seems to ring a welcome from the woods as if to say: 'I've come, I've come with the joyous months. With me are the green sward, the pale primrose, the tender anemone, the buttercup, and the golden daffodil. Rejoice whilst the youth of the year is with you!'

Nowhere did the glorious sunshine cast its rosy

blushes more brightly than over a certain old manor house, nestling in the heart of the country. It rested upon its ivied chimneys and upon its well-kept lawns and fine old garden, and enjoying the brilliance were Vanda and Adrian. Two years had sped since their father was laid in his lonely grave, but to the children the time had passed very happily. Tom had intended adopting both children, but Whanks would not hear of such an arrangement; and finally, when he was persuaded to occupy certain rooms in the house with Mr and Mrs Tom, the care and expense of Adrian's education was left, at his desire, to him.

On this sunny May morning the brother and sister were walking together for the last time for a long year. Adrian was going to Rome to study art; the long-desired ambition of his young life was about to be realised, and he was as full of hope as the spring day.

'Here come all the rest,' said Vanda, and they stood on the lawn to wait.

A strange group they looked. The tall, fragile figure of Vanda, the eager, restless boy, the blunt, white-haired Whanks, and the smiling Tom and his wife, all gathered together to make Adrian's last day at home a very pleasant one.

Through much trouble happiness had at last crowned their lives, and each felt that spring day how deep should be their gratitude.

The little group on the lawn disappears from view, the spring and summer has fled, and many more have come and gone, until it is May time again. The old house is gay enough to-day, people hurry hither and thither, the bells from the ivied tower ring out a merry peal, and the villagers stand in little bands to watch for the bride.

Vanda Castelli has given her fresh young womanhood to the care of James Herepath, and her brother, Castelli, the great artist, the idol of princes and people, had come from Rome to wish her God-speed.

And so she left the home which had guarded her so long, and with her maid Sally, now dignified with the name Sarah, entered upon a new life, with a fond husband by her side.

Whanks went out to America after Vanda's marriage, but before he went he told Tom the secret of his life.

'The man who ruined your life and Miss Leila's, the villain Herbert Clifford, was my brother. To make up for his dastardly crime, I have devoted my life to those she left behind. There is no need for me now, so I shall start once more, and feel at rest. I have done what I could.'

And so the curtain falls on those who have suffered, sinned, and died, and upon those who lived to rejoice.

There we must leave them.

# CHILD LABOUR.

ONCE more I have eschewed conventualism, and dared to put forth further details of some circus and acrobat life. I have not dealt with the pseudo-romantic in it, but have brought forth facts in many chapters which have actually occurred.

Fearlessly I am grappling with an unsuspected source of suffering, trusting in time to gain practical reform, and to save those who are at this present moment training under a *secret* and hideous system. There is little doubt that the disclosures made in *Ruby* and in *Slaves of the Sawdust* will sooner or later stir the public mind, and cause a demand for some simple but effective supervision during apprenticeship. For instance, the Act which protects children in our factories could be modified and extended to protect children in the 'show' business.

Putting aside the evil of such training and the hardships of the life, there is another phase to be discussed, which in a sense is more degrading, more contrary to humanity than even the cruelties practised on helpless girlhood by some mercenary masters, who force them to do feats which even tax the powers of male athletes. I allude to the iniquitous system of men waxing rich upon child labour. A certain class, who train girls for the ring, trapeze, as acrobats, or for 'high shows' and such like, live in luxury, entirely on the money earned by their young apprentices. It is the sad, overworked children who bring large salaries weekly to their master's pocket. Is it likely that he takes infinite pains to train them for their arduous feats excepting for his own selfish gains? It is no exaggeration to say openly that the master who thus trains is nothing less than a mere dealer in human flesh. There is not one iota of difference between the bland, smiling man who nightly introduces his weary apprentice to the public, and the slave dealers in the Eastern markets, for each amasses wealth from the unpaid labour of helpless fellow-creatures.

What is the remuneration during their long apprenticeship for these children who are so rigorously taught, that they may give passing pleasure to a thoughtless multitude? Food, which is usually of the best, so that their strength shall be sufficiently supported; clothes, both warm and comfortable—for would not chills and sickness ruin the show, and the master be the greater loser?—and some of the more generous occasionally give their apprentices a few shillings for pocket money.

This is all, for seven or ten weary years—ay, fifteen years in some cases—whilst they are earning large salaries for their exacting proprietors. Alas! for the workers there are few rewards. Yet as in every other occupation there are valuable prizes ready for those who have stamina and ability, but how many of all apprentices gain the prizes?

What the public should insist upon is registration, a periodical census of the numbers of apprentices and the numbers of those who are in the profession at the age of thirty years. More important still, the people should know what has become of the absentees. By this means it would be easy to trace how many were worked out at the end of their apprenticeship, and how many left the profession in disgust. It has been said to me by more than one person, 'Is it likely a master will part with a valuable apprentice because the term of indenture expires?' My reply is, that these men, with honourable exceptions, know perfectly well that their pupils would not remain with them, because the master could not afford to pay his late apprentice salaries equal to the amounts he, or she, has earned for him. Again, as these men live on unpaid labour, they arrange to have other apprentices following on to replace those who are out of their time.

As a rule the responsibility of training does not lie with the proprietors and managers who engage 'shows' for the entertainment of their patrons. Whatever their moral responsibility, there are few who trouble to inquire how the members of any particular troupe were brought to such perfection as to justify engagements at high salaries, or care that the sooner the hapless apprentice can earn for his or her master, the better for him. Quick perfection is the desideratum, so to that end the trainer works them morning, noon, and night.

Is it right that men should be allowed to live on child labour and eat the bread gained by so much suffering? Is it just that trembling children and growing girls should be slaving in the heat and glare of crowded circuses and music-halls night after night in all our great cities, and so that their masters may reap the harvest of severity?

'No! no!' the people cry with one voice. but they forget that it is the morbid taste of an inconsiderate public which is the cause of the evil, for it demands more and more difficult feats, and sad though it be, so long as there is a demand in the market, the supply will be forthcoming, as surely as in other commodities.

The men who are so degraded as to live on the earnings of childhood are not those from whom we can expect mercy while preparing the victims of their greed.

What will men not do for gain?

Before concluding, I wish to mete out justice to those in the profession who rightly deserve to be exonerated from blame, and to whose names no stigma can be attached. There are many such who have given me valued assistance in my work, who have stood by me in the fight, and who are ready now to support my efforts. To them I give my heartiest thanks.

> 'Ah, yet, tho' all the world forsake,
> Tho' fortune clip my wings,
> I will not cramp my heart, nor take
> Half views of men and things.'
> TENNYSON.

THE END.

COLSTON AND COMPANY, PRINTERS, EDINBURGH.

www.ingramcontent.com/pod-product-compliance
Lightning Source LLC
Chambersburg PA
CBHW030749230426
43667CB00007B/894